MARCEL PROUST

The Fictions of Life and of Art

LEO BERSANI

MARCEL PROUST

The Fictions of Life and of Art

NEW YORK

OXFORD UNIVERSITY PRESS

1965

PRINTED IN THE UNITED STATES OF AMERICA

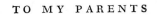

TO MY PARENTS

ACKNOWLEDGMENTS

This book has benefited from the kind assistance of many people. I am immensely grateful to Eléonore M. Zimmermann for her generous interest in my work on Proust; her encouragements and criticisms have been invaluable at every stage of my writing. Marcelle Gindre also made useful suggestions, and she and Richard Marienstras provided kind and patient help in the translation of many of the passages I quote from French writers. Conversations about Proust and about fiction with Hubert Dreyfus, Robert Garis, Joseph Pequigney, and Richard Poirier have been important, in a variety of ways, in the development and clarification of the ideas in this study. I am also indebted to my cousin Claire Bersani, who typed the manuscript, and to Claude André for friendly encouragement and aid in the final stages of my work.

I am thankful to the French Department, the President, and the Trustees of Wellesley College for granting me the leave of absence during which much of this book was written. Finally, permission to quote from the English edition of Proust's novel, *Remembrance of Things Past,* has been kindly granted by Random House, Incorporated.

L. B.

Cambridge, Mass.
March 1965

CONTENTS

CHAPTER FOUR

SOCIAL CONTEXTS: OBSERVATION AND INVENTION

CHAPTER FIVE

MARCEL'S VOCATION

MARCEL PROUST

The Fictions of Life and of Art

INTRODUCTION

It is quite possible that, to produce a literary work, imagination and sensibility are interchangeable qualities and that the latter can, without much disadvantage, be substituted for the former, just as people whose stomach is unable to digest food charge their intestines with this function. A man born sensitive to impressions but without imagination, might nevertheless write admirable novels. The suffering caused him by others, his attempts to forestall it, the conflicts provoked by his suffering and the other cruel person—all that, interpreted by his intelligence, might furnish the material for a book not only as fine as if it had been imagined and invented, but also as completely foreign to the author's reveries as if he had been absorbed in himself and happy, as surprising to him and as much the product of chance as an accidental caprice of the imagination.[1]

Proust's narrator curiously expresses in tentative and purely speculative terms, in this passage from Le Temps retrouvé, what we immediately recognize as an attempt to define his own literary enterprise. To substitute a history of the author's sensibility for the invented situations and characters of traditional fiction: it is this impatience with the very materials of story-telling, the wish to bypass imaginary plots and write a work of direct self-expression, that perhaps most sharply distinguishes Proust from earlier practitioners of the novel. Gaëtan Picon has rightly emphasized the originality of the Proustian point of departure.[2] For Balzac, Stendhal, Flaubert, and Henry James, the creative impetus is often a situation from which the novelist himself is absent: an anecdote read in a newspaper, a piece of gossip told by a friend,

3

a certain historical incident. It is in the telling of these stories that
the writer's individuality transforms, inevitably, the originally objective material, uses it as a medium of self-expression. But in
A la Recherche du temps perdu the primary and explicit aim of
the narrator when he begins to write is to portray as fully as possible the personality which other writers reveal by being interested in something else. Yet no sooner does the narrator set forth
a project of self-expression than he speaks of a writer presenting
the history of his own feelings as if he were inventing them, from
the distance and with the detachment of a man for whom self-
analysis would somehow have become "as surprising . . . and
as much the product of chance as an accidental caprice of the
imagination." The "admirable" works are those that are "imagined, invented," and in the book the narrator has in mind the
account of a sensitive man's suffering would appear "as completely foreign to the author's reveries" as if the author had, in
his life, been a happy man. Such a work would be novelistic and
directly autobiographical without really being either one. The
narrator's remarks suggest a constant tension between two forms
of expression, a struggle against personal confession within the
larger intention of confessing the self.

   Proust himself has, of course, written a work of self-analysis as
if the object of his analysis were not drawn directly from the history of his own sensibility. *A la Recherche du temps perdu* is an
extraordinarily dense exercise in introspection, and yet, by the
apparently simple device of using the main character of his novel
as the narrator, Proust has also, to a certain extent, detached himself from that character's life and point of view. The distinction
between Proust and his narrator (or Marcel) [3] has great importance and must be maintained in any discussion of the novel, for
it is on the basis of this distinction that a whole world of imaginary characters and events could be *invented* as the novelistic
framework for an *essai* of self-analysis. But Proust's narrator is
himself a writer, and his book is, as he says, the story of an "invisible vocation," [4] a vocation made visible and authenticated by
the work itself. The narrator's past has, therefore, a specific lit-

erary significance; his life presumably implies the book we are reading, and the book realizes the literary potentialities of his life. As a result, it is possible to trace, in great detail, the continuity between the kind of work he writes and aspects of his experience that may at first appear unrelated to that work. His subject is, in a sense, the problem he poses in the passage I have quoted: how has he been able to transform the history of his feelings into an "admirable novel"? The literary treatment of his past is, in fact, a constant exploration of the narrator's ability to re-create the self imaginatively, that is, of his resources as a novelist, and the processes of novelistic creation constitute one of the principal subjects of interest in *A la Recherche*. The story of a life whose meaning is fully realized only when that life is transformed into literature necessarily illustrates a progress from what is given in life to what is imagined and invented in art.

The narrator's interest in a work of self-analysis that would appear "as completely foreign to the author's reveries" as if his material were wholly invented is much more than the theoretical interest of a professional man of letters; the writing of this kind of work plays the crucial role of resolving tensions that almost make of his life a failure. His book does not, in fact, reveal a man "born without imagination," but one for whom a self-portrait has a special fascination, at the same time that he finds the self insignificant in comparison to some external "truth" or "reality." The sentences I have been discussing suggest a longing to escape from the self; the very distinction between works of sensibility and works of imagination implies the curious notion that certain men are capable of writing works completely alien to their own sensibilities. It is as if the narrator were intrigued by the paradoxical situation of the writer's being surprised by a self he will at the same time recognize. And it is perhaps the experience of having written his own work that makes Marcel suggest that literature can realize this paradox: he himself has (and I shall come back to this in more detail) invented a past which presumably existed when he began to write. What appeals to him in the literary form he proposes seems, therefore, to be that it can perhaps provide the writer with a highly desirable relation to himself.

Proust's novel is the history of the need for such a relation, a demonstration of the various forms this need has taken in the narrator's life. Marcel's painful dependence on his mother when he is a child, his love later on for certain women, his attitudes toward society, his intellectual habit of exhaustive analysis, his theories of art and time express, in various ways, a basic anguish about the nature of the self and its relation to the external world. They are, so to speak, different points along the "main line" of his personality, which can be defined as an extreme uncertainty about the stability of the self, a fearful fantasy [5] of losing the self unless it can be permanently fixed in some external picture. In a sense, his different experiences—of love, of society, of art—are strategies designed to relieve this anguish. I am not suggesting that the narrator's interest in art can be reduced to sexual fears and desires from his childhood, for it is obviously important not to confuse what may be the beginning in time of a certain need with the nature and significance of that need for a complex adult. Marcel's anguish as a man includes elements of the self other than sexuality; it is a concern about the stability and value of his whole being in its contacts with the world. Indeed, in the novel physical desire itself is exploited as a strategy to solve problems that are no longer merely sexual. The way in which Marcel falls in love or thinks about art constantly re-creates the original pattern, or "figure in the carpet," by a generous involvement of other parts of his personality. It could be said that his anguish about the self defines the "field" within which various other possibilities—such as love and creativity—can be expressed. The purpose of disengaging what seems to me the central obsession in Proust's novel is therefore not to reduce everything to that obsession, but rather to trace the continuity—which, as I shall show, is a process of invention and enrichment—between what is first presented as a crippling weakness and the freest, most creative activity in the narrator's life. The novel is, moreover, about this continuity, or rather it creates it: the metaphorical connections the narrator now establishes among different moments of his life give a psychological unity to what he had felt was the history of discontinuous personalities.

Now there has been recently in France much critical interest in disengaging the hidden springs of a writer's work, the unconscious or at least nonexplicit direction or intentionality discernible both in his work and in the rest of his life. The idea of nonreflective, implicit purposes is, of course, not a new one in either psychology or philosophy; in literary criticism it has given rise, in the last twenty years or so, as Jean-Pierre Richard has written, "to an exploration in depth, an elucidation of the work's hidden contents, in short, a kind of bringing forth of latent meanings." [6] The men who have been engaged in this sort of study by no means form a single school of critical thought; but in spite of considerable philosophical and temperamental differences, they share the wish to describe that level of mental life where the work of art has its origin—the profound and secret impulses that inform the whole work but which the language of the work does not explicitly express. The critic brings to light a particular psychological unity by disengaging an essential "theme," which Richard defines as "a concrete organizing principle, a fixed pattern or object, around which a universe would tend to crystallize and unfold itself." [7]

The "exploration in depth" presupposes a certain idea of what constitutes psychological depth, and much of contemporary French criticism is, at least implicitly, a philosophical statement on the nature of mental reality. In his book on Baudelaire published in 1947, Sartre applies the existential psychology developed in *L'Etre et le néant* to Baudelaire's life and work. He studies Baudelaire's "original choice," which Sartre defines as the attempt to see himself as if he were external to himself; Baudelaire's life is the history of the failure of this "project." [8] The descriptive vocabulary of Charles Mauron's "psychocriticism" is the vocabulary of psychoanalysis, and he looks in literary texts for "facts and relations which have, until now, gone unnoticed or been inadequately apprehended and the source of

which would be the writer's unconscious personality." Mauron
attempts to define "the involuntary associations of ideas beneath
the intentional structures of the text," and he moves from an
empirical study of these "networks of associations" to the hypoth-
esis of an inner dramatic situation which would constitute what
he calls the "personal myth" of a writer.[9] French criticism has,
however, as Mauron points out, consistently resisted Freudian
categories, in spite of an equally consistent interest in a psychology of depth or of the unconscious. The images of mental reality
proposed by Gaston Bachelard have generally found greater sympathy among the "thematic" critics than the hypotheses of psychoanalysis. The organizing principles Bachelard looks for in
poetry are certain attitudes toward, or "reveries" about matter, as
the titles of several of his studies indicate: *L'Eau et les rêves*,
L'Air et les songes, *La Terre et les rêveries de la volonté*, *La Terre
et les rêveries du repos*, *La Psychanalyse du feu*.[10] Mauron has,
it seems to me, asked some pertinent questions about this highly
personal psychology—which, he writes, seems to describe neither
conscious nor unconscious life, but rather "an incipient and confused consciousness"—but Bachelard's analysis of "sensory reveries" has undoubtedly played a crucial role in the development
of a criticism whose "themes" tend to be "category, form, concept
or quality (time, circle, depth, transparency)." [11] George Poulet's
work on the Proustian notions of space and time,[12] Richard's
study of Mallarmé's effort to solve "a problem of upward dynamic
movement" (". . . in a world whose laws are dispersion and
entropy, where can the initial impulse towards an ascending
movement be found?"),[13] and Jean Starobinski's study of Rousseau's attempt to restore transparency to an opaque world filled
with obstacles to communication [14] are impressive examples of
what has been called a "critique abyssale," a "study of hidden
physical or humoral sources." [15] Finally, Roland Barthes sets out
to find an "organized network of obsessions" in Michelet, and he
insists on what he calls the "substantial character" of a "theme"
in a passage that illustrates particularly well the transposition, in
thematic criticism, of explicit, intellectual expression in works of

art to a level of imaginary physical contacts with the world of matter:

> The substantial nature of the theme has two consequences: first of all, the theme rescues History. For example, politically, Michelet's point of view is by no means original, his ideas are typical of the *petite bourgeoisie* around 1840. But, once they begin to exist as themes, these commonplace ideas become specific experiences: Anglophobia is supported by a feeling of nausea in front of an excess and stagnancy of blood; Germanophilia, on the contrary, derives from his delight in a ceaselessly flowing substance, in blood-milk; machinism is discredited by the horror inspired by the Dry and the Sterile; and the Common People bring redemption insofar as they transcend the divisions of sex and are a union of the male idea and the female sentiment. The theme in Michelet thus has two roots: an historical root and an existential root. That is why historical criticism should not begin to study Michelet without having first of all established his thematic system.
>
> The theme also supports a complete system of values; no theme is neutral, and the world's substance is divided into beneficent states and maleficent states. In spite of what is generally thought, Michelet's moral philosophy is not at all rhetorical; it is derived from the body; History is judged by the laws of the flesh: Good is defined by virtue of its smooth, fluid, rhythmic nature, and Evil by virtue of its dryness and discontinuity.[16]

In spite of the brilliance of many of the studies I have mentioned, one can, it seems to me, take objection to these critics' use of the literary work. Curiously enough, it could be said that what interests them is what interested Sainte-Beuve: a portrait of the man *through* his life and work, and not necessarily a study of the work itself. Mauron is careful to point out the limitations of his method; in defining the place of psychocriticism in the great critical tradition, he writes: "Even when it has reached full maturity, psychocriticism would constitute only one wing—symmetrical to literary history—of criticism. But the study of creative language would occupy the center." [17] And Richard is aware that literature does not merely reflect certain inner structures, that it modifies and even creates them. His intention is to lead us back to literary forms as the "solutions" of a "human project," as "the ideal worlds where life attains its real happiness." [18] In an essay on Stendhal in *Littérature et sensation,* Richard points out that it is in his novels that Stendhal attains the balance sought for in his whole life between the opposite impulses to break down experience into separate, analyzable units, and to find the principle of harmony capable of giving continuity and wholeness to experience. This sense of the privileged role of literature in the writer's life does not, however, always lead to a study of the specifically literary qualities of the writer's work. For example, Richard considers Flaubert's ascetic attitude toward style as the crucial step in his search for an "ideal of hardness," for a clear, sharply defined form in which Flaubert can escape from a pathological fear of being drowned, of losing himself in a sort of undifferentiated liquid matter. At the end of his study, Richard notes that it might now be interesting to study Flaubert's novels to see if they actually fulfill the conditions for ideal form defined by his particular psychology. But, he adds, a study of the novels is not absolutely necessary to understand Flaubert's originality and greatness: "In effect, this greatness seems to me to consist, prior to any result, any written work, in a certain quality of inner tension. . . ." [19] Richard quotes from Flaubert's novels and Mallarmé's poems exactly as he uses biographical information—to illustrate an aspect of the man's inner world—and he often wholly neglects the stylistic and dramatic contexts of these passages in the novels and the poems. But, although it seems to me that Richard's study of Mallarmé, for example, is not entirely successful as an analysis of the particular appeal of Mallarmé's poetry, he is notably more sensitive to literary achievement than is Sartre in his study of Baudelaire. What might have been the most interesting chapter in Sartre's work is unwritten: a demonstration of the *poetic advantages* implicit in Baudelaire's "original choice." For if this choice accounts for so much of what Sartre obviously finds unsavory in Baudelaire's life and character, it is also by exploiting, as a poet, his particular psychological possibilities that Baudelaire was able to produce *Les Fleurs du mal*.

Even when the critics I have in mind limit themselves to the writer's work, their studies often seem too far removed from a direct experience of the work. They draw from novels or poems a kind of diagram of implicit mental structures, and the psychological history they uncover determines the structure of their critical essays. They describe a psychological drama pointed to by the literary work. Now it is clear that the critic distorts this drama by the very fact of articulating it. As Richard writes: "The difficulty of any structural description comes from our having to describe successively, one after the other, things which in fact exist together, simultaneously." [20] This difficulty is real enough, but it does not invalidate the critic's findings. To break down the writer's psychology into a logical progression is obviously to impose an artificial order on it, but this abstraction from the writer's inner life can, nevertheless, reveal the implicit logic of that life, its guiding principles and motivations. One could, it seems to me, more justifiably object to a neglect of the structure of the work of art; for the work is, in fact, the only concrete, visible expression of the mental structures the critic attempts to describe. The closest we can get to the writer's psychology is, then, not in an intellectual reconstruction of that psychology, but rather in a critical report of how we experience it there where it is actually expressed. A certain amount of abstraction from the work may be necessary, but it should be undertaken with the purpose of coming back to the work itself with the vocabulary best suited to make its organization and style intelligible.

It is this final elucidation of the writer's work that I find lacking in George Poulet's otherwise impressive studies of Proust. His analyses of time and space in *A la Recherche du temps perdu* have been extremely helpful to me, but Poulet's work does not give the impression that he is talking about Proust's *novel*. He is describing a drama that takes place—to use a favorite expression in French criticism—in a certain mental space, but what we miss is a description of the novelistic space filled with characters living

a variety of dramatic relationships with one another. This use of
the work of art to go beyond or behind the work is by no means
denied or disguised; a description of implied mental processes
may be presented as the legitimate object of criticism. Bachelard,
for example, writes that a phenomenology of poetic images requires that we participate in the activity of imaginative processes
rather than a description of poetic language.[21] Finally, the work
of Maurice Blanchot is the most abstract and, in the chemical
sense of the word, the purest version of this tracing of implied
mental spaces. Blanchot has written on specific writers, but he is
mainly interested in the ideal inner conditions of literary creation. His ambition is to work back to the source of literature, to
describe "the habits and structures of the mind which has built"
a literary work rather than the style and value of specific works.[22]

These aspects of recent French criticism have been mentioned
elsewhere. Richard himself and Yves Bonnefoy, in sympathetic
summaries of contemporary critical tendencies, have spoken of a
weakness both in formal analyses and in the judgment of literary
value in much of the work being done in France.[23] And Gaëtan
Picon, in the first volume of his *Introduction à une esthétique de
la littérature*, persuasively insists on the difference between a
study of the nature of a work of art and a judgment of artistic
value. What interests Picon is the possibility of arriving—through
a cultural consciousness, a comparison among works of art—"if
not at a universality, at least at an objectivity of taste." A literary
esthetic is impossible without the exercise of critical judgment;
for the work of art, ". . . existence is inseparable from value." [24]
This sort of emphasis on a critical responsiveness to specific texts
has, it seems to me, been made necessary by a body of work in
which the intellectual pleasure of investigating psychological
complexity is at times confused with the informed enjoyment of
successful literary expression.

The reader will easily recognize both Sartrean and psychoanalytic elements in my own approach to Proust, especially in the
psychological analyses of the first half of my discussion. I have,
however, not been tempted by the more or less specialized vocab-

ularies of existentialist and psychoanalytic criticism; Sartre's work, for example, has helped me mainly to locate and define the kinds of physical and mental events which, I feel, are likely to be crucial in giving shape to an individual history. But I have wanted especially, in my discussion of *A la Recherche du temps perdu*, to establish some of the connections between the narrator's personality and the sort of book he writes, and it has seemed to me that neither Sartre nor Mauron convincingly demonstrates how a certain psychological point of view might *serve* a discussion of literary form. I shall begin this study with an analysis of the narrator in Proust's work, but because the psychology I intend to examine is inseparable from a specific novelistic achievement, my main purpose will be to point out how certain psychological tensions are expressed and resolved in the writing of this particular work, in its special structure and style, its special strengths and weaknesses. For our experience of these tensions is first of all an experience of style, of dramatic incidents, and of characters of fiction.

A few remarks can serve to illustrate briefly how I understand this connection between the narrator's psychology and what we enjoy in reading the novel. Marcel's life is a series of disappointments; he has glamorous images of people before he meets them, and, as soon as they no longer seem mysterious to him, he loses most of his interest in them. The narrator remembers wanting to experience only what might be completely different from himself, and yet, because of his ambiguous attitude toward the self, it is the very difference in the people he meets that seems to disappoint him. They turn out, quite naturally, not to embody his fantasies about them, and, in a sense, he rejects them because they do not send back his own image to him. I shall be discussing this habitual response in greater detail, but I want to emphasize here that what interests us as we read the novel is not only that Marcel's fantasies prevent him, for example, from finding any happiness in society or in love; we also experience the luxuriously creative aspects of fantasy, how imaginatively satisfying his distortions of reality are. We have two characterizations of many of the people in the novel, and the differences between them not only indicate, say, the subjective nature that love has for Marcel, but also create two modes of fiction. Especially in the earlier volumes, character tends to be romanticized, removed from ordinary social reality. Gilberte, Madame de Guermantes, and Albertine are poetic images rather than psychologically probable individuals; their lives seem to contain the keys to enigmas of nature, art, and history. But, roughly from *Le Côté de Guermantes* on, they are stripped of their idealized personalities, and we see them mostly as limited, banal people in equally banal situations. The general fiction of the whole novel—that the narrator is remembering everything he is writing about—encourages us to accept these second characterizations as portraits of people observed in life. The narrator writes the romantic novel of what he desired, and the realistic, comic novel of what he saw. And each novel, to a certain extent, has its own characters. Marcel's peculiar psychology makes him particularly apt at experimenting with different ways of writing fiction, and the reader experiences the pleasures both of romantic creation and of realistic observation of character in the narrator's account of his failure to realize certain dreams.

It seems clear that the kind of study I am proposing must be made entirely on the basis of the evidence provided by the work itself. It would, of course, be absurd to claim that facts from a writer's life never illuminate his work; on the other hand, the writer *in* and *as* his work is not the same person as the writer outside his work. Our habit of saying: "I like Proust," or: "I find Anatole France boring" expresses both our implicit sense of this difference as well as a spontaneous confusion between a work of art and the man responsible for that work. We are certainly not saying that we "like" Proust in the way that we like our friends, and the metonymy we use to express our enjoyment of his novel, while it posits a non-existent figure (neither Proust the man nor his work, but a man who would be only his work), suggests how deeply we experience personality in art and how difficult it is for us to separate personality from biography. Proust himself, in his attack on Sainte-Beuve, makes, in somewhat different terms, the same distinction between the writer in his work and the writer as an object of biographical investigation. Sainte-Beuve's approach to literature "fails to recognize what we learn from even a slightly advanced degree of familiarity with ourselves: that a book is the product of a self different from the one we reveal in our habits, in society, in our vices. If we want to try to understand this other self, we can do so only by trying to re-create it deeply within ourselves." For Sainte-Beuve, the literary work is only one of many sources of information used to draw the moral and psychological portrait of the artist. He finds no question irrelevant to the understanding of the writer and his work: "What did he think of religion? How did the spectacle of nature affect him? How did he behave concerning women, or concerning money? Was he rich or poor; what was his diet, what were his daily habits? What was his vice or his weakness?" [25] It is not necessary to accept literally Proust's idea of the writer's two selves (an idea in which we recognize another version of his characteristic view of discontinuous, separate personalities in the same life) in order to appreciate the rightness of his objections to Sainte-Beuve's method. It can, after all, be argued that instead of using the artist's life to understand his work, a critic might, with more aptness, use the work to understand his life. For the writer's non-literary activities may express only a part of the individuality revealed in his work. The pressures of daily life necessarily reduce a personality to a more or less simplified expression; but a peculiar privilege of literary activity is the leisure it offers, leisure to give play to a range of feeling, of being that would never be tolerated in ordinary life. It is, then, useless to look to the writer's life for an explanation of what is in his books, for the conditions in which he writes those books allow him the freedom to express desires, fears, and interests that are either not at all or feebly and confusedly expressed elsewhere in his life. This is, I think, essentially Proust's argument against Sainte-Beuve: the writer's work is so deeply his life that it is foolish to expect his life to illuminate it.

The writer's biography may, on the other hand, help the critic to measure the distance between self-expression in art and self-expression elsewhere in life; it can indicate not so much the sources of an artist's work, as the psychological processes that separate imaginative life from "practical" life. George D. Painter presents his biography of Proust as precisely this sort of study, but while the first volume of his work is highly informative, it hardly suggests that the intention Painter announces in his foreword will be realized: "By discovering which aspects of his originals he chose or rejected, how he combined many models into each new figure, and most of all how he altered material reality to make it conform more closely to symbolic reality, we can observe the workings of his imagination at the very moment of creation." [26] And we have seen the dangers of the traditional biographical approach in several studies of Proust. If we look to Proust's life to understand *A la Recherche du temps perdu,* if we consider the book as simply another arrangement of the events of that life, we may very well be tempted—and this has been done—to correct the work: Albertine is "really" a man,[27] Marcel is "really" a snob,[28] his feelings toward his parents are "really" more aggressively antagonistic than he says.[29] Seen from this angle, an author is mercilessly "exposed," and his book can easily seem like an exercise in dishonesty, an attempt to make his life seem "better" than it actually was. Proust's distinction between the writer's two selves can be thought of as a way of pointing out that the work of art does not, in any simple way, reflect or distort reality, that the writer's life is only a partial realization of the possibilities dramatized in his work.

Moreover, this distinction between the artist's social personality and the self that goes into his work never becomes an absolute distinction between art and life. It is only superficially that art appears in Proust's novel as an escape from an unsatisfactory life; it is rather through art that his narrator lives most fully and most deeply, that he can satisfy his extraordinary appetite for experience. His profound pessimism, and his decision to exclude everything from his life except the book he discovers it is his vocation to write, should not deceive us. For both Proust and his principal character, art is first of all a psychological process present in all our responses to life; the work of art is the isolation and cultivation of a particular way of reacting to and acting on the world. It is creative because it creates more life than is possible outside of art. And, in a sense, the Proustian novel is precisely about the interpenetration of art and the rest of life, the consequences of a certain type of imaginative activity for the narrator's life and for his book. Marcel's experience of love, of society, and of works of art has a rich literary significance—not because he is uninterested in life, but because each kind of experience potentially contains the way in which it can be relived as purely literary expression. The time Marcel spends pursuing Gilberte and Albertine, or going into society, is not merely "lost time," although it appears to be partly that to the man who is no longer young and who anxiously wonders if he will have the time to finish the work he finally begins to write. In his love for Albertine, for example, Marcel not only suffers from his jealousy; he also discovers jealousy as a rich source of novelistic invention. And, as I shall show, the expression, in art, of his failure to possess Albertine is an act of self-possession, at the same time that the psychological security enjoyed from the perspective of memory allows him, while writing, to give more "reality" to Albertine than when he loved her.

If I had to try to sum up *A la Recherche du temps perdu* in one sentence, I would say that it shows how the disappointments the narrator suffers as a result of his extraordinarily rich imagination lead him to give up novelizing in life in order to reminisce about the way he used to novelize, in art. And the conditions in which imaginative fantasies are now elaborated make possible a re-creation of personality; but this new self has only a literary existence, and it can be understood not by reference to a personality operating under different circumstances and expressing itself in other activities, but rather by a study of the literary work. For the work of art does not reflect an already existing self; in a sense, it creates the man whose existence it reveals and contains. It is undoubtedly true that every act in a man's life is creative: to wish to do something and to act on that desire, for example, "compose" our personality in different ways. But, as I have suggested, a work of art seems to be not merely an addition to a personal history; it allows the self it creates to exist in a multiplicity of ways that would be contradictory and impossible in other kinds of behavior. The distinction made in ordinary language between "creative" writing and other types of writing suggests a vague but generally felt sense of this difference, of the greater range of self-creation allowed for in the life of the imagination. A cult of sincerity in art would therefore seem to reveal a peculiar misunderstanding of what artistic activity involves. The writer who claims he puts down only "what he feels" is strangely insensitive to the obvious fact that the act of writing creates new feelings, can never be simply a translation of states of mind that exist before the moment of writing. If we judge Rousseau on his own terms, we cannot avoid accusing him of "insincerity," and it is his own false premise that leads us to have moral reservations about a process of self-invention that is the heart of artistic activity. And we find that contemporary apostle of sincerity in art, Henry Miller, astonishingly naïve when, in the first pages of *Tropic of Cancer,* we read of his intention not to erase anything he writes—as if revision were necessary to make writing into an act of self-revision.[30]

A la Recherche du temps perdu is precisely such an act; the narrator, as Louis Martin-Chauffier has pointed out, does not rediscover his past, he invents it.[31] And the act of memory seems to involve such a liberal re-creation of the past, rather than a mere fidelity to past impressions, that some of the theoretical positions that inspired the narrator's work are made obsolete by the work itself. One of the most interesting aspects of the book is the contradiction between the narrator's subjectivist ideas—the inexorable "law" according to which all we can do is project images of ourselves on external reality—and what might be called the discovery of a diversified and distinct external world at the very moment when the narrator has presumably turned his back on everything except the world of his own impressions and fantasies. Objectivity is condemned as an illusion, but the narrator obviously feels confident of accurately reporting on the world outside of the self while he is apparently engaged in consecrating his self-imprisonment. The experiment in self-analysis is also a collection of universal laws. But to the extent that Proust's world illustrates and justifies these laws, we may find that it undermines *our* confidence in the narrator's ability to describe a world that does not merely reflect his own sensibility. I shall discuss, in my chapter on Marcel's life in society, the way in which dramatic variety is qualified in *A la Recherche* by an impressive series of psychological parallels between Marcel and the other characters, parallels which tend to blur individual distinctness of characterization and to reduce the Proustian universe to an allegorical representation of a single sensibility.

Proust's book has a particular richness, a multiplicity of directions which make it difficult to say anything definitive about the kind of novelistic world he creates. The conflict between the narrator's desire to possess a permanent image of himself and his conviction that value adheres only to what is not recognizable as belonging to the self creates a continual and unresolved tension between two kinds of literary works. On the one hand, Proust is one of the first modern novelists to challenge the conventions of psychological and social realism, to question the epistemological confidence of writers whose work depends on some measure of security about their sense of what constitutes "reality." The narrator defines, in his theoretical remarks, a literature of impressions, a deliberately subjective book whose only subject would be the writer's sensibility. On the other hand, Harry Levin is certainly right to study Proust as the last of the great French realists, and at the same time that Proust's narrator theorizes about a novel that would be faithful only to impressions, that would reflect his own experience of the impossibility of knowing anything outside of the self, he is also engaged in writing a work of acute social observation and criticism that continues, and in fact concludes, the tradition of Balzac, Stendhal, Flaubert, and Zola.[32] There is in *A la Recherche* what could be called a certain creative indecisiveness about novelistic form which is, of course, partly understandable in terms of a historical evolution of the novel, but which I shall be principally interested in examining as the literary consequence of the narrator's extreme uncertainty about the relationship between the self and the world. In realizing his project of self-possession through self-description, the narrator writes a work in which we see the novel as a document of realistic observation in the process of becoming a work in which the whole burden of literary expression would be carried by the *quality* of the narrative voice.

CHAPTER ONE

FANTASIES OF THE SELF AND THE WORLD

1. *"Je n'étais plus qu'un coeur qui battait"*

The experience Proust's narrator describes on the first pages of *A la Recherche du temps perdu* is commonplace enough for a man who has just awakened from a deep sleep; but Marcel's whole life has been characterized by the kind of uncertainty about the self which he describes here. The experience is one in which he loses his sense both of his own identity and of the identity of the external world. He recalls nights when his sleep was so heavy that when he awoke he did not know who he was or where he was: ". . . it was enough if, in my own bed, my sleep was so heavy as completely to relax my consciousness; for then I lost all sense of the place in which I had gone to sleep, and when I awoke at midnight, not knowing where I was, I could not be sure at first who I was. . . ." [1] He has to recognize the place if he is to know who he is; knowledge of the self, he suggests, depends on an ability to find the self in the external world. The narrator will come back often to the idea that by "looking inside," by attempting to define the self introspectively, we find only an "empty apparatus." [2] This statement by no means expresses his whole point of view on the processes of self-awareness, but it is important to see that he emphasizes, at the beginning of his work, the way in which the self relies, for its security, on a fixed scene in the outer world. By living in certain places, among certain arrangements of objects in the world, we materialize our identity in things outside of ourselves. To find the world familiar therefore involves a kind of familiarity with our past; an external scene and a particular, individualizing history simultaneously become available to us.

But there are moments when the external world is unrecognizable, when it becomes anonymous or unstable. Now the narrator
suggests that while we depend on the world's familiarity and
stability in order to recognize ourselves, what we see depends on
and reveals certain conditions *in us* at the moment of our looking
at the world. We may not be able to define these conditions ana-
lytically, but the stability or lack of stability we "find" in things
reveals nothing inherent about the nature of external reality;
rather, it tells us something about our own capacity to resist the
world's strangeness, its otherness, with a specific history and personality. The world is everything and nothing until a human decision fixes it, gives it meaning: "Perhaps the immobility of the
things that surround us is forced upon them by our conviction
that they are themselves, and not anything else, and by the immobility of our conceptions of them." But in sleep thought itself
becomes mobile; present and past mix, places become confused
with one another, and this leisurely moving around in our own
history can extend into the first moments after waking up. Because of the peculiar freedom the mind enjoys in sleep, Marcel
cannot locate the real bedroom in which he has been sleeping,
and, in the first moment of not being able to choose among the
bedrooms of his past, he is reduced to an elemental, purely physi-
ological existence: ". . . I had only the most rudimentary sense
of existence, such as may lurk and flicker in the depths of an
animal's consciousness; I was more destitute of human qualities
than the cave-dweller. . . ." [3]

The bedroom then begins to shift dizzily from one identity to
another. Because of the chance positions of his legs or arms when
he awakes, Marcel's body "remembers" different bedrooms it
associates with those positions. The passage is full of images of
movement: the narrator speaks several times of traveling, of the
sleeper moving in a world falling "topsy-turvy from its orbit," and
he describes the walls of the room as "whirling madly through
the darkness." With each new bedroom Marcel finds himself at
a different moment of his life. He experiences time as a rapid
succession of spatial arrangements. Between the different arrange-

ments there is only vertiginous movement; Marcel is dizzily whirled though the temporal "distance" that separates one bedroom from another. There is a suggestion of these distances being suppressed by a sort of melting of one picture into another: ". . . it often happened that, in my spell of uncertainty as to where I was, I did not distinguish the successive theories of which that uncertainty was composed any more than, when we watch a horse running, we isolate the successive positions of its body as they appear upon a bioscope." [4] The comparison is a curious one, for between the horse's successive positions there is, in effect, nothing, while there is a human duration between the various periods of Marcel's past, a duration which, however, he feels only as vertigo. The occasional continuity established from one place in his past to another involves a suppression of great stretches of time; the painful jump from one scene to another is eliminated, and many years are compressed into a somewhat blurred continuity of originally discontinuous scenes. This opening passage gives us a highly melodramatic example of the Proustian experience of time and space. I shall return to what has been analyzed—especially by Georges Poulet [5]—as the spatialization of time in Proust's world, the discontinuity among different points in space (and time), and the attempt to remedy this discontinuity by spatial juxtapositions. It is enough to point out here one aspect of this complex: the narrator's dependence, for self-identification, on a stable arrangement of things in space, and the precarious nature both of these arrangements and, consequently, of the stability of the self.

The opening passage of "Combray" is, of course, also important because, as the narrator tells us, each of the bedrooms he remembers brings back different moments of his past which, throughout the book, he will recall in more detail. But it is also a suitable introduction to this massive work in the sense that the psychological state Marcel describes suggests his deepest fears about the instability of his self in the world. A passage in *La Fugitive* illustrates particularly well the nature of this basic anxiety. Marcel and his mother are about to leave Venice, but

after seeing in the hotel register, among the names of expected
guests, " 'Baronne Putbus et suite,' " (Saint-Loup has recom-
mended one of the baroness's chambermaids to him),[6] Marcel
tells his mother that he intends to stay. His mother, angry, leaves
for the station without him; he quickly loses his desire for sexual
pleasure and, after several moments of intense panic at the idea
of being left alone in Venice, he rushes to the station and joins
his mother just as the train is pulling out. The description of the
sequence of Marcel's feelings is interesting. After saying that the
Baronne de Putbus's name made "feverish" his constant desire
not to lose permanently certain women, he writes:

> [All at once, the "sentiment" of all the hours of sexual pleasure
> which I was going to lose because of our departure raised this de-
> sire—which was, in my case, a chronic desire—to the level of a
> "sentiment," and drowned it in melancholy and vagueness;] I
> asked my mother to put off our departure for a few days; her air
> of not taking my request into consideration, of not even listen-
> ing to it seriously, reawakened in my nerves, excited by the
> Venetian springtime, that old desire to rebel against an imag-
> inary plot woven against me by my parents (who imagined that
> I would be forced to obey them), that fighting spirit, that desire
> which drove me in the past to enforce my wishes upon the peo-
> ple whom I loved best in the world, prepared to conform to their
> wishes after I had succeeded in making them yield. I told my
> mother that I would not leave Venice, but she, thinking it more
> to her purpose not to appear to believe that I was saying this
> seriously, did not even answer. I went on to say that she would
> soon see whether I was serious or not.[7]

The description begins in rather complicated abstract language: the sense of the sexual pleasures Marcel may miss "raises"
the more general desire not to lose certain women to the "height"
of a feeling, and "drowns" this desire in melancholy and vagueness. This peculiar kind of inner chemistry strikes us at first as
awkward and somewhat confused. We could, for example, object
to the use of "sentiment" twice; the second time the narrator
seems to want to insist on the special quality of a "sentiment,"

that is, the profounder effects it has on behavior than does a simple desire, and the first time he means simply the idea or image of the pleasure he would be missing. And what is this "sentiment" which is the product of an image of carnal pleasure added to a desire to keep certain women close to him? The sentence suggests rather heavily the intensity of Marcel's wish to stay in Venice—a "sentiment" apparently commits the whole personality, is a deeper, more solemn need than a "chronic desire"— as well, perhaps, as a certain confusion about the reasons for this sudden concentration of feeling. Why should Marcel's wish be smothered in melancholy and vagueness, which necessarily qualify the anticipation of pleasure? An answer is suggested in the conflict with his mother described in the following sentences. The melancholy and vagueness seem to anticipate his mother's resistance *and* his resistance to her. Curiously, the image of sexual enjoyment both activates a general desire for women into a specific act of aggressiveness and is presented as the cause of the languorous sadness that undercuts the aggressiveness. It is as if the subsequent struggle with his mother and the accompanying guilt were somehow part of the anticipated sexual pleasure. Indeed, the baroness is never mentioned again in the passage, and the intense "sentiment" quickly becomes a nastily resolute resistance to what he now recognizes as a purely imaginary plot devised by his parents to force him to obey. The connection of this with the sexual wishes mentioned at the beginning of the passage is underlined by the narrator's suggestion that the excitement caused in his "nerves" by the Venetian spring explains partly both his need for women and his need to struggle with his mother. Sexual energy lends itself at once to the equally intense and perhaps related energy of hostility.

Marcel orders a drink and sits on the hotel porch, where he listens to a musician, in a boat in front of the hotel, sing *Sole mio*. It is then that he feels the full effect of having defied his mother:

> The sun continued to sink. My mother must be nearing the station. Presently, she would be gone, I should be left alone in Venice, alone with the misery of knowing that I had distressed

her, and without her presence to comfort me. The hour of the
train approached. My irrevocable solitude was so near at hand
that it seemed to me to have begun already and to be complete.
For I felt myself to be alone. Things had become alien to me. I
was no longer calm enough to draw from my throbbing heart
and introduce into them a measure of stability. The town that
I saw before me had ceased to be Venice. Its personality, its
name, seemed to me to be lying fictions which I no longer had
the courage to impress upon its stones. I saw the palaces reduced
to their constituent parts, lifeless heaps of marble with nothing
to choose between them, and the water as a combination of
hydrogen and oxygen, eternal, blind, anterior and exterior to
Venice, unconscious of Doges or of Turner. And yet this unre-
markable place was as strange as a place at which we have just
arrived, which does not yet know us—as a place which we have
left and which has forgotten us already. I could not tell it anything more about myself, I could leave nothing of myself imprinted upon it, it left me diminished, I was nothing more than
a heart that throbbed, and an attention strained to follow the development of 'sole mio.' In vain might I fix my mind despair-
ingly upon the beautiful and characteristic arch of the Rialto, it
seemed to me, with the mediocrity of the obvious, a bridge not
merely inferior to but as different from the idea that I possessed
of it as an actor with regard to whom, notwithstanding his fair
wig and black garments, we know quite well that in his essential
quality he is not Hamlet.[8]

To feel alone means, for Marcel, not only the absence of another
person, but, most painfully, his own absence. He has lost his
sense of himself; he is nothing more than a beating heart and an
attention anxiously following the notes of *Sole mio*. It seems that
he is sad not simply because he has caused his mother pain, but
also because this means that his mother now has an unfavorable
image of him; he would like her to come back to console him for
having hurt her! He has, in fact, always depended on her willingness to provide a certain image of himself. At the Guermantes
matinée in *Le Temps retrouvé*, the guests around Marcel laugh
when he says to Gilberte that he will dine alone with her if she

does not find it too compromising to be seen alone with a "young man." "I realised that the remark that had made them laugh was one that my mother, to whom I was always a child, might have made in speaking of me. From which I noticed that, when I wished to form an opinion of myself, I took the same point of view as she." [9] This dependence on the mother's image of her child profoundly affects Marcel's life. When he feels he can no longer count on her image of him, as in the Venice passage, he also feels that his mother has taken away with her his support, his strength, his identity.

The corollary of this sense of being emptied of personality is the frightening anonymity of the external world. Identifying the world is impossible when self-identification *in* the world has become impossible: "Things had become alien to me. I was no longer calm enough to draw from my throbbing heart and introduce into them a measure of stability." Recognizing Venice— that is, something different from himself—depends on his projecting himself on the city, but, after Marcel's mother's departure, "I could not tell it anything more about myself, I could leave nothing of myself imprinted upon it. . . ." Now to "place" a part of the self on the world seems to be exactly what we do in order to make familiar and assimilate what is different from the self. We perceive similarities between things in the outer world and images of the world we already possess mentally. These images come from our past, and they constitute our imagination in the sense in which Proust's narrator generally uses the term: all our experience that is our history at any moment, everything that is not an object of present sensory perception.[10] And since a present experience can never be exactly identical with a past experience, recognizing something past in something present means finding more or less precise analogies. There is therefore perhaps no essential difference between mnemonic and the most elaborate imaginative processes. Both involve the metaphorical activity of identifying one thing by calling it something else; to recognize an object we have seen just a few moments ago is, for example, to make a very simple analogy, and there seems to be only a differ-

ence of "distance" from the original object between such simple
recognition and poetic metaphors. The function of metaphor is
therefore epistemological: we learn by assimilating through analogy. Poulet has analyzed the passage in which Marcel, in church
at Combray, "possesses" the hawthorns he sees on the altar
through an "imitation" acted out spontaneously as a metaphor:

> Higher up on the altar, a flower had opened here and there
> with a careless grace, holding so unconcernedly, like a final,
> almost vaporous bedizening, its bunch of stamens, slender as
> gossamer, which clouded the flower itself in a white mist, that in
> following these with my eyes, in trying to imitate, somewhere
> inside myself, the action of their blossoming, I imagined it as a
> swift and thoughtless movement of the head with an enticing
> glance from her contracted pupils, by a young girl in white, care-
> less and alive.[11]

Poulet notes that, through this imitation, ". . . something is
created which is still the material object, but it is now internal
rather than external; it is no longer a foreign and impenetrable
thing, but can be penetrated, recognized, identified, for it comes
from and is part of ourselves." [12]

Marcel's metaphor is the result of his effort to assimilate something outside of himself. The effort he makes is significant, for
the most elaborately metaphorical imagination—such as Proust's
—may, so to speak, be energized into great activity by the constant threat of a failure in the simplest kind of recognition.[13]
Ordinarily we find the world familiar without explicitly formulating the analogies that probably account for its air of familiarity.
The interest of the Venice passage is that it illustrates a failure
of recognition and therefore—in the broadest sense—of imagination; and this failure is properly defined as a kind of ontological
crisis, a sudden deprivation of self. Marcel can no longer "tame"
the potentially fearful aspect of what is distinct from the self because he can no longer use his memory and imagination to resist
the threat of otherness with images already familiar to the self.
He is overcome by the present; it is as if he had just been born,
and, without a personal past, he sees in the city only an anony-

mous mass of matter. He is, moreover, peculiarly susceptible to this sort of crisis. And, as I shall show, the importance of metaphor in the work he writes can largely be accounted for by the original helplessness of his imagination. The richness and density of his analogies are strategies designed to make analogies no longer necessary, to reduce the world entirely to the images the self already possesses.

The narrator's account of the Venice incident suggests the kind of emotional context in which he is likely to be unable to identify the self and the world. The connection between Marcel's loss of his mother, his sense of having lost himself, and the loss of the city is underlined a couple of pages after the sentences already quoted: ["Not only was my mother no longer present in Venice, but as I was now not calm enough to let my attention settle on all the things around me, even I ceased to be present in these things; what is more, they ceased to be Venice; as if I alone had been responsible for breathing life into the stones of the palaces and the water of the Canal."] The psychological sequence here is, then, an excited sexual anticipation, his mother's thwarting his wishes, a violent resistance to her will, and a devastating punishment. The punishment is a separation, or rather several separations. Not only is Marcel isolated from his mother; he is cut off from himself and, finally, from the external world. No longer able to project himself on the city, and finding the city intractable to any idea of it he may have, Marcel is reduced to a state of breathless panic. But in spite of the pain he suffers, he is fascinated by his very anguish. He knows that he is choosing to stay:

> I knew very well that in reality it was the resolution not to go that I had adopted by the mere act of remaining where I was; but to say to myself: "I am not going," a speech which in that direct form was impossible, became possible in this indirect form: "I am going to listen to one more line of 'sole mio'"; but the practical significance of this figurative language did not escape me and, while I said to myself: "After all, I am only listening to another line," I knew that the words meant: "I shall

remain by myself at Venice." And it was perhaps this melancholy, like a sort of numbing cold, that constituted the desperate
but fascinating charm of the song.[14]

There is something strangely appealing in this pain, something
that holds and fascinates Marcel. It is the charm of an old habit,
of a psychological drama first acted out in Combray, and whose
rhythms and patterns run through Marcel's experience from his
early childhood to the years he will spend writing the novel of
his past.

II. *Self-effacement and self-projection*

The narrator finds a special charm in the memories of his boyhood at Combray because, he writes, he had a faith in the reality
of the external world which he has since lost. After describing his
walks along the Méséglise and Guermantes ways, he explains:
"It is because I [believed in] certain things, in certain people,
while I was roaming along them, that the things, the people
which they taught me to know, and these alone, I still take seriously, still give me joy." [15] The "Combray" section communicates
the naïve intellectual enthusiasms of the narrator as a young boy,
his passionate openness to experience. He thinks of the world as
possessing truths about to be revealed to him; he lives with a daily
sense of imminent discovery. This is the first version of the idea
of secrets in the outer world, which will be developed in more
sinister modes in the later volumes. In the books he reads, in the
hawthorns along the Méséglise way, in the life of Gilberte
Swann, Marcel senses a precious and tantalizing reality lying just
beyond his reach. His mental energy is directed toward "the
secret of Truth and Beauty, things half-felt by me, half-incom-
prehensible, the full understanding of which was the vague but
permanent object of my thoughts." [16] For the boy, "reality" is
what is different from him, the mysteries in the worlds of nature,
society, and art. "I was not curious," he writes after speaking of
his desire to find in a storm at sea near Balbec "the true life of
nature," "I did not thirst to know anything save what I believed

to be more genuine than myself, what had for me the supreme merit of shewing me a fragment of the mind of a great genius, or of the force or the grace of nature as she appeared when left entirely to herself, without human interference." [17]

The man who is writing the book no longer looks at the world with such expectations; but it is important to see that the boy he describes has his attention turned, even painfully, anxiously so, to the future, to its exciting revelations. It could be said that he lives without a sense of time; he is convinced that life has not begun yet for him, that the only "real" things in his experience are those the future will bring. Indeed, he reacts with a peculiar sadness when it is suggested that what he has already done or felt "counts," that he has a past for which he is responsible. At the beginning of *A l'Ombre des jeunes filles en fleur*, Marcel's father, influenced by Monsieur de Norpois's indulgent attitude toward a literary career, seems inclined to let Marcel choose definitively to be a writer rather than a diplomat. " 'He is no longer a child,' " he says to his wife. " 'He knows pretty well now what he likes, it is not at all probable that he will change, and he is quite capable of deciding for himself what will make him happy in life.' " Marcel's reaction—a characteristic one whenever one of his desires has been granted—is to begin to doubt himself that he really does want to write:

. . . as an author becomes alarmed when he sees the fruits of his own meditation, which do not appear to him to be of great value since he does not separate them from himself, oblige a publisher to choose a kind of paper, to employ a fount of type finer, perhaps, than they deserve, I asked myself whether my desire to write was of sufficient importance to justify my father in dispensing so much generosity. But apart from that, when he spoke of my inclinations as no longer liable to change, he awakened in me two terrible suspicions. The first was that (at a time when, every day, I regarded myself as standing upon the threshold of a life which was still intact and would not enter upon its course until the following morning) my existence was already begun, and that, furthermore, what was yet to follow would not

differ to any extent from what had already elapsed. The second
suspicion, which was nothing more, really, than a variant of the
first, was that I was not situated somewhere outside the realm of
Time, but was subject to its laws, just like the people in novels
who, for that reason, used to plunge me in such depression when
I read of their lives, down at Combray, in the fastness of my
wicker sentry-box.[18]

Marcel's reaction to discovering himself in time is, then, a kind of
anxious resistance; he would like to remain the empty, expectant
receptacle of future truths.

This state of expectation poses, naturally, the problem of
knowledge: if certain parts of the external world contain the
secrets of reality, how can Marcel possess these secrets? By what
process can he come to know something different from himself?
For Marcel, the condition for knowledge is a total suppression of
the differences between the self and the world. Reading in the
Combray garden, the boy is painfully aware of the consciousness
of self standing between the truths he feels are contained in the
book and his excited receptiveness to these truths:

> [And my thoughts, were they not like another nest in the depths
> of which I felt that I remained buried,] even when I was look-
> ing at what went on outside? When I saw any external object,
> my consciousness that I was seeing it would remain between
> me and it, enclosing it in a slender, incorporeal outline which
> prevented me from ever coming directly in contact with the
> material form; for it would volatise itself in some way before I
> could touch it, just as an incandescent body which is moved to-
> wards something wet never actually touches moisture, since it is
> always preceded, itself, by a zone of evaporation.[19]

The self is an obstacle to possessing the truths hidden in the external world; the only real possession of these truths would be in
a total identification with the world that contains them.

There is, of course, a time in our lives when we have the illusion of an identity of being between the self and something
which is in fact different from the self. Every infant painfully
discovers his physical distinctness from his mother's body; he

must learn to give up an instinctive sense of continuity between himself and the external world. It would, of course, be impossible to remain blind to the fact of separation, but, to a certain extent, the lesson may never be accepted. We see in the way Marcel clings to his grandmother in his anguish at being in a new room the first night they spend at Balbec, that at moments when the world seems to threaten him, he calms his anxiety by thinking of his body as being one with hers:

> . . . I knew, when I was with my grandmother, that, however great the misery that there was in me, it would be received by her with a pity still more vast; that everything that was mine, my cares, my wishes, would be, in my grandmother, supported upon a desire to save and prolong my life stronger than was my own; and my thoughts were continued in her without having to undergo any deflection, since they passed from my mind into hers without change of atmosphere or of personality. And—like a man who tries to fasten his necktie in front of a glass and forgets that the end which he sees reflected is not on the side to which he raises his hand, or like a dog that chases along the ground the dancing shadow of an insect in the air—misled by her appearance in the body as we are apt to be in this world where we have no direct perception of people's souls, I threw myself into the arms of my grandmother and clung with my lips to her face as though I had access thus to that immense heart which she opened to me. And when I felt my mouth glued to her cheeks, to her brow, I drew from them something so beneficial, so nourishing that I lay in her arms as motionless, as solemn, as calmly gluttonous as a babe at the breast.[20]

Marcel, like an infant, finds the very source of his being in his grandmother's body; he is empty, without a sufficient will to live unless he attaches himself to this body, incorporates its strength. And at moments when the external world excites him rather than terrifies him, Marcel wishes for the same kind of oneness with it which he imagines having with his grandmother in this passage. There is, obviously, psychological continuity between his reliance on her strength in the Balbec hotel and his expecting to find a fulfilling, "nourishing" reality somewhere in the external world. In both the anguished need to touch his grandmother's heart and Marcel's exceptionally sharp sensitivity to the limited knowledge we can have of the world, there is clearly a persistent and fundamental need to merge with a source of strength outside of himself. What seems to me most significant here is not the narrator's intellectual awareness of the "slender incorporeal outline" of self-consciousness which prevents him from directly touching the substance of an external object, but rather the intensity with which this is felt as a privation. Marcel experiences his own subjectivity not merely as an obstacle to an accurate description of the world; more profoundly, it prevents him from *being* something else, condemns him to an incomplete, unfulfilling existence.

The fantasy of an identity between the self and the world can, however, be highly ambiguous. Superficially, Marcel seems only impatient with the self that keeps him from penetrating the "more real" life of nature; he is almost anxious to give up his own being in order to become something else. But he is also tempted by a paradoxical identification with something outside of himself which would *not* involve a loss of self. This fantasy is humorously suggested in the magic lantern passage at the beginning of "Combray." Golo uses the objects in Marcel's bedroom as bone structures for his body; he takes the form of whatever his image touches. But if his shape becomes that of the doorknob, the doorknob is also covered with his features: he remains Golo at the same time that he becomes something else.[21] He provides the narrator with a fanciful version of a peculiar relation between the self and the world, one in which each is absorbed by the other without, however, losing its individual identity. Throughout the novel we see Marcel's ambivalent feelings toward the value of his own personality and the value of what is entirely different from himself in a constant shifting from a fantasy of suppressing the self to a fantasy of suppressing the world. The passage describing his anguish in Balbec is a good example of this: he imagines identifying himself with his grandmother's strength by absorbing her. His need to be something wholly different seems equivalent to the need to transform something wholly different into himself.

The abundance of eating and digestion metaphors in *A la Recherche du temps perdu* has often been pointed out; they suggest this changing of a world of resistant matter into something more easily taken in and assimilated. When Marcel clings to his grandmother, he imagines becoming one with her by eating the substance of her strength. In fact, any kind of intimacy, bringing with it knowledge of the other person's secret nature, is imagined as physical assimilation. Marcel wonders for a long time about the taste of Albertine's cheeks; he speaks of being "famished" for her, writes that love tends to "the complete assimilation of another person," and notes with regret that ". . . other people are not comestible by way of conversation alone. . . ." [22] When Gilberte begins to call him by his first name, it seems to Marcel that, in this new closeness between them, she has taken his deepest individuality into her mouth by pronouncing his name:

> And when I recalled, later, what I had felt at the time, I could distinguish the impression of having been held, for a moment, in her mouth, myself, naked, without, any longer, any of the social qualifications which belonged equally to her other companions and, when she used my surname, to my parents, accessories of which her lips—by the effort that she made, a little after her father's manner, to articulate the words to which she wished to give a special value—had the air of stripping, of divesting me, as one peels the skin from a fruit of which one is going to put only the pulp into one's mouth, while her glance, adapting itself to the same new degree of intimacy as her speech, fell on me also more directly, not without testifying to the consciousness, the pleasure, even the gratitude that it felt, accompanying itself with a smile. [23]

Elsewhere in the novel the narrator suggests similarities between esthetic pleasure and the pleasure of eating. On the Méséglise way he prefers the pink hawthorns to the white ones largely because the former are more closely connected with the memory of tasting pink biscuits or crushed strawberries on cream cheese:

And these flowers had chosen precisely the colour of some edible and delicious thing, or of some exquisite addition to one's costume for a great festival, which colours, inasmuch as they make plain the reason for their superiority, are those whose beauty is most evident to the eyes of children, and for that reason must always seem more vivid and more natural than any other tints, even after the child's mind has realised that they offer no gratification to the appetite, and have not been selected by the dressmaker.[24]

Jean Pommier points to another passage in "Combray," where, as he says, the esthetic feeling is seen mainly as a derivative of the desire to eat, as a *pis aller*. The narrator is speaking of the buttercups along the Guermantes way:

For the buttercups grew past numbering on this spot which they had chosen for their games among the grass, standing singly, in couples, in whole companies, yellow as the yolk of eggs, and glowing with an added lustre, I felt, because, being powerless to consummate with my palate the pleasure which the sight of them never failed to give me, I would let it accumulate as my eyes ranged over their gilded expanse, until it had acquired the strength to create in my mind a fresh example of absolute, unproductive beauty. . . .[25]

The narrator does not, interestingly enough, say that the flowers' beauty is the cause of his pleasure; it is rather the pleasure he feels that makes them seem beautiful. And the perception of beauty is not, I think, a substitute for the desire to eat; it seems rather to accompany the satisfaction, on a non-physical level, of a desire to assimilate. The flowers are highly suggestive: not only does their color evoke the yellow in eggs, but in the sentence immediately preceding the passage just quoted, the narrator also mentions "the remote, incomprehensible features" of Combray in the past, which seem half hidden under the buttercups. In looking at the buttercups, Marcel sees more than the buttercups: they evoke images of food and of the local past. The brilliance of their surface perhaps takes on a slightly hallucinatory aspect, due both to the extensions Marcel's imagination gives to this surface and to the addition of oral energy to visual energy. The fantasy of eating egg yolks is the literal aspect of a larger process of assimilation: Marcel has "taken in" the flowers by adding to their physical presence his mental associations. His retrospective possession of the world when he writes his literary work is, as I shall show much later in greater detail, made possible by just this sort of progress from physical to metaphorical assimilation.

The fantasy of knowing by eating points to some of the ambiguities in the narrator's attitude toward the external world. As a boy he thinks of truth and reality as outside of himself; he is waiting for revelations meaningful enough to count as "life." He feels impatient with his own personality, with the consciousness of self that stands between his intensely expectant attention and the external sources of truth. But the eating images obviously suggest possession not only by passively becoming something else, but also by transforming what is desired into Marcel's system—on the literal level, his digestive system, and, psychologically and intellectually, the "system" of his individual style or point of view. Marcel's posture of expectation involves much activity, although he claims at times that he wants to bring nothing of himself to his contacts with other people and things. His desires to visit Balbec, to meet Madame de Guermantes, to be introduced to Albertine and her friends, are all accompanied by rather elaborate, specific images of what these experiences will be like. The Balbec he dreams of is a town of Gothic architecture and violent sea storms; the meeting with Madame de Guermantes is imagined as a contact with the mystery of the Merovingian age, and he expects her to personify the charm of his walks along the Vivonne, to be the living equivalent of a medieval tapestry or a stained-glass window; and he thinks of his meeting with Albertine as a doubly glamorous discovery of the life of the sea and the erotic immorality of cruel, sensual girls. The desire to empty the self of anything personal, to present a *tabula rasa* on which the great secrets of life can be printed, is accompanied by a wish to find the external equivalent of a picture carefully elaborated by, and revealing the nature of, his own imagination.

In a passage in which the narrator talks of his wish to visit the countries he read about as a boy—"an enormous advance towards the ultimate conquest of truth"—we see this hesitation between situating the object of his constant desire in the outside world or in his own imagination:

> Had my parents allowed me, when I read a book, to pay a visit to the country it described, I should have felt that I was making an enormous advance towards the ultimate conquest of truth. For even if we have the sensation of being always enveloped in, surrounded by our own soul, still it does not seem a fixed and immovable prison; rather do we seem to be borne away with it, and perpetually struggling to pass beyond it, to break out into the world, with a perpetual discouragement as we hear endlessly, all around us, that unvarying sound which is no echo from without, but the resonance of a vibration from within. We try to discover in things, endeared to us on that account, the spiritual glamor which we ourselves have cast upon them; we are disillusioned, and learn that they are in themselves barren and devoid of the charm which they owed, in our minds, to the association of certain ideas; sometimes we mobilise all our spiritual forces in a glittering array so as to influence and subjugate other human beings who, as we very well know, are situated outside ourselves, where we can never reach them.[26]

The degree of the narrator's sympathy with the boy's wishes is clear. It is true that he is describing a special period of adolescent exaltation in his life. But, by his use of the present and his generalizing of boyhood aspirations and disillusionments into a universal human fact, we see that the categories in which he thinks of his experience have not essentially changed since the time he is describing. Now the source of discouragement changes in the middle of the passage: at first he complains of hearing only "the resonance of a vibration from within" when he tries to reach the external world, but then he speaks of being disappointed at not finding in things "the spiritual glamor which we ourselves have cast upon them." The "charm" of things is in the images we have projected on them, but in nature the objects we desire are in a new atmosphere, detached from the private associations that make them appealing to us. Our deepest wish, the narrator suggests, is to find the incarnation of that which it seems impossible to know as a concrete, sensory experience: the contents of our imagination. External reality is disappointing *because* it is different, because it does not send back to us the material equivalents of our dreams.

Some of the intellectual consequences of these unsettled feelings about the relationship between the self and the external world are emphasized in Marcel's disappointment with the Balbec church he had been so anxious to see. The scene he had imagined—the foam of sea waves at the base of the church's tower, the statue of the Virgin that his mind "had carved a thousand times," an "ideal" statue "endowed with universal value"— is brutally replaced by a church of real stone about twelve miles from the sea, in the middle of a square crossed by trolley lines and surrounded by a café, a branch office of the Comptoir d'Escompte, and a pastry shop. The word "Balbec" no longer contains a Gothic church beaten by the sea, or truths about nature, history, and art; it will now evoke for Marcel a particular afternoon in which he saw a certain church in a certain village. And there is, in the tone of the narrator's description of his feelings as a boy, a note of lingering disappointment, a sadness at having had to recognize and accept the particular, contingent nature of things in which he had hoped to find timeless, universal truths. The boy tries to tell himself that what he is seeing is "far greater" than the photographs of the church he has seen, but the narrator adds that it was also perhaps less. The church seems like an "accident"; its stones can be measured, dirtied, defaced; they are subject to "the tyranny of the Individual." [27] His disillusionment is twofold and paradoxical: the church does not reflect his fantasies about it and, on the other hand, it is too much a part of the ordinary, contingent world with which he is already familiar.

Now Marcel has both a highly abstract turn of mind and an intense but distrustful sense of concrete reality. His way of thinking about his experience often seems Platonic: he feels that there must be eternal truths of nature, art, and love, truths more important than his experience of any particular countryside, painting, or woman. In his fantasies he is more excited by abstract categories than by specific people and places. Each person and each place carry with them the secret of a way of life—Albertine and the essence of the sea, Madame de Guermantes and the glamorous past of France, Madame de Stermaria and the soul of Brittany.[28] But the specific people and places are important, for he seems to feel that in certain parts of the visible world still unknown to him, the "ideas" are perfectly incarnated. While he conceives of truth as abstract and eternal, he also feels that any satisfactory contact with it must be through the senses, in the visible, external world. And the particular, temporal nature of this world defeats his expectations again and again. The experiences of involuntary memory presumably satisfy Marcel's need for a sensory contact with an extratemporal reality. But it seems to me that the conflict is never completely resolved, and even when the narrator is judging his early illusions as naïve, we see from time to time this persistently abstract and theoretical way of thinking about experience. Whatever is "realised," he says a few pages after describing his reaction to the Balbec church, is "sterilising." [29] All that is worthy of his attention loses its value as soon as it becomes an object of his attention. His ideas must have equivalents in direct sensory experience, but the equivalence is never perfect, and his ideas seem doomed to an abstract, entirely mental life.

But before being recognized as intellectually unacceptable, the external world is felt as dangerous. Marcel is painfully aware of the weak resistance he can make to new realities. He wants something totally new, a revelation, but, because of a sense of his own psychic fragility, he fears being submerged, overwhelmed by anything unfamiliar. At Balbec, what is essentially an intellectual disappointment in front of the church becomes acute anxiety by the time Marcel arrives at the hotel. In his new room, his body, as he says, remains vigilantly on guard; the new objects around him are hostile, insolently indifferent to his existence:

It is our noticing them that puts things in a room, our growing used to them that takes them away again and clears a space for us. Space there was none for me in my bedroom (mine in name only) at Balbec; it was full of things which did not know me, which flung back at me the distrustful look that I had cast at them, and, without taking any heed of my existence, shewed that I was interrupting the course of theirs. . . . I kept raising my eyes—which the things in my room in Paris disturbed no more than did my eyelids themselves, for they were merely extensions of my organs, an enlargement of myself—towards the fantastically high ceiling of this belvedere planted upon the summit of the hotel which my grandmother had chosen for me; and in that region more intimate than those in which we see and hear, that region in which we test the quality of odours, almost in the very heart of my inmost self, the smell of flowering grasses next launched its offensive against my last feeble line of trenches, where I stood up to it, not without tiring myself still further, with the futile incessant defence of an anxious sniffing. Having no world, no room, no body now that was not menaced by the enemies thronging round me, invaded to the very bones by fever, I was utterly alone; I longed to die.[30]

The narrator is describing this anguish from a position of security. A good many things have happened since that first night in Balbec—things ultimately connected with his decision to write —which make it possible for him to remember his fears with a certain humor. To describe his anxiety, he personifies parts of the room, talks of the clock making nasty remarks about him, remarks with which the curtains obviously agree. By talking of objects as if they were human, the narrator underlines, from a detached, more realistic point of view, the groundlessness of his anxiety. But he is far from dismissing the incident as insignificant. It illustrates, in spite of its humorous aspect in the more reasonable perspective of memory, a general truth about the relation between habit and our awareness of the external world, a psychological law summarized in the first sentence of the passage I have just quoted. And the narrator insists on the fact that he felt himself attacked in the deepest regions of the self; the odor of grasses penetrated, almost overcame his whole being. Marcel's fear (mentioned in a sentence I have not quoted) that the clock is making "uncomplimentary observations" about him is comical, but it also brings to mind his fears that the women he loves are laughing at him with their friends. The passage is another example of his peculiar vulnerability, the way in which, when he is placed in a setting for which he is not prepared, which he has not been able to represent to himself in advance, his resistance to the world disintegrates. He can make no connections between the dangerous present and a familiar past; his ability to find analogies, to make compromises and transitions, deserts him. This helps, of course, to explain the narrator's ambivalent attitude toward habit. Habit deadens his sensibility, makes his existence a kind of cliché; on the other hand, it protects him from the shock of an unfamiliar world, saves his personality from the assaults of a perhaps hostile and fearfully strong environment. As Samuel Beckett points out, the periods between the consecutive adaptations of habit "represent the perilous zones in the life of the individual, dangerous, precarious, painful, mysterious and fertile, when for a moment the boredom of living is replaced by the suffering of being." [31] It is precisely because the narrator's sense of self is so easily broken down that his most urgent need is to find himself reflected in the outer world, to substitute self-images for the potentially dangerous surprises of the world.

Self-recognition is, for Marcel, self-assurance. For the desire to find in the world only an image of himself is often the solution to his sense of the dangers for the self hidden in the world. We see in the *drame du coucher* incident described in "Combray," and in the narrator's generalization of his anguish as a child to the anguish of all men in love, the urgency of this need to force an image of himself on a hostilely different reality. Separated from his mother, who is downstairs at dinner with the rest of the family and Swann, Marcel feels he must make her come to him; but his anguish is already somewhat relieved when he thinks of his mother reading the note he has tricked Françoise into bringing to her:

At once my anxiety subsided; it was now no longer (as it had been a moment ago) until to-morrow that I had lost my mother, for my little line was going—to annoy her, no doubt, and doubly so because this contrivance would make me ridiculous in Swann's eyes—but was going all the same to admit me, invisibly and by stealth, into the same room as herself, was going to whisper from me into her ear; for that forbidden and unfriendly dining-room, where but a moment ago the ice itself—with burned nuts in it—and the finger-bowls seemed to me to be concealing pleasures that were mischievous and of a mortal sadness because Mamma was tasting of them and I was far away, had opened its doors to me and, like a ripe fruit which bursts through its skin, was going to pour out into my intoxicated heart the gushing sweetness of Mamma's attention while she was reading what I had written. Now I was no longer separated from her; the barriers were down; an exquisite thread was binding us. Besides, that was not all, for surely Mamma would come.[32]

It is the idea of his mother's *attention* that relieves Marcel; *he* is now downstairs too, an image of himself has penetrated into the forbidden atmosphere. The idea of physical pleasure is suggested both in what separates them and in what will bring them together: his mother is enjoying harmful pleasures, and the dining room, like an overripe fruit breaking its skin, discharges toward him the consciousness now filled with the words of his desperate note.

The narrator is, of course, aware of describing the feelings of an anxious child when he speaks of the evil pleasures being offered to his mother downstairs, and he adopts the child's point of view with the mixture of sympathy and gentle mockery characteristic of many passages in the early volumes. In the following paragraph, we see, however, that he thinks of the *drame du coucher* as prefiguring and already containing all the elements of anguish in love, which in Proust always means jealous love. He felt as a child that Swann would have made fun of his suffering if he had known about it. But, having since learned of Swann's love for Odette and having himself loved several women, he now realizes that these childish anxieties are "prep-

arations" for the adult's experience of love. As a child, he loves
Françoise for having ended the separation between him and his
mother; as men, we all feel a similar affection for the friend who,
at the dinner or theatre-party from which we are excluded, tells
the woman we love that we want to see her at once:

> How much we love him—as at that moment I loved Françoise—
> the good-natured intermediary who by a single word has made
> supportable, human, almost propitious the inconceivable, in-
> fernal scene of gaiety in the thick of which we had been imag-
> ining swarms of enemies, perverse and seductive, beguiling
> away from us, even making laugh at us, the woman whom we
> love. If we are to judge of them by him, this relative who has
> accosted us and who is himself an initiate in those cruel mys-
> teries, then the other guests cannot be so very demoniacal. Those
> inaccessible and torturing hours into which she had gone to
> taste of unknown pleasures—behold, a breach in the wall, and
> we are through it. Behold, one of the moments whose series will
> go to make up their sum, a moment as genuine as the rest, if
> not actually more important to ourself because our mistress is
> more intensely a part of it; we picture it to ourselves, we possess
> it, we intervene upon it, almost we have created it: namely, the
> moment in which he goes to tell her that we are waiting there
> below. And very probably the other moments of the party will
> not be essentially different, will contain nothing else so exquisite
> or so well able to make us suffer, since this kind friend has as-
> sured us that "Of course, she will be delighted to come down!
> It will be far more amusing for her to talk to you than to be
> bored up there." [33]

Separation—and this will, of course, be painfully true for Marcel
in his love for Albertine—seems to mean two things: the person
we love is enjoying unimaginable and evil pleasures, and she is
in an atmosphere hostile to us where she may be made to laugh
at us. What relieves the anguish caused by this idea is a kind of
knowledge. We "create" one of the moments that make up the
hours the loved one spends away from us; the threateningly
blank face of those pleasures is suddenly filled with our own
image when our friend tells the woman that we would like to

speak with her. And if she comes, we can partly imagine what she has been doing: her mysterious life away from us cannot be too different from, or too much more enjoyable than her life with us, since her image of that life has not prevented her from responding to her image of us.

The seemingly contradictory desires to penetrate a mysterious and fulfilling reality completely distinct from the self, and yet to find in the outer world the "charm" of his own reveries, are, in Marcel, two aspects of a single psychological process. His attitudes toward nature, society, and literature are analogous to his feelings about the women he loves. Somewhere beyond his personal experience an exotically mysterious life is being lived. For the child, this life consists of his mother's pleasures when she is away from him; as his intellectual life develops, a new but parallel vocabulary takes form, and somewhere hidden in nature or art is the truth or reality that will bring him definitive answers about life. But the yearning toward this unknown life or these unknown truths is experienced, to a large extent, as an extremely painful exclusion. Marcel feels hopelessly separated from what will calm him, or complete him, or, even, be the beginning of his "real" life, give him the necessary weight and content to exist in time. Now it seems that the idea of the real is so inextricably linked with the idea of the unknown that inaccessibility is the sign by which Marcel recognizes something worth knowing or possessing. As a result, the actual contact with Balbec, or with Berma's style of acting, or with the Guermantes circle, by the very fact of being an actual contact, destroys that sign of the unreachable which, for the narrator, adheres necessarily to truth. And his attempt to reduce the other reality to a reflection of himself is, in part, a solution to this painful sense of exile. This effort can be seen in the frantic need to implant his name in someone's attention, as well as in his elaborate fantasies of what it would be like to live with a certain person or in a certain place. Especially with someone he loves, knowing and therefore possessing the other person would mean believing that her life is really like his, a belief encouraged by the woman's ability to include his image along with her other images of experience. If the two sets of images can be contiguous in her mind, there is perhaps no essential difference between her life and his life. This obviously takes away the possibility of ever having that revelation of a marvelous, unimaginable reality that excites Marcel when he is very young; indeed, the narrator traces the stages of his loss of faith in finding any important truths in the external world. Not only do these truths fail to appear to Marcel; as we see in his relationship with his mother and with the woman he loves, the sense of a life different from his own is, finally, too painful to be kept, especially when that life seems full of forbidden pleasures, and to involve hostile mockery of him.

III. *The vulnerable self and its many deaths*

To be different, that is, to be individual, comes, then, to have connotations of sin for Marcel. Speaking of his unrealizable desire to possess Albertine's whole existence, he remarks that the "original sin" of certain women is personality itself: "And then, even more than their misdeeds while we are in love with them, there are their misdeeds before we made their acquaintance, and first and foremost: their nature." [34] This sin is what prevents the paradise of total identification; it is what makes both the self and the world dangerous and fascinating. And the individuality of the women he loves seems often to consist of their mysterious desires, or of their secret enjoyment of pleasures from which Marcel is excluded. But Marcel can also conceive of himself as causing pain because of pleasures *he* wants. In Venice, his desire for women is a sin that must be replaced by obedience to his mother. For this desire is immediately followed by the extinction of desire and the sense of a loss of being. Separateness, then, is not only feared; it is, to a certain extent, also wished for. In speaking of his mother, the narrator does not explicitly analyze this desire for separation. With Albertine he periodically feels the desire to be free of her, to begin a new life with other desires. But when she leaves him and, soon after, dies, he feels guilty about her death, wonders if, because of his constant talk about separation, he is not indirectly responsible for what has happened.

In "Combray" similar feelings are suggested. In spite of the rather vague chronology of this section—how old is Marcel at the times of the different episodes he describes? how far into adolescence is he by the end of the first volume?—it seems clear that the anxious need for his mother's kiss described on the first pages lasts well into his teens. He recalls adolescent sexual fantasies and experiences and then, at the end of "Combray," writes that his excited walks during the day alternated with his nightly anguish of having to go to bed and lose his mother's presence until the next morning. It is striking not only that the narrator seems to find nothing peculiar about this need lasting into his adolescence, but also that it continues at a time when Marcel is experiencing pleasures and fantasies that necessarily set up barriers between himself and his mother, that increase the distance between them. This is the time of a great physical and intellectual awakening for Marcel; his energies are far ahead of his capacity for expression, and he can, for example, articulate the enthusiasm he feels at certain impressions of nature only by waving his umbrella and shouting: "Zut, zut, zut, zut." Impressions of nature, and also the intense desire to see a peasant girl suddenly appear before him during his walks along the Méséglise way: the two kinds of exaltation seem essentially the same to him, nourish and intensify each other, ". . . and, my imagination drawing strength from contact with my sensuality, my sensuality expanding through all the realms of my imagination, my desire had no longer any bounds." But the exaltation soon turns into a bitter rage. From the toilet at the top of his family's home in Combray, he "implores" the Roussainville dungeon-keep in vain to send him a girl from the village; in vain he waits in his walks for a woman to appear from behind a tree,

> . . . and it was no longer in lightness of heart, but with sullen anger that I aimed blows at the trees of Roussainville wood,

from among which no more living creatures made their appearance than if they had been trees painted on the stretched canvas
background of a panorama, when, unable to resign myself to
having to return home without having held in my arms the
woman I so greatly desired, I was yet obliged to retrace my steps
toward Combray, and to admit to myself that the chance of her
appearing in my path grew smaller every moment.

The frustration is that he is thrown back on himself, on what
are for him the complicated and dangerous pleasures of mas-
turbation:

. . . with the heroic scruples of a traveller setting forth for unknown climes, or of a desperate wretch hesitating on the verge of
self-destruction, faint with emotion, I explored, across the bounds
of my own experience, an untrodden path which, I believed,
might lead me to my death, even. . . .

With a certain anguish, then, he discovers new pleasures in the
self, and he stops believing that his desires can exist outside of
himself, are shared by other people; they are only "the purely
subjective, impotent, illusory creatures of my temperament."
They seem no longer connected to nature, and external reality
becomes only the "conventional framework" in which he can
create these novels of desire.[35] The search for fulfillment outside
of himself, an angry disillusionment with a world unresponsive
to his desires, the turning back to an exciting but perhaps dangerous self: Marcel's later attitudes toward traveling, love, and
society, toward a life of social commitments and a life of cul-
tivating memory, repeat the rhythm and conclusions of this
adolescent drama.

The erotic and intellectual enthusiasms, the solitary pleasures
and the imaginary pleasures with the girl from Méséglise, make
up Marcel's daytime life at Combray, but the nights are given to
the *drame du coucher,* to the anguish of being separated from
maman. So violent is the shift of mood that the narrator dates
from this period his sense of independent, wholly discontinuous
personalities in his life:

And so it was from the 'Guermantes way' that I learned to distinguish between these states which reigned alternately in my
mind, during certain periods, going so far as to divide every day
between them, each one returning to dispossess the other with
the regularity of a fever and ague: contiguous, and yet so foreign to one another, so devoid of means of communication, that
I could no longer understand, or even picture to myself, in one
state what I had desired or dreaded or even done in the other.[36]

At Combray these discontinuous states are two antagonistic
needs: on the one hand, the need to have his mother at his side
at every moment, the fear, especially, of being alone at night
without her; on the other hand, the need to express and affirm
his own personality, to act on the world directly through his own
desires instead of through the protection of his mother. The excitement and the longing he describes clearly suggest the confused enthusiasm of the adolescent at the discovery of his own
strength, the experiments with different possibilities—intellectual
abstractions, romantic fantasies, erotic activity—of giving expression to his individuality. But his strength fails at night; he becomes just a "throbbing heart"; his self is with his mother and he
must have her in order to have it. And these states *feel* so different—the total helplessness coming immediately after the energetic
curiosities about nature and about women—that he comes to have
a kind of shocked view of time. Where is its continuity, can there
be such a thing as duration if he loses so suddenly all the projects
for life of the afternoon?

It is possible, I think, to find hints in the text of a psychological
connection between these two states. In the Venice passage the
link seems clear between the narrator's independence from and
resistance to his mother, and the immediate punishment of a loss
of self. There are at times suggestions of an abortive attempt to
break this tie. At Combray, in spite of Marcel's efforts to have his
mother with him at night, he partly approves of her resistance,
and, at the end of *Le Temps retrouvé*, the narrator significantly
speaks of the night she gave in and stayed in his room as a crucial
defeat for *his* life, not only for his mother: "It was that evening,

when my mother abdicated her authority, which marked the
commencement of the waning of my will power and my health,
as well as the beginning of my grandmother's lingering death." [37]
Marcel's mother encourages him to be less dependent on her,
although it is interesting that after her own mother dies she tries
to become more and more like her, as if it would be sinful to go
on expressing aspects of her character that do not remind her of
her mother's character.[38] There is, then, some indication that
Marcel is raised in a home where, in spite of the apparent good
sense of his parents, there is such a profound sense of oneness in
the family that both he and his mother cannot help but consider
their individual existence as a kind of guilty betrayal of family
love. The nasty hostility Marcel shows toward his mother in the
Venice scene suggests that his struggle for independence is only
partly successful. (This sort of rebelliousness is, incidentally,
more discreetly shown in A la Recherche than in Jean Santeuil,
where, for example, we see Jean brutally insulting his mother
and father in a fit of uncontrollable rage when they try to cure
him of his infatuation for Marie Kossichef.) [39] The passages from
"Combray" which I have been discussing do not present Marcel's
daytime state and his nighttime state as cause and effect, but the
evidence of the Venice passage, the persistence of the evening
anguish into adolescence, and, finally, Marcel's feeling that he has
completely lost his stronger self when night comes, certainly indicate the extreme fragility of his self-affirmations, and also imply
that the reason for this fragility is a fear of punishment. I shall
soon be considering in some detail a passage in which the narrator speaks of his love for Albertine as a punishment for a crime
against his family; and Albertine makes him suffer because her
elusiveness and mystery prevent him not only from knowing her,
but also from using her to objectify a stable image of himself.
Marcel never really loses the belief that his mother—and later the
women he loves—has the power to take away his strength, his
individuality. It is as if his efforts at independence were sinful
because they are, so to speak, attempts to transfer the possession

of himself from his mother to him. They are a kind of betrayal, partly wished for but also partly denied.

Marcel's attitudes toward time are a result of (and perhaps, in part, a solution to) these fears. He lacks a sense of duration; he has never experienced the passage of time because he cannot imagine his identity as something accumulating and persisting in time. He interprets the loss of his love for Albertine or for his grandmother as a death of personality: ". . . my life appeared to me—offering a succession of periods in which, after a certain interval, nothing of what had sustained the previous period survived in that which followed—as something . . . devoid of the support of an individual, identical and permanent self. . . ."[40] Marcel's identity is given to him in a series of pictures, but, as in space, there are gaps between the pictures, areas of emptiness.[41] If it is true that we measure time by a series of changing images, the faculty we call memory is what assures us that these pictures do have a continuity, that they make up the history of a single life. But the three thousand pages of memories in *A la Recherche du temps perdu* are written by a man who has lived most of his life with a peculiar infirmity of memory. The feelings experienced in certain settings seem to adhere to the external settings themselves; with the disappearance of the person or the place associated with a moment from his past, he laments the loss of a whole personality. There seems to be no overlap of feeling, nothing to convince him of a single, continuous history; between two moments in time he therefore finds the same discontinuity as between two points in space. Even after the Guermantes *matinée,* when images from the past come back with the feelings attached to them, Marcel still deduces the fact of a continuous personality in a peculiarly detached and intellectual way:

> When the bell [the Combray garden bell, which he hears ringing again] tinkled, I was already in existence and, since that night, for me to have been able to hear the sound again, there must have been no break of continuity, not a moment of rest for me, no cessation of existence, of thought, of consciousness of myself, since this distant moment still clung to me and I could

recapture it, go back to it, merely by descending more deeply
within myself.[42]

The fact that his past is still alive in him is an extraordinary revelation, for different desires and interests have always appeared
to him as different selves. In each situation Marcel takes a "still
shot" of himself, one he wants to keep for ontological reference.
To stop loving a woman, for example, means that his self is
"afloat" again, and the anguished doubts about his capacity to
resist the external world reappear. Time is melodramatically con-
ceived of as a series of deaths and resurrections; between two
states of mind there are a gap and a rebirth, not a process of
accumulation and development. And the emotional background
for this extreme weakness in Marcel's affective memory is perhaps in some feeling—illustrated in what he says about his daytime and nighttime personalities at Combray—of a psychological
and moral contradiction between two states of mind, a contradiction felt to be so great that the only way in which he can deal
with it is to shut off all communication between the two states,
to convince himself that they belong to two different people.

At the end of *Le Temps retrouvé*, when the narrator talks
about his decision to write his book, we find the same curious
mixture of attitudes toward the contents of the self. His reactions
here remind us of the mixed feelings of exhilaration and fear
when, as a boy, he discovered his strength at Combray. Part of
this strength seemed to him connected to death, his enthusiasms
made for a painful inarticulateness, and most of his life he has
felt a painful anguish when people have suggested that he has
been using his strength, making and defining a self for which he
is responsible. In *Le Temps retrouvé*, Marcel has at first a
"rational fear" of death: he wonders if he will have the time to
write his book. And one evening after the Guermantes *matinée*,
he has, indeed, an experience which suggests that his death may
be near. Out on a visit, he almost falls three times going down a
staircase, after which he feels that he no longer has any memory,
strength, thought, or indeed any existence at all.[43] He will con-

tinue writing, but from this evening on he will be as indifferent
to his work as to anything else in his life, and he will live with
the obsessive idea of death and a joyless need to rid himself of
this great weight of the past he is carrying in his body. He writes
that he was astonished to find himself indifferent to his sense of
weakness, to his remorse for having wasted so many years:

> . . . the truth is that, from the day when my legs had trembled
> so as I descended the stairs, I had become indifferent to every-
> thing; I craved nothing now but rest, while waiting for the long
> rest that would eventually come. . . . In reality, if I thought of
> my work and not at all of the letters to be answered, this was no
> longer because I recognised any great difference in importance
> between the two objects, as I had done in the days of my idleness
> and then in the time of my active work up to the evening when
> I was obliged to seize hold of the railing of the staircase. The
> organisation of my memory and my preoccupations was closely
> bound up with my work, perhaps because, whereas the letters
> were forgotten immediately after being received, the idea of my
> work was in my mind, always the same, in a perpetual state of
> development. But it also had become irksome to me. . . . Since
> that day on the staircase, nothing concerning the social world,
> no happiness, whether it came from [people's friendship,] the
> progress of my work, the hope of fame, any longer penetrated
> to my consciousness except as such a pale ray of sunlight that it
> no longer had the power to warm me, put life into me, give me
> any desire whatsoever; and even at that, wan though it was, it
> was still too dazzling for my eyes and I preferred to close them
> and turn my head toward the wall.[44]

But how can the energy for an enormously complex literary
construction come from such tired indifference? The writing of
the book appears even more mysterious when we read that the
idea of death has become a conscious, constant preoccupation:
". . . now the thought of it adhered to the deepest stratum of
my brain so completely that I could not turn my attention to
anything without first relating it to the idea of death and, even
if I was not occupied with anything but was in a state of com-

plete repose, the idea of death was with me as continuously as the idea of myself." [45] In deciding to write his work the narrator renounces any kind of future for himself except a literary future; what is striking in these passages, however, is his distance from even this kind of life. And if we are to take what he says seriously, the main impetus to writing seems to be a frightened need to unload himself of the oppressive weight of his past, that is, of his self. On the last two or three pages of the novel he speaks of being frightened at the thought that the bell of the garden door at Combray is still ringing in him, and he becomes dizzy at the idea of all the past on which his present self must "balance" itself:

> There came over me a feeling of profound fatigue at the realisation that all this long stretch of time not only had been uninterruptedly lived, thought, secreted by me, that it was my life, my very self, but also that I must, every minute of my life, keep it closely by me, that it upheld me, that I was perched on its dizzying summit, that I could not move without carrying it about with me.
>
> The date when I heard the sound—so distant and yet so deep within me—of the little bell in the garden at Combray was a landmark I did not know I had available in this enormous dimension of Time. My head swam to see so many years below me, and yet within me, as if I were thousands of leagues in height.[46]

The narrator, who has had such a weak sense of his own past that only recently he made the guests of the Princesse de Guermantes laugh by speaking of himself as a young man, does, however, at that party, discover his past, feel its full weight for the first time, and we see, so to speak, how "weighty" the consequences are. He sees himself—and all men—precariously balancing themselves on stilts, raised dizzily away from the ground by the stretches of time in their pasts, finally to be brutally thrown down by death.

The writing of the book, then, seems to be a painful but necessary discharging of all this past, a chance to externalize it, to control and lessen the dizziness. The narrator feels himself "pregnant with the work" which, he knows, *is* his past, and "which I was carrying within me," [47] and the conventional metaphor of the writer giving birth to the world of his imagination seems to be, for him, a conscious physical oppression. There is, in fact, a process suggesting the stages of pregnancy: the joyful conception of the idea at the Guermantes *matinée,* the weakness and dizziness on the staircase some time later, and a painful delivery. The discoveries which give him an identity, which temporalize and give continuity and stability to all the separate pictures of the self with which he has always lived, have, then, something terrifying about them. Having lived for so long without a sense of the past, he is now overwhelmed by this past. There is too much self; to "find" it is his salvation, but it is also the beginning of death, for the future is now both impossible and unnecessary. The joyful revelation will be begun by a man who feels himself already dead.[48] But the writing of the work turns out to be not merely a painful delivery of the old self; the future is discovered as a chance to invent the past, to recognize the self at the same time that he creates it, exposes it—this time without fear—to new identities.

CHAPTER TWO

THE ANGUISH AND INSPIRATION OF JEALOUSY

1. *The mystery of other people's desires*

In the reassurance and illusory permanence of the maternal glance, Marcel has found his most reliable source of self-recognition. New places and new people are always threatening to overcome him with what seem to him hostile wills, and in each case he has to be assured of his power to resist by imposing on the world an image of himself he can recognize. His mother has a timeless image of him; no matter what he becomes, he will always be for her the child to whom she will respond in the same loving way. Marcel looks for a similar kind of sympathy from the other women he loves. The loved one's inattention induces panic; to deal with what he thinks of as a menace to his individuality, Marcel adopts strategies to make of the loved one a reflection of his fantasies about her.

As a child at Combray, Marcel's anxiety is relieved when he feels that, through his letter, he has penetrated his mother's attention. With all the women who interest him later in his life, we find the same specific need to see their glance turn to and include him. At Carqueville one day with his grandmother and Madame de Villeparisis, Marcel sees, as he leaves the church, some girls from the village near the old bridge. He finds one of them particularly desirable, not so much because of her beauty, but because she seems somewhat detached from the others, seems to dominate and even scorn them. Indeed, this elusiveness is the real object of desire (and the source of anxiety), and the narrator characteristically underlines the possession beyond physical possession that he wanted: "But it was not only to her body that I

56

should have liked to attain, there was also her person, which abode within her, and with which there is but one form of contact, namely to attract its attention, but one sort of penetration, to awaken an idea in it." But the idea awakened must be a favorable one, it must be "her admiration, her desire," and strong enough so that she will keep a memory of him until he can come back. He speaks to her, carefully referring to the Marquise de Villeparisis and her carriage with two horses. But, in saying these words, he finds that his desire and interest fall:

> . . . suddenly I had a great sense of calm. I felt that the fisher-girl would remember me, and I felt vanishing, with my fear of not being able to meet her again, part also of my desire to meet her. It seemed to me that I had succeeded in touching her person with invisible lips, and that I had pleased her. And this assault and capture of her mind, this immaterial possession had taken from her part of her mystery, just as physical possession does.[1]

Attracting the girl's attention both begins and ends the "relationship"; it includes and acts out Marcel's basic needs and his most intense satisfactions. He has made her notice him, and this calms him, gives him "un grand apaisement," the word he uses more often than any other to describe the physical well-being, even the physical pleasures he finds with the women he desires. There has been a kind of non-sexual contact which, however, follows the rhythm of a sexual experience: the desire, the awakening of desire, the penetration, and the appeasement. But it has been an "immaterial" possession, and the calm comes not from Marcel's having found any pleasure in approaching the girl, but in watching the pleasure he gives her. The whole experience is seen essentially as a struggle between two willful detachments. The really elusive presence in the passage is Marcel's, and his goal is reached when he has brought the girl close enough to him so that now *he* can retreat and watch her interest with calm indifference.

It is the "fugitives," the "êtres de fuite" [2] who attract Marcel, and Albertine and her friends are, of course, the major examples of such elusiveness. The girls on the beach at Balbec seem to have "a sincere contempt for the rest of humanity"; they move like magnificently free and elegant birds down the beach, indifferent to everything but their own group. Their life seems full of secrets to Marcel, essentially erotic secrets, for he writes that in none of his fantasies about them did he imagine that they could possibly be "virtuous." And his most urgent concern is to find out what he looks like from inside such an "inhuman" world; he wonders if one of the girls who seems to have glanced at him actually noticed him, what he could have represented to her, from what "universe" she was looking at him.[3] The narrator underlines here how intimately the ideas of knowledge and possession are linked to overcoming disdain in others, a disdain so powerfully and painfully felt that it can be conquered only by a kind of digestive assimilation of the other person's individuality:

> And since, whenever the idea of women who are so different from us penetrates our senses, unless we are able to forget it or the competition of other ideas eliminates it, we know no rest until we have converted those aliens into something that is compatible with ourself, our heart being in this respect endowed with the same kind of reaction and activity as our physical organism, which cannot abide the infusion of any foreign body into its veins without at once striving to digest and assimilate it. . . .[4]

In *A la Recherche du temps perdu* the mystery of other people's personality is generally dramatized as the mystery of their desires, which usually means their sexual desires; and when Marcel feels himself to be the object of those desires, his sense of mystery, and his interest, tend to disappear. Marcel's goal in love is, therefore, to "penetrate" the woman's attention, and he uses physical desire as the best way of fixing that attention, of immobilizing her glance. Now it may seem extraordinary that in a work where sexual pursuit takes up so much of many characters' lives, we have very little sense of lovers actively desiring the people they pursue. For sexuality is both important and unimportant in the novel. We seldom find physical love as something pleasurable in itself in Proust's world. What Marcel desires, for example, is not Albertine, but rather knowledge and control of Albertine's desires. Physical desire and pleasure give the most unmistakable signs of an attitude—simplified, but certain and uncontrollable. Marcel admires Saint-Loup in the restaurant at Rivebelle, where the latter sees behind the indifferent masks of all the women to whom he has made love the memory of the pleasure he caused, the part of himself they have taken on all the "unknown ways" they have traveled since he knew them.[5] Marcel wants much more than physical possession, but physical possession is the short-cut to what he wants. It is a way of completely taking over another consciousness; by occupying completely someone else's attention, Marcel finds a visible proof of his own individual existence.

Marcel's anxiety as a man is, therefore, not exactly a sexual anxiety, but rather a concern about the stability and value of his whole being and its relationship with the outer world. The fear of losing the self is not the same thing as, say, a fear of castration, precisely because Marcel's anguish can no longer be simplified to such a physically literal fear, but now involves elements of the self other than sexuality. But because it is through sexuality that possession and loss—of others and of the self—are most dramatically experienced, it often seems, in A la Recherche, that the mystery of other people's personalities is merely a sexual mystery, and curiosity about the lives of others is expressed as voyeurlike ambitions. With Gilberte, Marcel still seems able to think of her personality as including various sorts of desires; in the later volumes—and especially with Albertine—his questions become almost entirely sexual. He locates the mystery of personality in the way a sexual desire is felt, and what begins with Albertine as a curiosity about a whole way of life connected with the sea ends up as an agonized curiosity about the way Albertine feels when she is imagining or actually experiencing sexual pleasure with a woman. And, compared with this need to know about Albertine's sexual habits, other kinds of curiosity seem to Marcel hardly to express any desire for knowledge at all:

Since what is called aesthetic curiosity would deserve rather the name of indifference in comparison with the painful, unwearying curiosity that I felt as to the places in which Albertine had stayed, as to what she might have been doing on a particular evening, her smiles, the expressions in her eyes, the words that she had uttered, the kisses that she had received.[6]

The first step in Marcel's investigations is to find out if Albertine *is* sexually attracted to women, and he spends years attempting to learn what she did in certain places, how she behaved with certain women. And the reader comes to feel, especially in *La Prisonnière* and *La Fugitive*, that bribery and constant lying are the only appropriate methods of breaking down the mystery of personality: Marcel pays Aimé to find out what Albertine did in Touraine, and he tries to trick Andrée into admitting Albertine's Lesbianism. These strategies do not lead to any certain proof, but they give the impression that for Marcel, and for Proust, the only unknowable part of another person's life is, as Jean-François Revel has said, his or her "schedule." And this emphasis on sexual desire as the essence of personality tends to make the narrator think of his contacts with others in terms of melodramatic, conclusive revelations. Even in relationships where he is not himself deeply involved, Marcel often sees other people as puzzles to be solved, and he is happy to find a key that makes a whole personality intelligible: Charlus's homosexuality makes his personality as clear as a sentence in which letters arranged at random suddenly fall into wholly coherent patterns;[7] Princesse Sherbatoff's name makes her "social personality," which Marcel had been unable to define when he first saw her in the train, as easy to figure out as a guessing game when the missing word is given.[8] And, after Albertine's death, when Aimé writes that he has found out that Albertine used to go to the baths at Balbec with several women, the narrator emphasizes his sense of asking questions about the essence of Albertine's personality in seeking such information:

To understand how deeply these words penetrated my being, the reader must bear in mind that the questions which I had been asking myself with regard to Albertine were not subordinate, immaterial questions, questions of detail, the only questions as a matter of fact which we ask ourselves about anyone who is not ourselves, whereby we are enabled to proceed, wrapped in an impenetrable thought, through the midst of suffering, falsehood, vice or death. No, in Albertine's case, they were essential questions: "In her heart of hearts what was she? What were her thoughts? What were her loves? Did she lie to me? Had my life with her been as lamentable as Swann's life with Odette?" And so the point reached by Aimé's reply, even although it was not a general reply—and precisely for that reason—was indeed in Albertine, in myself, the uttermost depths.[9]

But this does not mean, as Revel maintains, that Proust sees no real mystery in other people's personalities.[10] It is true that Marcel devotes most of his energy to trying to find out how Albertine spends her time, but he does this in order to know what kind of desire is separating her from him, to possess the images that possess Albertine.

The need to become familiar with Albertine's desires is so intense that the activity of loving turns out to be something like a compulsive intellectual investigation. And the detective-story atmosphere is sustained by the imagination for crime that the fragile self develops: Marcel's mother is enjoying "mischievous pleasures" downstairs with Swann and the rest of the family; [11] the narrator enters Charlus's brothel to prevent a "horrible crime"; [12] and, in his attempts to find out Albertine's sexual secrets, Marcel feels he is preventing her from doing something evil.[13] Now if Albertine hides her desires from Marcel, one possibility of finding out about those desires is for Marcel himself, in a sense, to hide, deliberately to let Albertine satisfy her desires while he watches her. By extreme attention, he can perhaps "follow" her desires as she satisfies them. This is obviously a sexual parallel to Marcel's staring at the hawthorns in the Combray church, attempting to imitate "the action of their blossoming" in order to penetrate their essence, and finding the metaphor in himself that "repeats" the form of the flowers.[14] But with Albertine, Marcel's quest for knowledge becomes frankly unsavory. In his jealousy all his curiosities about everything in life are concentrated in the single wish to watch the expression on Albertine's face as she has sexual pleasure with another woman:

> All the curiosity that I had felt about her life in the past when I knew her only by sight, and on the other hand all my desires in life were blended in this sole curiosity, [the way in which Albertine experienced pleasure, to see her] in company with other women, perhaps because thus, when they had left her, I should have remained alone with her, the last and the master. And when I observed her hesitations, her uncertainty when she asked herself whether it would be worth her while to spend the evening with this or that girl, her satiety when the other had gone, perhaps her disappointment, I should have brought to the light of day, I should have restored to its true proportions the jealousy that Albertine inspired in me, because seeing her thus experience them I should have taken the measure and discovered the limit of her pleasures.[15]

But Albertine is dead, and Marcel tries to break down the mystery of her homosexual desires by repeating them imaginatively himself, or by using substitutes for Albertine. Looking at Andrée after Albertine's death is a way of getting closer to Albertine's desires. If she did have homosexual feelings for Andrée, then the latter's face is the image that awakened Albertine's desires, and by finding Andrée beautiful himself, Marcel can perhaps approximate what it felt like for Albertine to want her.[16] He also arranges the kind of scenes he thinks must have been common in her life. He watches two laundresses have relations with each other in a house of prostitution, and he has the impression of hearing Albertine's pleasures, of witnessing what is for him the wholly mysterious phenomenon of feminine sexuality:

> [As she was being caressed, one of the girls suddenly began to make a sound which I at first was unable to identify, for we can never understand exactly the meaning of a sound we have not heard before, one which expresses a sensation we have not experienced. If we are in the next room and cannot see anything,

we may take for uncontrollable laughter the noise caused by the suffering of a patient who is being operated on without having been put to sleep; and as for the sounds made by a mother who has just been told that her child is dead, if we do not know the facts, it may be as difficult for us to provide a human translation for these sounds as when we hear the noise that comes from an animal, or a harp. We need some time to understand that the sounds made by the patient and the mother express something which, by analogy with what we ourselves may have felt (and which is, however, quite different), we call suffering, and it also took me a certain amount of time to realize that the noise I was hearing expressed something which, once again by analogy with very different sensations I had experienced myself, I called pleasure. And this pleasure must have been very strong indeed to have had such an overwhelming effect on the person who was experiencing it, strong enough to make her speak this unknown language which seemed to express and comment upon all the phases of the exquisite drama being lived by the little woman, of this drama which was hidden from my eyes by the curtain which always prevents everyone else from seeing what goes on in the most intimate and mysterious parts of each person's life.] [17]

II. Jealousy and the tortured imagination

But it is precisely this "mystère intime" of another person that the jealous lover tries—hopelessly and with exasperation—to penetrate. Indeed, the lover's interest is born of the anguish caused by that mystery, and needs anguish to be sustained. Now the nature of jealousy depends both on the desires of the anxious investigator and on the desires he is attempting to understand. Suffering varies according to the limits within which the loved one's desires can be imaginatively apprehended. Proust dramatizes brilliantly the ways in which the lover tries to familiarize himself with the images that appeal to the loved one, to feel how these images attract and pull the other person into certain forms of activity. The differences between particular jealousies are differences between imaginative capacities.

In the various examples of jealousy in the novel, the narrator

suggests two kinds of imaginative identification with the loved
one's desires that are possible for the jealous lover. Either he can
identify himself with the group of people with whom the woman
finds her pleasure, or he may find that, in a general way, what
gives her pleasure is also what gives him pleasure. If Albertine
loves Saint-Loup—and this is the "normal" jealous situation—
Marcel does not share her desire, since he himself does not pursue men; but his jealousy is still bearable, because she is looking
for a kind of pleasure *he can give*. The image attracting her is the
image of a man, and so the nature of her desire does not absolutely exclude the possibility of Marcel's becoming the object of
that desire. Her desiring glance may reflect him again, for what
she sees with desire is not essentially different from his own body.
The narrator insists on the fact that the idea of Albertine's having
relations with other women is much more painful to him than the
idea of her betraying him with Saint-Loup. The difference is one
of imaginative possibility for Marcel. The jealous man, he writes,
has to experiment with different kinds of suffering: ". . . in
jealousy we have to some extent to make trial of sufferings of
every sort and degree, before we arrive at the one which seems
appropriate." [18] Albertine's Lesbianism is more painful to Marcel
than her possible relations with men because it is more difficult
for him to participate in her desires for other women: "This love
of woman for woman was something too unfamiliar; nothing
enabled me to form a certain, an accurate idea of its pleasures,
its quality." [19]

The kind of identification Marcel can make with Albertine's
Lesbian desires only aggravates his suffering. First of all, because
of the pleasures he himself has known with women, he feels he
has a particularly painful insight into the attractiveness of
feminine images for Albertine. His own desires are being repeated, but turned against him:

> I myself, with the help of my own love of women, albeit they
> could not have been the same thing to Albertine, could more or
> less imagine what she felt. And indeed it was already a first de-
> gree of anguish, merely to picture her to myself desiring as I had

so often desired, lying to me as I had so often lied to her, preoccupied with one girl or another, putting herself out for her, as I
had done for Mlle. de Stermaria and ever so many others, not to
mention the peasant girls whom I met on country roads. Yes, all
my own desires helped me to understand, to a certain degree,
what hers had been; it was by this time an intense anguish in
which all my desires, the keener they had been, had changed
into torments that were all the more cruel; as though in this al-
gebra of sensibility they reappeared with the same coefficient but
with a minus instead of a plus sign.[20]

Both Marcel and Albertine are, in their desires, facing in the
same direction, toward women, but there is no chance of her
turning *to* him. She is, so to speak, next to him, looking at and
responding to the same images as he. She wants what he wants,
which is something different from him. Unable to recognize himself by analogy in what she desires (as he might have done with
her desire for Saint-Loup), he has no hope of becoming the
object of that desire. Moreover, although Marcel is sensitive to
the attractiveness that Albertine may find in women's images, he
cannot identify at all with the kind of pleasure Albertine may
conceive of having with other women. They both desire women,
but their bodies are satisfied in different ways. Marcel's desire for
women is necessarily felt as a possibility of specific sensations,
and his thoughts about Albertine's Lesbianism involve the painful paradox of finding the same images attractive but for un-
imaginably different reasons of physical pleasure.

The narrator shows other forms of jealousy, similarly based on
the possibilities of imagining the loved one's desires, in several
characters in the novel, especially in Saint-Loup and Charlus.
Some of Proust's readers feel that the revelation of Saint-Loup's
homosexuality at the end of *La Fugitive* is a disagreeable *coup de
théâtre,* a gratuitous "spoiling" of his character. But this aspect of
his personality is suggested indirectly in several ways throughout
the novel: in the narrator's mentioning, in his first description of
Saint-Loup, something "effeminate," [21] in Robert's violent reaction to the man who propositions him on a street in Paris (are

we to think that he leaves Marcel a minute later to seek out the
man and arrange a meeting with him, away from Marcel?), and
especially in his jealousy of Rachel. In restaurants or at the theatre, Robert often notices the attractive men before Rachel does;
he points one out to her, begging her not to look at him, thereby,
the narrator says, bringing the other man to her attention. And
Rachel finds sometimes that Robert has "such good judgment in
his suspicion" that she often betrays him with someone she never
would have noticed if it had not been for him.[22] This peculiar
way of encouraging Rachel to betray him is intelligible as an expression of intense jealousy. Saint-Loup begins by acting the role
of Rachel: he picks out the desirable men. The first movement of
his jealousy, then, is to identify with Rachel's desire; like Marcel
sharing Albertine's desire for women, Saint-Loup, during those
first moments in a public place, "puts on" Rachel's desire and
focuses on a specific masculine image before she does. Robert's
love for Rachel is by no means a cover-up for his homosexuality,
but an intimate connection between this love and his homosexuality is suggested. If Saint-Loup's immediate awareness of the
handsome men around him suggests that even during his affair
with Rachel his homosexuality was already expressing itself—if
only indirectly—we also see, in his behavior with Rachel, what
might be called the heterosexual function of this homosexuality.
According to the Proustian definition of intimacy, he is closer to
her when he shares her desires, even though this may mean, ultimately, that he will no longer desire her. In the narrator's theoretical statements, homosexuality tends to be traced to genetic
causes, to a kind of biological mistake—a woman is given a man's
body, and vice versa—but the portrait of Saint-Loup's jealousy is
evidence of a more psychological approach. The narrator is, of
course, by no means saying that Saint-Loup's painful love for
Rachel is the cause of his homosexuality, but he does dramatize
Saint-Loup's expert sensitivity to masculine beauty as the desperate activity of a heterosexually active imagination. He thus qualifies his own melodramatic view of the freakishness of homosexuality. Saint-Loup's homosexually directed attention is one way

of not being excluded from what Rachel may be doing. But this activity itself seems to make the jealousy more frantic, as if, in responding to the attractiveness of men in imitation of Rachel, he began to play the role of a woman and therefore excluded himself from her attention by the very means designed to penetrate it.

The complication of roles being played is even greater in the scene at Rachel's theatre in *Le Côté de Guermantes*. It is here that we see the most elaborate strategy of the loved one: she hides her desires in such confusion that the jealous lover is completely defeated, cannot even begin to imagine these desires. Robert feels that Rachel is paying attention to a young male dancer wearing red make-up on his cheeks and a costume of a black velvet cap and a hortensia-colored skirt, and who, in the midst of the crowd of reporters and society men backstage, is skipping and gesturing with such grace that, for Marcel, ". . . it was as restful and as fresh a spectacle as watching a butterfly straying along a crowded street to follow with one's eyes, between the strips of canvas, the natural arabesques traced by his winged capricious painted oscillations." Saint-Loup and Rachel quarrel, and she deliberately admires the dancer, is impressed especially by the feminine grace of his hands: " 'Isn't he too wonderful with his hands,' " she cruelly says to Saint-Loup. " 'A woman like me couldn't do the things he's doing now.' " And the dancer smiles "mysteriously" at Rachel when she asks him if his hands are as expert with women, at the same time that she suggests the pleasure they could have together because of what is feminine in his grace: " 'You look just like one [a woman] yourself, I'm sure I could have a wonderful time with you and a girl I know.' " [23]

The situation is, obviously, a hopeless one for Saint-Loup's jealousy. Not only is he unable to prevent Rachel from almost making an assignation with the dancer; the kind of imaginative identifications with specific pleasures which jealous lovers always seek in *A la Recherche* are also impossible. Saint-Loup cannot even ask questions possible for Marcel when he thinks of Albertine and Andrée, for Swann when he thinks of Odette and For-

cheville, for Charlus when he thinks of Morel and other men.
What sort of roles are being played here? Is Rachel attracted to
the dancer as she would be to another man, such as Saint-Loup?
Is she attracted by women or by men in costume and wearing
make-up, men who remind her of women? Or is it only the friend
she refers to who looks for her pleasures with other women, or
with men reminding her of women? And how does Rachel conceive of pleasure taken at the same time with another woman and
a feminine man? The images of desire are inextricably embroiled
in a literal and psychological costume play: the man would be
playing the role of a woman for Rachel or her friend, or for
both, and they would partly play the role of a man with a man
looking like a woman. And the main characters here are professional actors; the scene takes place in a theatre and the passage
begins with Marcel's reflections on the "ephemeral vivid personalities which the characters are in a play," personalities which,
once a performance is over, disintegrate into the actors' real lives,
a faceless text, and rubbed off make-up. And, the narrator adds,
this "dissolution . . . makes us—like the dissolution of a dear
friend—begin to doubt the reality of our ego and meditate on the
mystery of death." [24] The conclusion is unexpected and somewhat melodramatic at the end of the first paragraph of this section, but it is justified in the dramatic context of the whole
passage. The scene between Rachel and the dancer raises, in a
sinister way, the question of playing roles, of a kind of make-
believe, as a stimulus to sensual pleasure. And with her promise
of introducing him to her friend, there is even provision for a
kind of audience, or at least for a situation in which each of them
can be both actor and audience, since the cast would be larger
than necessary for the "production" of physical pleasure. But the
interplay of different roles is too confusing for a clear choice of
role on the part of the excluded jealous lover. What image is he
to try imaginatively to find attractive? In Rachel's desire itself
there seems to be a continual hesitation not only between masculine and feminine images, but also between masculine and feminine images playing roles not ordinarily associated with them.

What is the desire that would give the key to Rachel's self, to possessing her again?

Saint-Loup's anger is not spelled out explicitly in this way, but it is, first of all, clear that the whole scene is about the psychological implications of assuming certain roles. Both in Marcel's thoughts about actors and in Rachel's mysteriously suggestive remarks to the dancer, the reality of the self is seen as doubtful; the question, ultimately, of the death or deaths of the personality is raised. And Saint-Loup's reaction is extraordinarily violent: within a few minutes' time, he physically attacks two people. Neither the journalist who refuses to throw away his cigar nor the homosexual who accosts Saint-Loup in the street has caused his jealous anger, but the anger they may have provoked for other reasons is certainly increased by his exasperation with Rachel. And the homosexual's proposition comes at a particularly appropriate moment for Saint-Loup's anger: Rachel's behavior with the dancer was full of implications of homosexuality. It is also at least probable that Saint-Loup leaves Marcel so abruptly in order to meet the man who propositioned him. This need to have intimate relations with another man would dramatize, by its very nature, a possibility of entering into, of imitating the general area of theatrical, role-playing sexuality from which Rachel has excluded him. Finally, theatricality is treated in the passage as a strategy by which others are made to suffer. The narrator introduces the theme of cruelty in the incident of the friends Rachel has planted in the audience and who laugh off the stage the young singer whom Rachel hates. And she feels such uncontrollable sadistic pleasure in making Saint-Loup suffer that she points him out to the dancer and says: " '. . . Look, he's hurt. . . .' " [25] Rachel's cruel mystifications are essentially strategies of an "être de fuite." The mobility and uncertain nature of her desires make possession impossible; her desires, and therefore her personality, do not stay fixed; they move exasperatingly among different images, and so escape imitation and apprehension. Her mysterious suggestiveness with the dancer makes her inaccessible to Saint-Loup; what makes him suffer is that she has cruelly deprived him of strategies for possessing her. He is reduced to threatening not to give her a necklace he had promised and to turning away from her and making two other people feel the violence of his anger.

In Charlus's jealousy of Morel, we see the same attempt to possess someone through imaginative identification with other desires or objects of desire. Morel is perhaps the most "slippery" character in the novel; his behavior unpredictably steers back and forth among several contradictory, equally obsessive concerns. Willing to do anything for money, but putting his reputation at the Conservatoire even above money, sermonizing his brother for having treated their sisters badly, passing from a desire to seduce and then abandon Jupien's niece to a real tenderness for her and then to a nervous rage against her—the peculiar range of his feelings and behavior makes it hard to identify with his desires, and so to identify him. "He resembled," writes the narrator, "an old book of the middle ages, full of mistakes, of absurd traditions, of obscenities; he was extraordinarily composite." In a sense, Morel is more elusive than Albertine. The latter's kindness to Marcel, her admiration of him, her remarkable docility reveal themselves with enough consistency so that, in spite of Marcel's anguished sense of her mysteriousness, the reader may feel that he has a clearer image of her attachments and needs than Marcel seems to feel is possible. But in Morel, the desire for money, cynicism, irresistible sadistic impulses, artistic and moral principles all live together in a chaotic, disconnected way that makes the narrator think of his personality as "a sheet of paper that has been folded so often in every direction that it is impossible to straighten it out." [26] Morel's sexual pleasures seem to have the same kind of indeterminacy: ". . . he was sufficiently fond of both women and men to satisfy either sex with the fruits of his experience of the other," [27] but what is the part of calculation, and how does Morel imagine pleasure? In his sexual pleasures, his ambitions, and what he considers his moral point of view, he jumps from one desirable image to another in a way that makes impossible the kind of tentative but nonetheless thorough explanation of motive, of an inner atmosphere, which the narrator gives us with most of the other characters.

What is an intellectual mystery for Marcel is a source of tortured jealousy for Charlus. As always with Proust's lovers, the baron's happiness or unhappiness depends on the degree to which he can dominate, possess Morel. The narrator characteristically presents this as a general law: "For the possession of what we love is an even greater joy than love itself." [28] Charlus approves of Morel's marriage to Jupien's niece because he sees in it a way of increasing Morel's dependence on him. The girl, he thinks, will be an extension of Morel's personality, a more reliable version of him than Morel himself; she will admire and need the baron. The marriage is, for Charlus, mainly a way of creating new needs in Morel—having to do with a family, their apartment, his future—which will be visible, clear, and which only Charlus can satisfy. It is a way of immobilizing Morel, of substituting for his mysterious desires other desires set up by Charlus himself. Charlus has a kind of comical pride at Morel's successes with women. He does not seem to see Morel as turning away from him in these successes; it is as if in Charlus himself there were a strong enough fantasy of being a woman so that he can identify with the feminine image Morel finds attractive, and therefore, paradoxically, not consider the latter's heterosexual desires as a betrayal. The narrator, however, offers another, more conventional explanation of Charlus's lack of concern: homosexuals consider love for a woman as "something different, which occurs in another animal species (a lion does not interfere with tigers)," and so this love "does not distress them, if anything, reassures them." This explanation is a striking example of the discrepancy we sometimes find in the novel between dramatizations of certain kinds of behavior and the narrator's theoretical analyses. The passage seems to me to be a combination of nastiness toward homosexuals ("normal" pleasures are inconceivable to them; they absurdly see women as another "species") and of complicity with them and defiance of a hostile audience (homosexuals are proudly indifferent to the claims of heterosexuality;

women cannot make them suffer). Above all, it does not take into
account the implications of Charlus's unconscious imitation of
women. Indeed, in the same passage we see another example of
this imitation. Women's admiration for Morel provides an opportunity for Charlus to make a public statement of his own admiration; his supposedly disinterested report to Marcel and Brichot
of Morel's successes gives him a chance to use, or rather to usurp
the woman's privilege:

> "But do you know, my dear fellow, he has women," he would
> say, with an air of disclosure, of scandal, possibly of envy, above
> all of admiration. "He is extraordinary," he would continue.
> "Everywhere, the most famous whores can look at nobody but him.
> They stare at him everywhere, whether it's on the underground
> or in the theatre. It's becoming a nuisance! I can't go out with
> him to a restaurant without the waiter bringing him notes from
> at least three women. And always pretty women too. Not that
> there's anything surprising in that. I was watching him yester-
> day, I can quite understand it, he has become so beautiful, he
> looks just like a Bronzino, he is really marvellous." [29]

There is "possibly envy" too, and in Charlus the narrator suggests
a fundamental confusion between the desire to have and the desire to be. The image of virility is both an object of sexual desire
and a model to be imitated: the gracious woman alternates in
Charlus with the militant, severe male. Morel's appeal to women
gives the baron the chance for a double identification—with the
women who pursue him and, at least in the form of envy and
admiration, with the virile Morel.

But, like Saint-Loup with Rachel, Charlus discovers in Morel's
life mysteries of sexual pleasure even more confusing and anguishing for him than Rachel's cruel elusiveness is for Robert.
The baron opens by mistake a letter sent to Morel by the actress
Léa, "notorious for her exclusive interest in women." The letter
is passionate, filled with expressions whose "indelicacy prevents
us from reproducing it here." Léa makes fun of Charlus in the
letter, as well as of an officer who is keeping her. She speaks of
several other women who seem to be friends of hers and Morel's,

and she addresses Morel only in the feminine (" 'Grande sale, va!'," " 'Ma belle chérie' "). Charlus, never having suspected that Morel even knows the actress, is stupefied, but what makes his suffering unbearably sharp is the impenetrable mystery the letter creates. For Charlus the expression "en être" means to have homosexual desires like his, but Léa writes to Morel:

". . . Of course you are so, my pretty, you know you are." [". . . Toi tu en es au moins, etc."] . . . What most disturbed the Baron was the word 'so.' Ignorant at first of its application, he had eventually, at a time already remote in the past, learned that he himself was 'so.' And now the notion that he had acquired of this word was again put to the challenge. When he had discovered that he was 'so,' he had supposed this to mean that his tastes, as Saint-Simon says, did not lie in the direction of women. And here was this word 'so' applied to Morel with an extension of meaning of which M. de Charlus was unaware, so much so that Morel gave proof, according to this letter, of his being 'so' by having the same taste as certain women for other women. From that moment the Baron's jealousy had no longer any reason to confine itself to the men of Morel's acquaintance, but began to extend to the women also. So that the people who were 'so' were not merely those that he had supposed to be 'so,' but a whole and vast section of the inhabitants of the planet, consisting of women as well as of men, loving not merely men but women also, and the Baron, in the face of this novel meaning of a word that was so familiar to him, felt himself tormented by an anxiety of the mind as well as of the heart, born of this twofold mystery which combined an extension of the field of his jealousy with the sudden inadequacy of a definition.[30]

"The sudden inadequacy of a definition": the importance the narrator gives to the intellectual problem—as well as the humorous aspect of the baron's confusion—do not make Charlus's suffering seem abstract or reasoned; he rather underlines the loss of all control over this suffering when the mind can no longer work at getting used to certain definite painful images. Charlus suddenly finds that the language he has always used to identify himself is also used to identify sexual desires and plans from which he is totally excluded. For Léa's letter sets up an unsolvable problem for Charlus's imagination: by what images and identifications can the homosexual man actively calm his jealousy of another homosexual man who finds his pleasure with Lesbians? When Morel's activity is with heterosexual women, as I have said, the baron is calm and proud: he can both "envy" Morel's success in playing the virile role by which he, Charlus, has attempted for years to dominate aristocratic society, and he can identify with the women who find this virility irresistible. But Léa's letter reveals a wholly different situation. Morel presumably enjoys pleasure with women who desire principally women, and who seem to treat him like a woman. The "play" here is a perfect parody-imitation of the ordinary heterosexual relation. In her letter Léa says, essentially, that for a man to qualify as a homosexual, he has to be attracted to women. A man and a woman desire each other; but the man knows that the woman wants another woman, and she finds him desirable both, it seems, because she can think of him as a woman and because he shares her kind of desire for women. This last suggestion gets to the heart of the convoluted roles being played here: Charlus would have to feel what it is like to be a man being treated like a woman who desires women acting like men. How exactly does Morel conceive of his satisfactions in these relations? And it is just as impossible for Charlus to identify himself with Léa and her friends. The baron's homosexuality consists of his simply playing the two roles of an ordinary relationship: he would like to be both the virile seducer and the worshiping woman. But how to imagine being a woman playing the role of a man and wanting a man for the reasons that men usually want women? We can think of Charlus as having a man's body but psychologically behaving like a woman, or, as the narrator sometimes suggests, as essentially a woman forced to play the role of a man because of a physical "mistake." But what he can never do is to play the role of a man in the particular, artificial way possible for a Lesbian, that is, as a contradiction of a physical fact. He is completely excluded from Morel and Léa's world; his own role-playing is naïvely simple and wholly inadequate to the kind of labyrinthine distortions suggested by Léa's letter.

III. Strategies to immobilize the "êtres de fuite," and "les joies de la solitude"

The impression Proust's lovers have of the lives of those they love is similar to Marcel's confusion, which he describes in the first pages of the novel, when he awakens in the middle of the night not knowing where he is or who he is. Like the objects in the bedroom, the images of the loved one and of the loved one's attitude toward the lover dizzily shift among various combinations. In both cases questions of identity are involved: without a reliably fixed, immobile image in the outer world, possession of others and of the self is impossible. Identities disintegrate into several unconnected pictures; attempts to project or recognize the self in visible external scenes are frustrated by the elusive metamorphoses of these scenes. The dizziness described at the beginning of "Combray" is the physical symptom of a general instability of being which Marcel tries to cure in various ways. The only satisfactory strategy will be the writing of the novel itself, but we see in the life being described other tentative, "wrong" solutions.

In Marcel's love for Albertine there is a wide range of tactics designed to turn her attention and desire toward him, or by which he at least hopes to possess her by understanding or sharing her desires. Marcel is almost grotesquely comical in some of these strategies, comical in the unpleasant way that Racine's unhappy lovers often are. In Racine the lovers state their passion to those they desire much more directly than in Proust; in the latter there are no violent outbursts of desire and jealous accusation. Occasionally in Racine characters try to give an impression of indifference to the people they desperately love; but these attempts to imitate the loved one's indifference are only silly parodies of indifference, and no one else is fooled for a moment. Pyrrhus is only ridiculous when he tries to convince Phoenix that he no longer loves Andromaque, and we sympathize with the confidant's impatience with this sad nonsense. In Proust, such scenes are frequent, especially in the stories of Swann's love for Odette and Marcel's love for Albertine. The strategy is an awkward imitation of the loved one's behavior. Marcel thinks he discovers in what Albertine has told him a sinister web of lies; he adopts what he takes to be her tactics and forces himself to be insincere with her about his feelings. Sincerity would be dangerous: once certain of his need for her, Albertine might think she could have both the material advantages he gives her and her freedom. To make himself seem less of a prisoner, he lies and threatens, tells her they will have to separate, that he will quickly forget her. But he is unconvincing in the role she plays with such ease. He worries, first of all, that she may believe him and, indifferent herself and encouraged by his indifference, may leave him. But, like Odette with Swann, Albertine seems to see through the make-believe and to translate all the poses of indifference into the frantic, insincere threats they really are. And there are signs that she gets tired of the game; for some time before she leaves him at the end of *La Prisonnière,* she seems discouraged and disillusioned. It is as if Marcel's expensive gifts no longer seemed worth the exhaustion of accounting for every minute of every day, of perhaps pretending not to know that he has people spying on her, of submitting to the constant cross-examinations and acting as if they were not inspired by a desperately possessive jealousy. Marcel wonders how calculated Albertine really is: does she leave him knowing that he will make concessions before she does, that she will be able to come back and do as she pleases? His game really works only on himself, and, in the heavy, often oppressively dense analyses of *La Prisonnière,* he describes the way he gets used to the idea of separation by talking about it so much, how his lies slowly accustom him to the idea of living without Albertine.

Finally, the most futile aspect of all Marcel's strategies is that if they worked, he would no longer be interested in Albertine. Now the remarkable thing about the portrait of Albertine is that we have several clear, sharp images of her at the same time that certain of her desires and attitudes remain wholly mysterious. Her mild, almost lazy sensuality, her envy of the rich, her intellectual pretensions, her admiration and tenderness for Marcel are all presented without much ambiguity. But what seem to be her lies, her intimacy with women Marcel knows to be Lesbians, the obscene expression she uses in a moment of impatience constantly half-reveal a side of which Marcel can never quite be sure. But it is for this side that he "loves" her; if he were sure of possessing her, he would no longer want her. "We love only what we do not wholly possess." [31] This is Proust's version of the Pascalian idea of *divertissement*: Marcel acts as if he wanted total possession of Albertine, but his love is only the activity toward possession. For Marcel, personality—his own and that of others—is by definition what has not happened or has not yet been revealed; it is in its essence a secret. Even if there is no objective reason for him to be jealous of Albertine, you might say that he has to ask her to make him believe that there is. If she persuaded him of her faithfulness, he would not have, in her reliable love for him, the fixed image of himself he needs, for this image is by nature something that others cruelly withhold from him.

Albertine's and Odette's perhaps unconscious strategies are masterful. They first become part of Marcel's and Swann's habits; both men, before loving them jealously, come to expect the women's presence as a predictable, regular part of their lives. And then the other side suddenly appears. Alongside of an uninteresting reliability there seems to be a mystery, a part of the woman's life that is never given. And the habit becomes love, a desperate need for total possession. For the men lose their advantage as soon as they want to use it. To be sincerely indifferent is a condition of being loved; feigned indifference is only the embarrassing strategy of a bad actor, an invitation to the woman to use the man as she likes. And Marcel's and Swann's strategies are ultimately ridiculous because of the absurd expectations these strategies imply. They act as if, by lying about their own feelings, they could change the woman's feelings. Albertine and Odette may be frightened into caution, but they cannot be frightened into love.

". . . Elstir when he gazed at them had no need to bother about what the violets were doing." [32] But Odette, Rachel, Morel, Albertine, unlike the flowers studied by the great painter, are always moving away from the lover's attention, and their flight is intentional, secretive. The suffering of Proust's lovers comes from their not being able to make those they love "sit" permanently for them, give up their freedom and live like models posing in a studio. *La Prisonnière* records Marcel's attempts to immobilize Albertine, and this experiment ranges from a rather sinister use of her to a poetic feeling for a quiet, familylike existence. Albertine is most fully Marcel's "prisoner," he has least to worry about what she is doing, when she is sleeping. There are several pages in *La Prisonnière* where he describes his happiness watching her sleep. Sleep realizes, to a certain extent, the possibility of love: "[When I was alone, I could think of her, but since she was not there I could not possess her;] when she was present, I spoke to her, but I was too far absent from myself to be able to think." Possession is impossible without the other person's presence, but, characteristically, Marcel seems almost to find experience unreal unless he can reflectively define and digest each impression as it occurs. A painter, by deliberately immobilizing an object or a human figure, enjoys a physical presence at the same time that he can leisurely think about the source of his enjoyment; a docile model offers itself to his devouring attention. With Albertine, Marcel satisfies this double need when he watches her sleep. Her body no longer gives signs of intentions hostile or indifferent to him; he can watch her, and lie next to her, thinking of her as a beautiful but mindless part of nature: "I felt at such moments that I had been possessing her more completely, like an unconscious and unresisting object of dumb nature." [33] The women Marcel loves seem to get in the way of the pleasure they might give him; their presence disturbs the playing out of exciting fantasies about them. He needs the stimulus of another body, but it is as if he wanted quickly to take a picture of the other person and then be alone to enjoy its beauty. The narrator elaborately prepares mentally for every physical contact; before kissing his mother or Albertine, he tries to concentrate lucidly on what he is about to do, so that he will know what he is enjoying. In the comical description of his kissing Albertine in *Le Côté de Guermantes,* we see how the mere movement of his face toward her, the rearranging of perspectives and the weakening of visual and olfactory perceptions as his face presses against hers, spoil the kiss for him. He wants a motionless, complete image of Albertine which his intelligence and all his senses could enjoy in leisure. His pleasure is never in the unpredictable quality, in the sensual surprises of an actual physical contact; it is rather in totally possessing, controlling a mental picture of the object of his desires. And there are even suggestions that when he and Albertine make love, the form that his pleasure takes is much the same as when he is alone.[34]

Asleep, Albertine becomes a thing subject to his scrutiny, to his appreciation, and also to his physical caprices. For he says that, lying against her unconscious body, he would sometimes enjoy "a pleasure that was less pure." Interestingly enough, it is at such moments that Marcel can best express his real tenderness for Albertine. He can love her most gently now because it is really he who is at rest; he is no longer able to see in her eyes the signs of elusiveness that spoil his pleasure and make him cruel when she is awake. The whole passage is, incidentally, a good example of how an abstractly sinister piece of behavior can be presented without any of the conventional attitudes toward it. There is not the slightest concession to a moralistic point of view on what the narrator is describing. Not only is it clear here that Marcel uses Albertine's body without the slightest scruple; there is in his language no insincere or equivocal concern with a public judgment of his behavior. And it is, in fact, true that for Marcel such incidents are his purest expression of love. He acts on his desires to make Albertine suffer when she is awake and responding to him, when her activity exasperates him; it is her immobility that appeases and humanizes him. Indeed, the sexual experience itself seems to be a particularly mild form of pleasure, less exciting than tranquillizing: "For this I had no need to make any move-

ment, I allowed my leg to dangle against hers, like an oar which
one allows to trail in the water, imparting to it now and again a
gentle oscillation like the intermittent flap given to its wing by
a bird asleep in the air." The whole passage has images taken
from the calm aspects of nature: the "mysterious emanation" of
Albertine's sleep is "soft as a breeze from the sea, fairylike as . . .
moonlight"; her breathing has the slow, majestic movements of
sea waves; her body occasionally trembles "as the leaves of a tree
are shaken for a few moments by a sudden breath of wind." This
dehumanization of Albertine, instead of implying any guilty or
violent pleasures for Marcel, simply gives him the completely
satisfactory sense of enjoying a peaceful countryside: "Her sleep
brought within my reach something as calm, as sensually delicious as those nights of full moon on the bay of Balbec, turned
quiet as a lake over which the branches barely stir, where
stretched out upon the sand one could listen for hours on end to
the waves breaking and receding." [35] Proust's novel has many
scenes of distorted and agitated sexuality; it is, however, important to see that such sexuality is usually distinct from sensual
pleasure. Charlus being beaten by a soldier is mainly concerned
with his *idea* of making himself a willing victim of brutal mas-
culinity. And certainly, for Marcel, a very great sensuality is
almost always satisfied in a non-sexual, quiet, even domestic way.

La Prisonnière is, therefore, not only the account of Marcel's
tortured jealousy. He hesitates between an anguished curiosity
about what Albertine may be hiding from him and a calm and
deep sense of the peace and even the beauty of their life together.
There are many moments like the ones when he watches Albertine sleep, moments when, because of her presence in the house,
he has a physical sense of great well-being, of pleasurable *apaisement*. He speaks of the "domestic, almost conjugal bliss" that he
enjoys with her; [36] while Albertine lives with him, Marcel can
express fully that domestic, or domesticated, sensuality which
brings him the greatest happiness. If her presence is, in one sense,
a kind of eviction of his mother, a betrayal of the moral values of
Combray and a foray into a mysterious world of forbidden sex-

uality, Albertine is also partly Combray-ized. She comes to know and obey Françoise's "code," she gives the appeasing good-night kiss of Marcel's mother, and, especially, she makes it possible for Marcel to go back to the pleasures that made of much of his life at Combray a childhood paradise. These are the pleasures of a family existence, with the rest of the world shut out; they consist of walks and rides in the country, evenings of listening to Albertine play the piano, long mornings in bed listening to her sing in the next room. And Marcel savors this life of warm, quiet intimacy. This is the happiness of Combray in the daytime, a happiness always associated with being close to nature. Robert Brasillach insists on the simplicity of this joy—the joy of being outdoors and in good health—and, as Germaine Brée has said, Combray is born of a deep harmony the individual finds with the world and happiness.[37] Even in Paris, Marcel lives his existence as a series of country scenes: Albertine's eyes remind him of the sea, her singing awakens memories of birds singing in the woods. Marcel's tender attentiveness to the weather repeats, more fully and poetically, his father's proud meteorological observations at Combray. Outside of the moments of jealousy, which seem to correspond to the painful nights of his childhood, Albertine re-creates a part of Combray for Marcel, the same calm family life in the country that was Illiers for Proust, Etreuilles for Jean Santeuil.

In the last volumes of *A la Recherche du temps perdu,* the search for pleasure takes more and more the exotic, dangerous forms of Sodom and Gomorrah, but the only convincing scenes of achieved pleasure are those that repeat the domesticity of Combray. Such passages complete, with great density and detail, a seemingly non-Proustian statement from *Jean Santeuil,* one, however, which reflects the simple happiness that will retreat more and more before the desperate, theatrical pleasures of Charlus: "Things are so beautiful simply because they are what they are, and existence is so much calm and beauty diffused all around them." [38] Repelled and anguished by the mysteries he always suspects in any object of sexual desire, Marcel takes refuge in these

innocent pleasures of family life. The enjoyment of such moments is felt as intensely as if it were a rescue from danger and
evil. Indeed, the pleasures given by each of the five senses, as if
to compensate for the frightening or unsatisfactory experiences
connected with sexuality, become extraordinarily acute in other
kinds of situations. The sounds of sexual pleasure made by Charlus and Jupien make Marcel think of murder; but the Paris
street sounds, the cries of different vendors, inspire long and
amused analogies with various kinds of music. The sexual scenes
he sees at Montjouvain and in Charlus's brothel are scenes of
sadism and, with Mademoiselle Vinteuil and her friend, of prof-
anation of a parent; but Marcel stares with intense pleasure at
the hawthorns, waiting to see the truth they hide. His lips are
inadequate to give him the taste of Albertine's cheeks, and when
he kisses her his crushed nose can no longer take in her odor; but
the odors of his Aunt Léonie's apartment and the taste of the tea-
soaked *madeleine* give him the security of a protective family life
and even a kind of religious felicity. Finally, to touch Albertine
when she is awake is to be reminded of her "untouchable," elusive thoughts and desires; but to touch her body when she is
sleeping gives him the same quiet and deep pleasure as the "scar-
let shower of anemone-petals" which the sun seems to spread
out on the carpet of his room at Balbec, "among which I could
not resist the temptation to plunge my bare feet for a moment." [39]

After his return with Albertine from his second stay in Balbec,
Marcel seems to spend most of his life in bed, although there is
no indication that any physical infirmity forces him to stay in his
parents' apartment. But this apparent renunciation of experience
is actually an enrichment of experience. Going into society has
bored him; visiting new places has been disappointing; and his
love for Albertine is making him see the dangers of attaching
himself to another person, the fatigue of the painful and useless
investigations into which his jealousy forces him. In the moments
of respite from his jealousy, Marcel feels indifferent toward Albertine and wishes that she were no longer there so that he could
travel and see new places, meet new people. The morning that

Françoise brings him Albertine's letter of goodbye, his old dreams of Venice have come back and his restlessness has become a specific plan to go to Italy without Albertine. But such desires seem to be another version of *divertissement*. The pleasures of traveling, of meeting new women, are really pleasures only as desires, not as experiences of actual contact with new places and people. Marcel sometimes speaks as if Albertine were preventing him from living more fully; but what she really does is to create that atmosphere of domestic tranquillity in which he can live what is for him the fullest, most satisfactory life: the life of desire and fantasy, and, especially, of remembering past desires. The time with Albertine, although it is filled with anxieties and desires that keep Marcel from writing, is in several ways a preparation for writing, a try-out of the imaginative processes he will use later on for his book. The following passage is a particularly good example of the way in which Marcel instinctively understands the idea of growth not as an accumulation of new experiences, but as a re-creation and an *approfondissement* of past experience:

> Françoise came in to light the fire, and to make it draw, threw upon it a handful of twigs, the scent of which, forgotten for a year past, traced round the fireplace a magic circle within which, perceiving myself poring over a book, now at Combray, now at Doncières, I was as joyful, while remaining in my bedroom in Paris, as if I had been on the point of starting for a walk along the Méséglise way, or of going to join Saint-Loup and his friends on the training-ground. It often happens that the pleasure which everyone takes in turning over the keepsakes that his memory has collected is keenest in those whom the tyranny of bodily ill-health and the daily hope of recovery prevent, on the one hand, from going out to seek in nature scenes that resemble those memories, and, on the other hand, leave so convinced that they will shortly be able to do so that they can remain gazing at them in a state of desire, of appetite, and not regard them merely as memories, as pictures. But, even if they were never to be anything more than memories to me, even if I, as I recalled them, saw merely pictures, immediately they recreated in me, of me as a whole, by virtue of an identical sensation, the boy, the youth

who had first seen them. There had been not merely a change in the weather outside, or, inside the room, the introduction of a fresh scent, there had been in myself a difference of age, the substitution of another person. The scent, in the frosty air, of the twigs of brushwood, was like a fragment of the past, an invisible floe broken off from the ice of an old winter that stole into my room, often variegated moreover with this perfume or that light, as though with a sequence of different years, in which I found myself plunged, overwhelmed, even before I had identified them, by the eagerness of hopes long since abandoned. The sun's rays fell upon my bed and passed through the transparent shell of my attenuated body, warmed me, made me as hot as a sheet of scorching crystal. Whereupon, a famished convalescent who has already begun to batten upon all the dishes that are still forbidden him, I asked myself whether marriage with Albertine would not spoil my life, as well by making me assume the burden, too heavy for my shoulders, of consecrating myself to another person, as by forcing me to live in absence from myself because of her continual presence and depriving me, forever, of the delights of solitude.[40]

The vague nature of Marcel's physical weakness helps to keep him constantly in that stage of the activity of *divertissement* in which the objects of desire still seem desirable. He is prevented from actively going after what he feels would make him happy, so he is never disillusioned by an actual realization of desire, and yet he is well enough to feel that the images he finds agreeable are not merely inner pictures, but attainable and fulfilling realities in the outer world. He has taken the anguish out of *divertissement* by managing never to get beyond the projects, the desires themselves; but the intensity and excitement of desire are kept because his physical state permits him to feel that there is something more than his desires. Pascal justifies *divertissement* as evidence of man's need for God. Unable to bear solitude, terrified of death, and miserable without the satisfactions only God can give, man deceives himself into thinking that various finite goals will make him happy. His life is a series of pursuits, disillusionments, and renewed pursuits. But this very restlessness is for

Pascal a sign that there is a need in man for a fulfillment that nothing finite can give; if it does not prove the existence of God, it at least testifies to the need for God in man. Proust and his narrator are just as convinced as Pascal that to reach the objects of our desire is always disappointing, but rather than use this to justify a renunciation of the world and a search for God, Proust makes the state of desire itself into the absolute satisfaction. Marcel encourages his illusion that he wants something outside of himself in order to enjoy more fully what is already a part of himself: his memories, the pictures of his past. At the time of his life described in *La Prisonnière*, the illusion still seems necessary. The narrator has not yet explicitly seen that the only possible possession, and therefore the only peace and happiness, is possession of the self; there is still the lingering idea from Combray that the "true" and the "real" are hidden somewhere in the outer world, and in the paragraph following the one I have quoted Marcel speaks of his desire to be free of Albertine in order to explore the streets and cities where he may meet new women. But he is beginning to see that to live alone is not only the *pis aller* made necessary by the elusiveness of external reality, but is actually the only way of having those satisfactions he has until now expected to be revealed to him from the outside.

The narrator rediscovers "the delights of solitude" at different moments of his life, and each time they are enriched by the participation of a greater part of his being: the physical pleasure in the toilet at Combray, the excited identifications with fictional characters when he reads in the garden at Combray, the processes of remembering and desiring and beginning to articulate whole periods of his life—the time spent in Combray, in Doncières—while he lies in bed in *La Prisonnière*, and, finally, still in bed, the literary use of these memories, their transference from a perishable brain to indestructible art. These solitary pleasures take place, so to speak, within that "field" of possible behavior traced by an old fascination with the self; but all the narrator's faculties, his resources of fantasy and, later, his linguistic power, will contribute to enrich and transform this self-absorbed activity into a

more complete and articulate commitment to experience than
would have been possible for Marcel in an active involvement
with anything outside of himself. This is, in a way, only to say
that he is an artist and that his work will be his fullest commitment. What the work does is to situate this truth psychologically,
to give the dramatic facts that both make the act of writing a
necessary choice for Marcel and, above all, an opportunity for
a complete use of self.

IV. *From the lover's anguish to the novelist's possessions*

Marcel's love for Albertine, even that part of it that makes his life
most artistically unproductive while he is living with her, will be
artistically useful in other ways. He comes to see the novelistic
potentialities of certain of his emotions, and, in a sense, his whole
book is about the similarities and differences between the novelistic imagination when it is used in life and when it is used in
literature. When Marcel is in love with Albertine, jealousy stimulates his imagination in a way that produces nothing but suffering. Everything that she says and does and that other people say
about her sets off various more or less "fictional" situations in his
mind. He tries to explain to himself why she wants to go to
Madame Verdurin's the evening Morel is to play there, why she
leaves him to go to her aunt's in Touraine; he wonders about the
nature of her friendship with Mademoiselle Vinteuil, or the
meaning of a grimace or a smile.

The analysis of Marcel's love for Albertine is rich in implications about the kind of futile richness imagination has in life.
The novels we construct are necessarily arbitrary, may have nothing to do with the reality we are interested in knowing. We are
always having to guess about other people's feelings and often
about what they may or may not have done. We imagine several
possibilities about reality, and we try to settle for what seem to us
the most reasonable or probable ones. This fictional quality of
our ideas about other people is present even under the best conditions of openness and confidence. Even if we imagine someone

who would speak to us freely and sincerely of his or her deepest and most private feelings, not very much would really ever be given to us; we would still have to guess what it is like to feel what is called love or fear from the viewpoint of another body and another history. And when someone hides intentions or feelings, we are reduced even more to our own resources of dramatizing *our* fantasies as real possibilities for someone else. We are, in such cases, closer to a purely novelistic process, for we are deprived of an at least general confirmation and approval of our ideas as corresponding to something outside of us, as a report as well as a fantasy.

In nature our creative participation in reality is even more radical. The connections we establish among different parts of a natural scene, the harmonies we see, the relations among colors and shapes can never be traced to a specific intention realized in nature before we choose to see them there. Sartre, discussing the hypothetical character of what he calls our "dreams" on certain motifs vaguely outlined by nature, points out that even a belief in universal providence would not guarantee any specific intention outside of the human viewer. *I* see the harmony of blue and green in the picture of water and grass, but each color can be independently explained by physical factors (for the water, for example, depth of the river, swiftness of the current, quality of the soil) which make the harmony of blue and green seem purely fortuitous: "The matching of hues can be intentional only as something accidental, it is the meeting of two causal series, that is, at first sight, the result of chance." [41] The world is not an intended puzzle with any one key to it, and each one of us, so to speak, lives his own novel about the meanings of life.

Now an emotion such as jealousy creates a situation in which the imagination, desperately and gratuitously rich, cannot settle for any one story. For there is an elusive reality beyond our imagination, and our aim, precisely, is not to invent a story, but to hit on the right version of certain real facts. Proust insists on the paradoxical nature of jealousy. Because it is an essentially investigating attitude, the jealous man, on the one hand, is all attention;

he wants to catch and register facts about other people. On the other hand, because he can never be sure of what these facts are, and because he has an urgent, obsessive need to know, he may, while apparently watching the world, lose himself in the confusing variety of solutions he inevitably imagines. The Proustian system of multiple motivations (the "soit que . . . soit que . . ." type of sentence to explain a piece of behavior), and, especially, the agonized moving from one painful mental picture to another illustrate how the desire merely to absorb certain facts results in a proliferation of conjectures that make external reality seem more ungraspable than ever. The intense urgency felt in jealousy has the disastrous effect of crippling the pragmatic faculty that usually qualifies the attention we give to the world; Marcel, completely attentive, is also completely gullible.

There is an interestingly similar treatment of jealous curiosity in a recent novel by Alain Robbe-Grillet. In *La Jalousie* [42] we see the world from the point of view of a husband apparently anxious to discover if his wife—referred to only as A . . .—is having an affair with another man, Franck. The husband is never referred to directly; his psychology is expressed entirely through descriptions of external reality. There is no analysis of the emotion of jealousy, only a picture of the world as it looks to a jealous man. In part, Robbe-Grillet's technique suggests the husband's attempt to be objective, to prevent his own feelings from interfering between what he sees and his anxiously receptive consciousness. But this attempt at a correct reading of reality only makes the ambiguities of what he sees more starkly evident. The painstaking descriptions reveal nothing but the obsessed point of view from which they are made. The angle of vision, the choices of what is described, the patterns of recurrent description, the kind of detail entered into all describe the emotion of jealousy, and perhaps not at all the "truth" about A . . . and Franck. And subjective fantasies invade the descriptions themselves in the guise of objective descriptions: the husband "looks at" scenes he cannot possibly have seen—such as Franck killing the centipede in the hotel bedroom where he may have spent a night with

A . . .—with the same scrupulous attention as when he is describing their behavior in his presence on the terrace or in the dining room. Finally, the habit of attention becomes so generalized that its original purpose is defeated, and the ambiguity of the whole of reality, not merely of the relationship between A . . . and Franck, comes to obsess a mind now "jealous" of the whole universe's "secrets." The husband pathologically pays attention to everything; he compulsively describes his whole world —the house, the lines of banana trees, mosquitoes flying around a lamp. The jealous man thus comes to have an unbearable sense of the unknowable nature of all reality, of the fact that any description we make of the world both reflects a particular point of view and is necessarily inadequate to describe a complex, constantly changing world. This is a truism we all admit theoretically, but which seldom bothers us because we know that we can actively affect the world without having exact knowledge about it. *La Jalousie* is a pathological study precisely because the jealous husband has lost the knack of ignoring the essential inappropriateness of our statements about reality to reality itself. He has reached a kind of untenable epistemological honesty, and this is his madness. Jealousy creates an unappeasable need to know, and the processes by which knowledge is sought in *La Jalousie* demonstrate that what we call knowledge corresponds not necessarily to external fact, but rather to the nature of a particular need to know.

Proust's techniques, range of interest, and talent are, of course, very different from Robbe-Grillet's, but his narrator's jealous investigations are as futile as those of the husband in *La Jalousie*. Having refused to accept any one, possibly false view of Albertine's attitude toward him, Marcel accepts many views, which may all be partly true, but which may also be completely false. The novel we are reading gains great psychological richness and density because of the way the narrator thus imaginatively explores people's lives, but Marcel suffers because for him, a character living in the world of the novel, his fantasies are never adequate to the reality that dramatically provokes them. But he

comes to realize the artistic usefulness of his failure. The jealous
man's interpretations of a woman's behavior may all be false, and
therefore useless for possessing her. But certain of his fantasies
can be chosen as the reality of another person's life—someone
living only in the world of the novel. Anything the novelist
chooses to say is "true" because people's lives are exactly equivalent to his fantasies about them. The world of the novel is an
intended, purposeful one, and in that world people's capacity for
life is limited to the novelist's inventive capacity. What he says
about his world creates that world; what he says about the real
woman who may have betrayed him can only be a stab in the
dark about a world to whose existence he is unnecessary. The
fantasies of jealousy can thus be turned away from the real
woman and dramatized in a work of art: "Jealousy," Marcel
writes toward the end of Le Temps retrouvé, speaking of his
book, "is a good procurer who, when there is an empty space in
our picture, goes out into the street and gets us the good-looking
girl we needed." We are no longer in love with the woman, but a
remark she makes awakens for a moment the old suffering and
curiosity, and the anguished imagination swiftly creates several
situations that might explain her remark: "The brushes, drunk
with infuriated love, paint and paint." [43] The suffering of jealousy is being used as a moment of *inspiration;* characters, situations, ideas come in a rush to the novelist, he has the passage he
seemed incapable of writing. Proust marked this passage "Capi-
talissime": it suggests one of the most important strategies by
which a dead end in Marcel's life comes to nourish his art.

But the experience of jealousy gives the narrator the idea of
writing a novel in which expectations encouraged by earlier fiction will, to a large extent, not be satisfied. Novelists before
Proust generally take an omniscient point of view; it is the fullness and reliability of their knowledge which remind us how far
we are from life. When Fielding, Balzac, and Flaubert analyze
their characters' motives, we know that these *are* their motives,
and part of our pleasure is precisely in this relaxing illusion of
having captured a mind, of its holding still while we look at it.

Characters' doubts about each other remind us of our own imperfect knowledge in life, and the most unrealistic situation "in" the novel is actually the conditions in which we read the novel. Because we share an omniscient author's point of view—a god's point of view in the world of the novel—our relationship to the characters perfectly satisfies a fantasy of ideal possession. We know that a character's existence does not depend on us (so he is not only a creature of our fantasy), and yet his existence is fully contained in our awareness of him. In life, as the narrator writes in "Combray," we have only images of other people's feelings; but beyond these images there is a whole world we can perceive only with our senses, and which is therefore largely opaque to us, which "offers a dead weight which our sensibilities have not the strength to lift." But in fiction other people are reduced entirely to these images: "The novelist's happy discovery was to think of substituting for those opaque sections, impenetrable by the human spirit, their equivalent in immaterial sections, things, that is, which the spirit can assimilate to itself." The act of reading satisfies the double requirement of the desire for possession as Marcel defines it: these people about whom we know so much are "out there," distinct from us, but their reality is inert, a question of print on a white page; they become actively alive only when a reader internalizes them completely. "After which it matters not that the actions, the feelings of this new order of creatures appear to us in the guise of truth, since we have made them our own, since it is in ourselves that they are happening, that they are holding in thrall, while we turn over, feverishly, the pages of the book, our quickened breath and staring eyes." [44]

The narrator's remarks can, it seems to me, be developed further; they encourage us to think of the reading and writing of novels as experiences and experiments in gaining a certain power over the self and the world. For the novelist, the people whose lives he possesses so securely had their beginnings in him, and the range of experience he defines and possesses as he writes is, of course, his own. He enjoys a kind of power over his own personality by "distributing" himself among various parts of his novelistic world. But to the extent that his self-dramatization proceeds from a desire to possess what is different from the self, the novelist may be tempted to consider the world he is inventing as if he were discovering it outside of himself. He wants, as it were, to become the reader of his novel, to have his work return to his imagination as if it had not begun there. He would then be transforming what is actually a self-revelation into a triumph of his dream of possessing others. Actually, the very nature of storytelling suggests this need to substitute the self for the world by making it appear as independent of the storyteller as is the world. The novelist possesses himself as he can never possess the world, and yet he has made himself look like the world. He has become what he ordinarily finds outside of himself: other people, dramatic incidents, various physical settings. And when novelists present their stories as if they were taken from "real life," the convention they are obeying perhaps owes its strength to the peculiar pleasure given by this superficially easy, but deeply subtle lie. Proust's narrator is, in ways I shall discuss more fully later on, a victim of that lie about his own story, although he apparently intends to prevent himself from enjoying such illusions. He continually reminds us that the only possession possible for the artist is self-possession and thus seems to recognize implicitly that what the writer does in his work is to give to other people parts of himself they would never have possessed if he had not first of all had the hopeless ambition of possessing others. It is therefore only for his public that the novelist realizes this ambition: the lives of his characters are different from the reader's own life, but they are not really lived unless the reader agrees to incorporate them into the history of his imagination.

But, as readers, we also have a peculiar way of undermining the novelist's gift. The curiosity we feel about people in life may carry over into our reading of the novel. If we find the characters convincing representations of human beings, it may not be easy to control fantasies of what their lives are like *beyond* what is given to us. Since we novelize so constantly about the world around us, filling in the gaps of our knowledge about others with our own needs and projects, we may forget that such novelizing is a bad way to read a novel. We are tempted to talk about characters of fiction as we would about people we know. And since these characters have no physical presence to remind us that the external world is essentially unknowable, beyond our reach, our conjectures about them may seem as real as what the novelist actually gives us, since both are mental realities. With people we know in our lives, we may make mistakes and indulge in fantasies that are irrelevant to what they are or what they have done, but there *is* more to their lives than we can ever seize by being attentive to their behavior. And we not only try to look behind and beyond what they say and do; we also try to imagine other ways of behaving, what would have happened if someone had acted differently, why someone did this and not that. But such questions are, of course, misplaced when they are asked about characters in a novel. We can, certainly, analyze a character's behavior, draw conclusions about him that are not explicitly spelled out, but this is not the same thing as wondering about parts of his life that are nowhere expressed in the novel. For his life is entirely within the novel and he cannot "really" be anything that is not somehow accounted for by the language in which he exists. But we easily take these people of fiction for real people, and it almost seems that the novelist's success can partly be measured by the extent to which he passes off his verbal creations as the real thing, and seduces us into forgetting that his creative powers are, after all, only linguistic.

Now in much modern fiction the reader is deliberately encouraged to feel that the world of the novel can be as elusive as the world of the rest of his experience. The "dear reader" geniality of the traditional omniscient author expresses a fundamental sympathy for the public. The pleasant, personal tone of the narrator in addressing his audience suggests his willingness to give this marvelously available, final, and defined world to his readers. The more he explains his characters, the more, so to speak, he compassionately discourages the reader's imagination; we are not overly tempted to add our own inventions to the story, and it is easier to resist the desire to create as well as possess the people whose lives are so generously given to us. When, however, some of the late nineteenth-century writers rebel against the tradition of the omniscient author, the narrative points of view with which they experiment in their novels radically change the relationships between the narrator and the reader and between the reader and the characters. Flaubert is the first novelist to protest emphatically against the persona of the chatty author, but in his novels he by no means gives up the privileges of omniscience. If an important part of his achievement is in the special kind of narrative perspective from which he tells his stories—his ambiguously ironic and sympathetic attitude toward characters such as Emma Bovary and Félicité—he never questions, by his technique, the reader's right to enjoy conditions of ideal knowledge and possession in reading fiction. This traditional enjoyment is much more seriously threatened by the narrative techniques of Proust, Gide, and Henry James. By writing stories in which the narrative point of view is limited to the awareness of characters within the world of the novel, they seem to be forcing the reader into frustrations similar to those he experiences in life. We see only as much as what James calls the "center of consciousness" sees; the world of the novel passes through the imperfect reflecting consciousness of a character, who is not the creator of that world, in much the same way as the reader sees life only as it is reflected through his particular point of view.

I shall presently be discussing in detail Proust's use of Marcel and the narrator to tell his story; it may help to emphasize the interest and complexity of what Proust does if, as a conclusion to these general remarks, I consider an extreme use of the center-of-consciousness method, again taking Robbe-Grillet's *La Jalousie* as an example. The technique has great potentialities for perversity, and they are fully exploited in *La Jalousie*, in which the method is expertly used to tease the reader. In the novel, A . . . and Franck talk about a novel they are reading (and which the husband has not read); the story seems to have parallels with what may be their own story, and the reader wonders if they are using it to discuss their own complications in front of A . . .'s husband. The narrator, having, obviously, more literary sophistication than they, remarks that they never judge the quality of the novel, that they discuss the characters as if they were real people, whom they know, and they enjoy imagining what might have happened in the novel if the characters had behaved differently. We are apparently being told that Franck and A . . . read unintelligently: they let their novelistic imaginations wander too much while they are reading a novel. This meaning, however, can only exasperate us, since Robbe-Grillet has written a novel in which he is constantly tempting us to make the same kind of mistake as A . . . and Franck. They are undoubtedly reading a less experimental novel than we are, but much of the experimenting with which we have to deal seems intended to trick us into the mistakes they make with more traditional fiction. We cannot be entirely certain which of the narrator's descriptions are fantasy, and which represent things the jealous husband actually sees in the external world. The result is that, in a sense, we are more mystified than he. Not only do we never know the "truth" about A . . . and Franck; there is no way of being sure to what extent the husband is a prisoner of his obsessive images. And on every page it seems that we are being provoked into asking all the irrelevant questions about a work of art: do Franck and A . . . spend the night together when they go into town, is Franck slowly poisoning his wife, does the husband finally kill A . . . ?

But if we resist being teased into asking such questions about non-existent things "beyond" the narrative surface, what kind of relationship *is* possible to the characters in this novel? What critical questions and analyses are relevant to what Robbe-Grillet has done? James saw clearly enough the special enjoyment possible from such a novel. We have the advantage over the center of consciousness of having, as he cannot have, his wondering as an object of our attention, as something to appropriate, to look at and know as we never can with our own wondering in life. And indeed, at the same time that Robbe-Grillet tantalizes us with all the uncertainties of his characters' behavior, he has organized the narrative point of view into such a complex puzzle of recurrent descriptions, with more or less important variations each time, that he is really making loud claims on what is evidently for him the right kind of attention. The patterns of the narrative point of view itself are to be deciphered. But although the novel gives us a striking sense of how the world looks from the point of view of a jealous mind, the fact that this mind is almost entirely reduced to one obsessive emotion makes the work rather thin—at the same time that we are expected to take a good deal of trouble to make the narrative intelligible. We cannot always distinguish between what is actually seen and what is a jealous fantasy; we have no idea of the temporal relationship between the incidents described and the description of these incidents; and, finally, we can hardly say that a "character" is suggested when this character's density consists entirely in a compulsive attention to certain details. By perversely trying to make us bad readers, Robbe-Grillet is revitalizing some basic truths about the differences between life and art, about the nature of reading. It is, however, a serious weakness in what might have been a brilliant if limited achievement that Robbe-Grillet expects us to continue to be interested in technique when he is no longer satisfying our interest in psychology.

The psychological and social contexts in which Proust portrays the jealous lover are, of course, incomparably richer. And literary technique is both unobtrusive and a matter of great importance in *A la Recherche*: the narrator, no longer in pursuit of Albertine, must translate his experience of jealousy into certain decisions he now has to make as a writer. We see that he denies himself the satisfaction of creating an imaginary Albertine who could be possessed more easily than the woman who has made him suffer; he presents his jealous fantasies *as* fantasies, and the ambiguities that tortured him in life become the subject of his art. He remembers Albertine's elusiveness and wonders about her secrets a second time. But by recalling his anguished curiosity about the women he has loved, the narrator seeks to fix and possess the even more painfully elusive image of himself. His interest in new novelistic techniques to portray love are inspired not only by a desire to be faithful to his experience; they are strategies of self-possession. The narrator's literary choices affect, moreover, both the nature of this self-possession and, retrospectively, his relation to the world. His experience of love reveals, as I have shown, certain aspects of the novelistic imagination; the work in which he exploits the novelistic richness of that experience also allows him to create a world where imaginative fantasy is no longer a sign of helplessness, but rather an instrument of ideal control and possession.

CHAPTER THREE

THE LANGUAGE OF LOVE

I. *The loved one's absence from the lover's desires*

Unable to possess himself by directing and immobilizing the desires of the women he loves, Marcel nevertheless discovers in the activity of loving an image of his persistent needs. He comes to feel that the lover's jealousy is essentially self-jealousy, and that the woman herself, from the first stages of excited fantasy about her to the last pains of jealousy, is relatively unimportant, merely an occasion for the acting out of certain characterizing needs in the lover. In *La Fugitive,* the narrator explains the "minute place" the loved one occupies in our anxiety about her: "The fact is that the person counts for little or nothing; what is almost everything is the series of emotions, of agonies which [certain chance circumstances] have made us feel in the past in connexion with her [le processus d'émotions, d'angoisses que tels hasards nous ont fait jadis éprouver à propos d'elle] and which habit has attached to her." [1] Love is an anxiety which a fortuitous group of circumstances attaches at different moments of our lives to different people.

Ortega y Gasset remarked that *Un Amour de Swann* shows us every kind of feeling except love.[2] With Swann and later with Marcel we have stories in which the experience of love has few of the elements that much of the literature before Proust has trained us to expect in a story about love. It is not that idealistic definitions of love had not already been questioned. What is peculiar to Proust, it seems to me, is the explicitness and thoroughness with which he attacks the fundamental assumption of certain idealizing portraits of love. In the medieval courtly epics and lyrics, for example, as well as in Corneille, Rousseau, and Claudel, love includes moral admiration; the lover's personality is ennobled by his passion for someone worthy of being loved. Love thus realizes and intensifies a profound harmony between the self and the world: the lover *knows* the object of his love, and his responses are governed by moral qualities he rightly perceives. Corneille's characters occasionally speak of the mysterious *je ne sais quoi* which is at the beginning of love, but this blind initial response always turns out to be morally right, and what is dramatized is not the irrational aspect of love, but rather the merits that make the lovers approve their apparently blind choice as an instinctive appreciation of the loved one's value.

In Rousseau's *La Nouvelle Héloïse,* Saint-Preux loves Julie because she is the woman most worthy of being loved he has ever known. Her virtues are the cause of his love, and his perception of them determines the strength of his love and the form it takes. Julie in the middle of her family, idolized by the whole community as she fulfills every social duty with spontaneous generosity and justice, so effectively controls Saint-Preux's feelings by her noble qualities that his love for her is both increased and largely purified of sensual temptations when he has lived for a time in the Wolmar household. If it is true that there is a certain rebellious sensuality in the second half of *La Nouvelle Héloïse,* this current is much weaker than has often been said. Sexual passion is almost entirely replaced by the very real passion for virtue —for the calm pleasures of domestic life—which even gives a certain life to the sermonlike descriptions of the ideal household. To think of Rousseau as tending naturally to glorify a basically anti-social, destructive passion, and forcing himself to write an apology for marriage, is to misunderstand the nature of Julie and Saint-Preux's love. What Julie realizes in church the day of her marriage is that physical passion is only the illusion of nature; she discovers the heart of Rousseauistic thinking when she sees that what is most profoundly natural in man is also moral and social. When she writes that it was better for her not to marry the man she loves passionately, she is thinking not of what her love for

Saint-Preux has been but of a kind of love that intrudes into the story mainly as a fear, albeit as a curiously moving and persistent one: the fear of the potential blindness of passion, of the dehumanizing indifference of the lover to the moral personality of a person he or she seeks merely to possess at any cost. In *La Nouvelle Héloïse,* Rousseau transcends the profound discomfort and confusion over sensuality which we find in the *Confessions* both by glamorizing his neurotic impulses into an image of a great but forbidden passion, and by concentrating most of the sensual energy of his characters in the milder pleasures of domestic life and enthusiastic friendships.

Racine's dramatization of love as a debasing passion contrasts sharply with the courtly and romantic images of ennobling love. The people loved in Racine's plays are by no means base, but the lover's feelings have, in a sense, become completely detached from the loved one's moral worth. The activity of loving makes Racine's characters blind to everything except the violent need to possess, at any cost, a certain "object." The pathetic appeals of Andromaque and Junie are powerless to humanize Pyrrhus' and Néron's passion; the loved one is, finally, irrelevant to the passion he or she inspires. The lover is overwhelmed by feelings he may despise for a person he may not wish to love, and the exasperating irrationality and irresistible force of his passion give love the awesome aspect of a supernatural mystery, of a curse inflicted by the gods. Love in Proust's world is a much more prosaic affair; there are no avenging gods, no sense of a fatal passion, not even the glamor of violence. It is as if we had a deliberately clinical reduction of Racinian love to a certain imbalance between the self and the world, to a kind of pathological mistake on the part of the lover. But like Racine and the classical moralists, Proust sees nothing ennobling in love; the courtly tradition of the moral inspiration of love is completely foreign to his sensibility. Proust's lovers are, like Racine's, intensely unhappy in love, they are unable to resist their feelings, and they find themselves capable, perhaps not of murder, but of lying, bribery, and tyrannical behavior in order to possess their "prey."

What interests Proust is to get at the cause of this misery. Whereas in Racine a basic unresponsiveness to the loved one is only implied by the lover's brutal treatment of the person he or she pursues, Proust centers his analysis on the relationship between the lover's feelings and the person who is presumably the object of those feelings. Swann and Marcel suffer not so much because of the indifference or unworthiness of the women they love, but essentially because of the loved one's irrelevance to the lover's feelings. The irrationality of Marcel's love for Albertine is not that he pursues someone who is perhaps indifferent to him; it is rather that her possible indifference is enough to awaken in him the desire to possess her absolutely. The narrator thus comes to feel that when he most intensely needs someone else, he is, in reality, astonishingly unaware of the other person, and seems to be pursuing an elusive fantasy in himself. His responses to the world are perhaps only responses to the self. The Proustian critique of the idealistic tradition in the literature of love, and his particular contribution to the tradition of a deeply pessimistic view of love are, therefore, aspects of the narrator's anguished feelings about the self and the world. Love renews and intensifies his painful sense of the mystery of personality and the elusiveness of the external world.

Nothing could be more different from Marcel's failure to "see" Albertine than the clarity and distinctness with which Julie's image appears to Saint-Preux in *La Nouvelle Héloïse*. Alone at Meillerie, Saint-Preux has no difficulty evoking her life in great detail; as he thinks of her daily occupations, he sees again how worthy she is of being loved, and his love grows as he recognizes and affirms all that is lovable in her: "I always picture you attending to duties which make you even more deserving of my esteem; and my heart melts with delight when I think of your inexhaustible goodness." [3] Marcel, on the other hand, knows he is in love with Gilberte and Albertine because he notes in himself obsessive images and intentions in all of which they play central roles, but as vaguely outlined objects of pursuit rather than as clearly seen causes of his love. When he is with Gilberte on the

Champs-Elysées, he tries desperately to fix an image of her he can take home with him, but when he is alone he is so busy planning how he will let her know about his love that he has no time to think of her. With Albertine, his love is a frantic curiosity, and when she leaves him, Marcel recognizes the strength of his love in his inability to do anything but imagine ways of finding out how she felt when she left, and of forcing her to come back:

> To carnal pleasure I did not even give a thought at this moment; I did not even see, with my mind's eye, the image of that Albertine, albeit she had been the cause of such an upheaval of my existence, I did not perceive her body and if I had wished to isolate the idea that was bound up—for there is always some idea bound up—with my suffering, it would have been alternately, on the one hand my doubt as to the intention with which she had left me, with or without any thought of returning, and on the other hand the means of bringing her back.[4]

There is much activity from which Albertine is, then, absent; thinking about her turns out to be thinking of the details of a plan to have Saint-Loup try to bring her back to Paris:

> . . . what I myself called thinking of Albertine, was thinking of how I might bring her back, of how I might join her, might know what she was doing. With the result that if, during those hours of incessant martyrdom, there had been an illustrator present to represent the images which accompanied my sufferings, you would have seen pictures of the Gare d'Orsay, of the bank notes offered to Mme. Bontemps, of Saint-Loup stooping over the sloping desk of a telegraph office at which he was writing out a telegram for myself, never the picture of Albertine.[5]

And even at the moments when Marcel is not working out schemes to bring Albertine back, he realizes how much he wants her not so much by the suffering he feels when he has a clear image of her, but by his bursting into tears when he thinks of or sees things connected with their life together, such as Incarville or the Verdurins, the piano she used to play for him or the car he bought for her. In a sense, Marcel "deduces" his love for Albertine from his frantic behavior to get her back and from the pain caused by things associated with her.

Marcel discovers, then, that his violently possessive love for Albertine is compatible with an almost total ignorance of, and even inattentiveness to, Albertine. The experience of love thus reinforces his doubts about the possibility of authentically knowing what is different from the self. If the image of Albertine is so consistently absent from his need to possess her, it is at least probable that *what* he needs to possess does not correspond to the real girl he is pursuing. And he finds further evidence for the unimportance of the loved one when he compares his love for Albertine with his infatuations for Gilberte and Madame de Guermantes. The similarities among these different experiences make it seem as if he had always been pursuing the same woman. To us these similarities may point to a serious inflexibility in Marcel's personality, to an inability to get beyond a narrow range of obsessive responses. The narrator characteristically finds in this repetitiveness evidence of a universal psychological law. Certain basic needs of our personality reappear in every aspect of our behavior: ["Our slightest desire, while it is a unique chord, contains the fundamental notes out of which our whole life is built."] [6] The women he pursues after Albertine's death are, he writes, all substitutes for her, and he suggests that the various activities in a man's life are attempts to satisfy a "désir premier" present in seemingly unrelated desires:

> Andrée, these other women, all of them in relation to Albertine—as Albertine herself had been in relation to Balbec—were to be numbered among those substitutes for pleasures, replacing one another, in a gradual degradation, which enable us to dispense with the pleasure to which we can no longer attain, a holiday at Balbec, or the love of Albertine (as the act of going to the Louvre to look at a Titian which was originally in Venice consoles us for not being able to go there), for those pleasures which, separated one from another by indistinguishable gradations, convert our life into a series of concentric, contiguous, harmonic and gradu-

ated zones, encircling an initial desire which has set the tone, eliminated everything that does not combine with it and spread the dominant colour (as had, for instance, occurred to me also in the cases of the Duchesse de Guermantes and of Gilberte).[7]

The lover impatiently eliminates what does not harmonize with a basic persistent desire in his desires for different women; in his urgency to satisfy a profound need in himself, he obscures what is irrelevant to that need in each of his loves, thus hiding from himself the uniqueness of each woman. The lover's apparent purpose is to penetrate the mysteries of another life; in reality, he adds to the mystery by obsessively repeating a "processus d'émotions, d'angoisses" from his own past. But, characteristically, the narrator comes to consider what might have been only a source of profound discouragement as a chance to penetrate the mysteries of the self:

> I had guessed long ago in the Champs-Elysées, and had since established to my own satisfaction, that when we are in love with a woman, we simply project into her a state of our own soul, that the important thing is, therefore, not the worth of the woman but the depth of the state; and that the emotions which a young girl of no kind of distinction arouses in us can enable us to bring to the surface of our consciousness some of the most intimate parts of our being, more personal, more remote, more essential than would be reached by the pleasure that we derive from the conversation of a great man or even from the admiring contemplation of his work.[8]

The lover has only to look at himself rather than at the women in order to possess what is, after all, the real object of his pursuit. To write about love should, then, presumably be to write about a process of painful self-discovery. Or, more precisely, it is in the reflection on a failure of self-possession that the self is discovered; the detailed memory of that failure outlines an individuality that could never be satisfactorily reflected in the woman's eyes.

11. *The self as an "appareil vide": a critique of psychological analysis*

In remembering his own jealous behavior and that of others, the narrator suggests the ways in which novelistic characterization should reflect his experience of love as a monologue masquerading as a dialogue. When, in *A l'Ombre des jeunes filles en fleur,* he notes that Albertine resembled Gilberte in her "craze for amusement," he sees in this similarity a sign of the persistence of certain tastes in himself, and he outlines how a novelist might express this self-characterizing activity of falling in love:

> They are, these women, a product of our temperament, an image inversely projected, a negative of our sensibility. So that a novelist might, in relating the life of his hero, describe his successive love-affairs in almost exactly similar terms, and thereby give the impression not that he was repeating himself but that he was creating, since an artificial novelty is never so effective as a repetition that manages to suggest a fresh truth. He ought, moreover, to indicate in the character of the lover a variability which becomes apparent as the story moves into fresh regions, into different latitudes of life. And perhaps he would be stating yet another truth if while investing all the other persons of his story with distinct characters he refrained from giving any to the beloved.[9]

These suggestions for novelists are given in the conditional tense; they are presented as if they were speculations that occur to the narrator as he is writing about his own experience with Gilberte and Albertine. It seems, however, obvious that, to a certain extent, the narrator's sense of what he himself is doing leads to his theoretical conclusions about what a novelist "should" do in portraying characters in love. But there is by no means a simple equivalence between what he writes in the many theoretical passages in the novel and his actual dramatizations of himself and Albertine, or of Swann and Odette. The narrator's theories have not really caught up with his practice; they seem to describe more adequately his intentions before writing than the actual achievement of his work.

To re-create our "true life," we must resign ourselves to "giving up our dearest illusions, ceasing to believe in the objectivity of what we have ourselves built up, and instead of lulling ourselves for the hundredth time with the words, 'She was very sweet,' reading behind all this, 'I enjoyed having her in my embrace.'" [10] Although it is not true that the narrator gives "no character" to Albertine, he can, as I have shown, describe his feelings for her and yet speak very little about her. He seems to want to find the language adequate to the "processus d'émotions, d'angoisses," to what he also refers to as the "obscure deities" [11] in himself that are the real causes of love. His literary problem is, therefore, to find a vocabulary of self-description. It is interesting that in spite of this intention to analyze the self, Proust's narrator raises serious objections to the traditional language of introspection. Sartre has often used Proust as a scapegoat for his attacks on this language of psychological analysis in fiction. What is remarkable, given Sartre's obvious distaste for Proust, is how often passages from A la Recherche du temps perdu could be used to illustrate Sartre's psychological and stylistic ideas. The view of love proposed in L'Etre et le néant as a conflict in which the lover tries to force the loved one to choose him absolutely (as a way of justifying his very existence) seems, in many respects, a summing up of the Proustian picture of love. And the Sartrean argument that consciousness has no content, that it is an activity transcending toward objects, is anticipated in Marcel's surprised realization that he does not discover his love for Albertine by introspective analysis of his feelings, but by noticing both the effect on him of certain objects associated with her and his frantic plans to keep her a prisoner in his parents' apartment.[12] In fact, in one passage the narrator questions the whole process of introspection as a means of finding out anything about the self, and we find something close to the Sartrean view that consciousness is a void except insofar as it can project itself into objects in the outer world: ["Now, since the self is constantly thinking numerous things, since it is nothing more than the thoughts of these things, when by chance, instead of having them as the objects of its attention, it suddenly turns its thought upon itself, it finds only an empty apparatus, something unfamiliar, to which—in order to give it some reality—it adds the memory of a face seen in a mirror."] [13] The idea of the self as an "empty apparatus" is, of course, implicit in Marcel's anguish about the nature of his personality; I have discussed his dependence on stable reflections of himself in the outer world. To affirm the uselessness of introspection, the void the mind finds when it tries to analyze and discover itself, would, then, seem a natural consequence of this anguish. It is, however, true, for reasons I shall presently discuss, that the narrator's novelistic procedures qualify and even contradict the lessons of experience that lead to his writing a novel, and the self so meticulously analyzed in the narrative of *A la Recherche* is anything but an "empty apparatus." But what Sartre fails to mention is the nonanalytic bias of this massive work of analysis, the thorough dramatization, for example, of love not as a state of analyzable feelings, but as a specific kind of activity of the self *in* the world. Much of his own critique of a static, wholly inner concept of emotion is already dramatized in the love affairs of Proust's characters.

The main fault the narrator finds with intellectual self-analysis is that it obscures the "désir premier," interrupts a psychologically necessary process. It hides rather than expresses the real cause of behavior; such analyses are often used to deceive the self and, it is hoped, others. The narrator questions the value of all intellectual reporting on character, and he insists on the reliability of more active agents of characterization, on, especially, the truthfulness of the body. The portrait of Legrandin in "Combray" is a good example of this. The Legrandin constantly inveighing against snobs is an obstacle that obscures, in his own eyes and, for a long time, in the eyes of Marcel's family, important physical evidence of what he really is. For the truth of his character is in fact expressed in the way he tells his lies; by watching him lie, Marcel finally discovers a striking example of what Georges

Piroué has called "the authenticity of the false." [14] When Marcel, whom Legrandin has invited to dinner, asks him if he knows the Guermantes, two Legrandins answer:

> . . . Legrandin the talker would reply, "No, I have never cared to know them." But unfortunately the talker was now subordinated to another Legrandin, whom he kept carefully hidden in his breast, whom he would never consciously exhibit, because this other could tell stories about our own Legrandin and about his snobbishness which would have ruined his reputation for ever; and this other Legrandin had replied to me already in that wounded look, that stiffened smile, the undue gravity of his tone in uttering those few words, in the thousand arrows by which our own Legrandin had instantaneously been stabbed and sickened, like a Saint Sebastian of snobbery:
>
> "Oh, how you hurt me! No, I do not know the Guermantes family. Do not remind me of the great sorrow of my life." And since this other, this irrepressible, dominant, despotic Legrandin, if he lacked our Legrandin's charming vocabulary, shewed an infinitely greater promptness in expressing himself, by means of what are called 'reflexes,' it followed that, when Legrandin the talker attempted to silence him, he would already have spoken, and it would be useless for our friend to deplore the bad impression which the revelations of his *alter ego* must have caused, since he could do no more now than endeavour to mitigate them.

We know only the passions of others, the narrator goes on to say; what we know about our own passions we learn from other people: "Upon ourselves they [our passions] react but indirectly, through our imagination, which substitutes for our actual, primary motives other, secondary motives, less stark and therefore more decent." [15] And, more generally, it is not only shame or vanity that accounts for these self-deceptions. The narrator speaks, for example, of the "invisible beliefs" that allow us to be blind to our real desires. As long as he feels certain that Elstir is going to introduce him to Albertine, Marcel feels indifferent toward her; it is only when the chance to meet her has been lost—

and with it the certainty that he is about to realize his wish—that he realizes how important this meeting is for him. In the same way, the narrator adds, we are indifferent to death because we really do not believe in it; or we think we no longer love a woman because we feel certain of possessing her.[16] The circumstances of self-deception vary, but the unreliability of our self-analyses is a permanent fact.

In reflection we thus construct a convenient or flattering self-image, and in one passage Proust's narrator goes so far as to suggest the total superfluity of all intermediate analyses that set up abstract categories between our needs and our behavior. During his second stay in Balbec, Marcel alternately moves toward Albertine and away from her, qualifying his claims of affection for her with claims of his indifference, in a "rhythmical oscillation which leads from a declaration to a quarrel," and the purpose of which is to mystify and dominate Albertine. Telling her he loves someone else, he suddenly pities her—she is, understandably enough, confused—and he feels like kissing her. He looks at her from "a standpoint that was purely human," with a compassion which, he writes, might have been shallower if he did not also love her, but which makes his jealous love momentarily vanish. But then he questions the usefulness of distinguishing this movement of pity from his moods of anxious love: "[. . . within the movement of withdrawal which constitutes one of the two elements of the rhythm, of what use is it to make a further distinction for] the refluences of human pity, which, the opposite of love, though springing perhaps unconsciously from the same cause, produces in every case the same effects?"[17] The distinctions set up by the vocabulary of conscious analysis—the shades of feeling that differentiate love from pity, passion from tenderness, and so forth—reflect what are perhaps only minor accidents, circumstantial trimmings on the main circuit from the unconscious to behavior. They tend to obscure not only the more profound consistency of the lover's behavior, but also the "désir premier" which his behavior is an attempt to satisfy.

The narrator's impatience with what could be called his secondary feelings of pity for Albertine is somewhat like Sartre's refusal to grant any importance to the good intentions of a character such as Garcin in *Huis clos:* Marcel's compassion no more prevents him from trying to imprison Albertine than Garcin's patriotic feelings save him from acting like a coward. It is, however, not difficult to see why Sartre finds Proust so irritating. When Sartre criticizes the language of psychological analysis, it is because he believes that consciousness is fully expressed in its projects with regard to things outside of itself. The Sartrean novel looks, of course, nothing like the Proustian novel. The intellectual density of *A la Recherche du temps perdu* is meaningless from Sartre's point of view; he finds nothing internal that would justify such density of analysis. Proust, however, seems to hesitate between two points of view on the contents of mental life. I have quoted a passage where the narrator writes that the self consists of an awareness of things outside of the self; if it tries to become the object of its own thought, it finds only an "empty apparatus." But immediately after the passage from *La Fugitive* in which the narrator emphasizes that thinking of Albertine always meant thinking of ways to make her come back, he criticizes men in general for rushing into "action" instead of pursuing "knowledge":

> Just as, throughout the whole course of our life, our egoism sees before it all the time the objects that are of interest to ourselves, but never takes in that Ego itself which is incessantly observing them, so the desire which directs our actions descends towards them, but does not reascend to itself, whether because, being unduly utilitarian, it plunges into the action and disdains all knowledge of it, or because we have been looking to the future to compensate for the disappointments of the past, or because the inertia of our mind urges it down the easy slope of imagination, rather than make it reascend the steep slope of introspection.[18]

The nobler choice is, obviously, "the steep slope of introspection"; it is, in fact, the choice on which the narrator acts in writing his work. And the self which the work reveals is not mainly a group of thoughts about other things, of projects to be realized

in the world. Marcel's discovery of the self as an "empty apparatus" seems to be not a philosophical certainty that will dictate certain novelistic techniques, but rather an anguishing proof of his
dependence on the external world, a dependence from which he
seeks to free himself in his work. His principal goal is, precisely,
to fill the void of consciousness with a self he can permanently
possess. If the narrator is as mistrustful of psychological analysis
as Sartre, it is not that he believes that mental life consists only of
projects that transcend the self; these projects are reliable signs,
guideposts that help to get beyond the inadequate analyses of
ordinary introspection to profounder analyses of unconscious patterns. Marcel finds in his behavior a sort of diagram of an essential self, certain "fundamental notes" that seem to indicate an
elusive but permanent individuality. His objection to analytical
language is, essentially, that it is ordinarily used to construct a
false self and to hide the real self. Marcel's experience shows him
the kind of mistakes ordinarily made in introspection; but he piti-
lessly exposes the errors of introspection in himself and in others
in order, finally, to be able to analyze the self accurately. For
Sartre a man can be accurately described by a description of his
behavior; Proust's narrator describes his behavior in the hope of
constructing a self without projects. The idea that the self exists
only through its activities in the world is a disturbing one for
Marcel; and if he insists on these activities in, for example, his
love for Albertine, it is with the purpose of deducing from them
a "désir premier" which does not depend on them, which is an
independent mental reality.

III. *The "notes fondamentales" from the perspective of memory:
psychological analysis reinstated*

How, exactly, does the narrator understand this original desire,
the "fundamental notes" of his personality which characterize his
desires for various women? What kind of language does he use to
describe this deeper self, and, especially, what are the conditions
in which psychological analysis can be trusted as an instrument

of self-knowledge? The basis for a persistent pattern of desire in
the narrator's life is suggested in his account of the crucial moment when he feels that he must possess Albertine's life. She
tells him, in the train going from La Raspelière to Balbec toward the end of his second stay at the resort, that she is a close
friend of Mademoiselle Vinteuil and of Mademoiselle Vinteuil's
Lesbian friend, and the "crystallization" of Marcel's love that
immediately takes place is presented as the accomplishment of a
just punishment:

> At the sound of these words, uttered as we were entering the
> station of Parville, so far from Combray and Montjouvain, so
> long after the death of Vinteuil, an image stirred in my heart, an
> image which I had kept in reserve for so many years that even if
> I had been able to guess, when I stored it up, long ago, that it
> had a noxious power, I should have supposed that in the course
> of time it had entirely lost it; preserved alive in the depths of my
> being—like Orestes whose death the gods had prevented in order
> that, on the appointed day, he might return to his native land
> to punish the murderer of Agamemnon—as a punishment, as a
> retribution (who can tell?) for my having allowed my grand-
> mother to die, perhaps; rising up suddenly from the black night
> in which it seemed for ever buried, and striking, like an Avenger,
> in order to inaugurate for me a novel, terrible and merited exist-
> ence, perhaps also to making dazzlingly clear to my eyes the fatal
> consequences which evil actions indefinitely engender, not only
> for those who have committed them, but for those who have
> done no more, have thought that they were doing no more than
> look on at a curious and entertaining spectacle, like myself, alas,
> on that afternoon long ago at Montjouvain, concealed behind a
> bush where (as when I complacently listened to an account of
> Swann's love affairs), I had perilously allowed to expand within
> myself the fatal road, destined to cause me suffering, of Knowl-
> edge.[19]

What is interesting in this curiously rhetorical passage is the
narrator's use of his past—a past in which Albertine had no part
—to describe the suffering Albertine causes him. The full strangeness of Proustian love is only too evident here. The memory of

the Lesbian scene at Montjouvain takes on the aspect of a deserved punishment for a family "crime" when it makes Marcel love Albertine because of her possible association with that scene. It is the pain this association causes him that transforms his feelings for her into the intensely jealous love of *La Prisonnière* and *La Fugitive*. And the narrator insists on how Albertine's remarks make a part of his past alive for him; he discovers his love for her at the same time as what he calls the "noxious power" of a past image. He learns, in a sense, something about how accidents in the past do not simply remain in the mind as memories irrelevant to our main interests, but can, actually, be the stuff from which a personality and a fate are built. He has tended, as I have shown earlier, to think of his past as dead; the self has seemed to him a series of unconnected personalities, and memories merely intellectual vestiges from another time, unrelated to what he is now. What happens in the train is somewhat like the moments of involuntary memory: Marcel has a revelation of the powerful presence of the past in him. The incident is, in a sense, even richer than the *madeleine* experience or the involuntary memories in the Guermantes *hôtel* in *Le Temps retrouvé*, for it illustrates in a more specific way, psychologically, both how the past makes necessary certain responses in the present and also how his future has been prepared for by his past. As a boy, Marcel, already obsessed with the elusiveness of the external world (from the mother he cannot possess entirely to the great realities hidden in nature) saw at Montjouvain a particular form of elusiveness, of interest and activity from which he—his masculine image—would necessarily be excluded. He of course did not understand that at the time, but when his anguished need to possess an image of himself in the external world is played out as the pursuit of a woman, Lesbianism is, so to speak, available in his mind as the particular kind of elusiveness that will make him suffer. An elusiveness he will also look for: having sinned against his mother and grandmother both by his tyrannical possessiveness and his selfish indifference, he can, by pursuing Lesbians, punish himself for his desire for independence by a hopeless, anguished pursuit of indifferent women.

Something profound in Marcel's personality is, then, revealed in his pursuit of a certain kind of woman, or, more exactly, in a certain type of desire that seems to characterize him. I have been, in my analysis, more explicit than the narrator in seeking out the guilt, the ambivalent attitude toward the self that seem to lie at the origin of these recurrent "fundamental notes." He sees clearly enough that he equates love with the romantic illusions or the anguish to which apparently elusive women give rise in him, but—and I shall return to this—he makes a universal law of his own experience, and does not analyze the particular psychological tensions that make *him* pursue such women. The *Sodome et Gomorrhe* passage is exceptional in the sense that it does suggest the complex psychological drama behind the necessity for anguish in love. Generally, the narrator sees patterns of similarity in his behavior rather than the causes behind the patterns. He sees, for example, his anguished need for his mother as a child not as the basis for his later behavior in love, but merely as a prefiguration of love, to which such anguish is "predestined." The possible causal importance of this childhood need is brushed aside when he suggests that his painful dependence on his mother is mainly irrelevant to his relationship with her, and belongs to adult love: ". . . when, as had befallen me, such an anguish possesses one's soul before Love has yet entered into one's life, then it must drift, awaiting Love's coming, vague and free, without precise attachment, at the disposal of one sentiment to-day, of another to-morrow, of filial piety or affection for a comrade." [20] The narrator does, on the other hand, speak of becoming more and more like certain members of his family, of spontaneously imitating their behavior: he sermonizes Albertine in the same language his parents used with him when he was a child, and he even finds himself repeating Léonie's tactics with Françoise in his efforts to dominate Albertine.[21] But he insists less on the specific psychological reasons for this imitation than on a general law of heredity (". . . the more we become ourselves, the more [our family traits] are accentuated"), a kind of genetic continuity from generation to generation.[22]

To point out what seem to me the limits of the narrator's awareness is simply to say that, beyond a certain point, he dramatizes facts about himself of which he is intellectually unaware. There is, naturally enough, an unconscious background which, somewhat as Legrandin's snobism reveals itself to Marcel through his behavior, is offered to the reader not in any explicit statements, but in the various signs—narrative organization, style, dramatic incident—of Marcel's literary behavior. His lucidity, as it is, seems highly courageous: in a sense, he deprives himself of the illusion of freedom by insisting on the necessary patterns that every desire in his life expresses. Such patterns have, of course, considerable appeal for Marcel; being certain of a continuity between past and present brings a relief more satisfying than any hope of unpredictable variety in the future. His self-analysis is not a therapeutic purging of his anguished need for self-possession; it is the activity of self-possession that succeeds where all the narrator's other activities have failed.

It is primarily the perspective from which the narrator analyzes his feelings that both makes possible this self-possession and determines the nature of the self he constructs. Retrospective analysis provides, first of all, a certain distance from the tensions being described, a distance that facilitates a kind of intellectual resolution of these tensions. In general, the narrator tells us explicitly that he almost never thought of Albertine herself, sums up and reflects upon the thoughts he did have, and concludes, from these reflections on his experience, that love is subjective and the woman loved insignificant. There is little or no attempt to place us at the emotional point of view of the past; the dramatic discovery of important truths about love is swallowed up into a retrospective analysis of past moments from the point of view of the truths deduced from them. What is being lived in the narrative is not, for example, the moments of anguish when Marcel learns that Albertine knows Mademoiselle Vinteuil and her friend, but rather the moment of intellectual satisfaction enjoyed in analyzing what happened then. On the one hand, the psychological continuity is clear between the narrator as he writes about the incident and the man whom Albertine's remarks shocked into suffering: neither one seems to find anything aberrant in the idea of Albertine's Lesbianism as a just punishment for his crimes. On the other hand, the suffering is no longer present, and we see what the narrator calls in *Le Temps retrouvé* the use of analysis as an escape from suffering: "When life walls us in, our intelligence cuts an opening, for, though there be no remedy for an unrequited love, [we can find some release by acknowledging our suffering, even if we only draw from it] the lessons it has to teach." [23]

The way out is, quite naturally, not without its pleasure. The latter is suggested, in the *Sodome et Gomorrhe* passage, by the use of certain elaborate, eloquent turns of phrase. At a distance, the drama takes on a certain ritualistic dignity; the narrator evokes Greek tragedy, speaks with solemnity of "an Avenger," and ends an extremely long sentence with the recherché construction: "la voie funeste et destinée à être douloureuse du Savoir." The Proustian sentence almost never gives us a direct and simple evocation of a past scene; the scene is used essentially as a basis, or even as a pretext for an elaborate verbal construction, for the creation, within the syntactical labyrinth, of metaphorical worlds around historical fact. Immediately following the passage I have quoted, we read:

> And at the same time, from my bitterest grief I derived a sentiment almost of pride, almost joyful, that of a man whom the shock he has just received has carried at a bound to a point to which no voluntary effort could have brought him. Albertine the friend of Mlle. Vinteuil and of her friend, a practising and professional Sapphist, was, compared to what I had imagined when I doubted her most, as are, compared to the little acousticon of the 1889 Exhibition with which one barely hoped to be able to transmit sound from end to end of a house, the telephones that soar over streets, cities, fields, seas, uniting one country to another.[24]

And, a few pages later, the narrator speaks of the daily renewal of suffering he was able to predict for himself after the ride from La Raspelière to Balbec:

> The light of the approaching sunrise, by altering the appearance of the things round me, made me once again, as though it shifted my position for a moment, yet even more painfully conscious of my suffering. I had never seen the dawn of so beautiful or so painful a morning. And thinking of all the nondescript scenes that were about to be lighted up, scenes which, only yesterday, would have filled me simply with the desire to visit them, I could not repress a sob when, with a gesture of oblation mechanically performed which appeared to me to symbolise the bloody sacrifice which I should have to make of all joy, every morning, until the end of my life, a solemn renewal, celebrated as each day dawned, of my daily grief and of the blood from my wound, the golden egg of the sun, as though propelled by the breach of equilibrium brought about at the moment of coagulation by a change of density, barbed with tongues of flame as in a painting, came leaping through the curtain behind which one had felt that it was quivering with impatience, ready to appear on the scene and to spring aloft, the mysterious, ingrained purple of which it flooded with waves of light [et dont il effaça sous des flots de lumière la pourpre mystérieuse et figée.] [25]

The symbol of the narrator's "bloody sacrifice"—the morning sun suddenly flooding the curtains with light—is given a rich series of religious, scientific, and artistic references that dignify and make less violent the association with blood. And, with rather irritating virtuosity, the narrator fixes our attention at the end of his involved comparison not on the curtain bathed in the flaming rays of the sun, but on the deliberately vague and tantalizing "pourpre mystérieuse et figée" that is no longer visible. Finally, the original emotion can be attenuated by prosaic references as well as by heightening and brilliance. The analogy of his actual suffering and the suffering he had imagined with the telephone and the "little acousticon of the 1889 Exhibition" puts the shock he is describing into the same category as a kind of banal, naturally detached public amazement at the "wonders of science."

Nathalie Sarraute, in *L'Ere du soupçon,* writes that Proust observes groups of memories, sensations, and feelings at rest, after they have played themselves out; he describes their positions "as if they were stars in an immobile sky." Madame Sarraute herself aims, in her novels, at suggesting "the swarming of innumerable sensations, images, sentiments, memories, impulses, small abortive acts" which lie behind a character's language and which express the confused, unanalyzable, and immediate response of the whole mind to present experience. Our verbal awareness is never adequate to this inner reality, a reality that may be more faithfully indicated by bodily signs than by intellectual analysis. Nathalie Sarraute notes that these inner "groups" often appear suddenly in Proust in a revealing look or word; I have already mentioned these uncontrollable signs by which characters in *A la Recherche du temps perdu* express profound interests, needs, and fears which, so to speak, skip the mental area of analytic reduction and act directly, through the body, on the world. But generally, Nathalie Sarraute goes on, Proust's narrator explains these psychological phenomena as a series of causes and effects: "Only rarely (I refrain from saying never) did he try to relive them and to have the reader relive them in the present, while they are being formed and throughout their development as tiny dramas, each one with its own peripetias, its mystery, and its unpredictable ending." [26]

Indeed, an important consequence of the distance Proust's narrator maintains from the incidents he is describing is the elaborate use of an analytic language he seems, theoretically, to reject. I have considered a passage in which he suggests the uselessness of distinguishing, for example, between pity and jealousy in his love for Albertine, since they both have the same results in behavior and may have the same unconscious causes. It is interesting that in the passage from *Un Amour de Swann* which Sartre quotes as an example of Proust's "symbolic chemistry"— and of the failure of intellectualist analysis to hide the irrational, magic basis of psychic causality [27]—the narrator, speaking of the moments when Swann's angry jealousy of Odette changes into a calm tenderness, makes precisely the kind of distinction which, at other places in the novel, he calls unprofitable:

> For the moment that Swann was able to form a picture of her [Odette] without revulsion, that he could see once again the friendliness in her smile, and that the desire to tear her away from every rival was no longer imposed by his jealousy upon his love, that love once again became, more than anything, a taste for the sensations which Odette's person gave him, for the pleasure which he found in admiring, as one might a spectacle, or in questioning, as one might a phenomenon, the birth of one of her glances, the formation of one of her smiles, the utterance of an intonation of her voice. And this pleasure, different from every other, had in the end created in him a need of her, which she alone, by her presence or by her letters, could assuage. . . .
>
> And so, by the chemical process of his malady, after he had created jealousy out of his love, he began again to generate tenderness, pity for Odette.[28]

The fact that Marcel is speaking of Swann here rather than of himself is unimportant: the same kind of abstract, almost allegorical language (in this inner drama, jealousy adds to love a desire to take Odette away from others) is frequently used when Marcel recalls his own experience of love. When he recalls, in *La Fugitive*, the way his forgetting Albertine actually increased his painful need of her for a time, he suggests complicated relations and fusions among independent inner entities: ". . . my suffering went on increasing day by day instead of diminishing, not that oblivion was not performing its task, but because by the very fact of its doing so it favoured the idealisation of the regretted image and thereby the assimilation of my initial suffering to other analogous sufferings which intensified it." [29] This inner world is agitated, heavily populated; and the kind of analytic density we identify with Proust involves, in large part, a meticulous detailing of the various "moves" made by these psychological abstractions, the displacements, new formations, and disappearances in the rich allegorical world of the mind. The narrator speaks, for example, of the conflict between his desire to find out about Albertine's Lesbianism and his wish to believe that she never had relations with other women:

> And so I sought—and, in course of time, managed—to rid myself of the painful certainty which I had taken such trouble to acquire, tossed to and fro as I still was between the desire to know and the fear of suffering. Then my affection might revive afresh, but, simultaneously with it, a sorrow at being parted from Albertine, during the course of which I was perhaps even more wretched than in the recent hours when it had been jealousy that tormented me.[30]

In the same volume, the narrator carefully traces the three stages in his forgetting Albertine; the complicated reshiftings of jealousy, tenderness, forgetting, and indifference; the new states born of alliances among different feelings; the slow fading out—with occasional rebirths—of certain emotions in the inner constellation.[31]

The passages quoted above are typical of the "crowded" later volumes, and the inner world they describe is filled with animated abstractions. This sort of analysis is more frequent in the novel than the precise linking between past and present that we have in the passage where Marcel learns of Albertine's friendship with Mademoiselle Vinteuil. Even there, his anguish at discovering Albertine's connection with Mademoiselle Vinteuil and her Lesbian friend comes to us tranquillized, in eloquently metaphorical language. In the past he was already sensitive to "the joy of a great discovery" which accompanies our worst suffering,[32] and the literary version of Marcel's pain is dominated by a now relatively detached interest in his pain. Feeling is similarly intellectualized in the passages of psychological analysis. What was either bodily pain in the presence of certain images connected with Albertine, or the busy schemes to keep her a prisoner or make her come back to Paris becomes, in the narrative, a point of departure for abstract, wholly internalized patterns of response. An intermediate mental area between Marcel's unconscious and his behavior is constructed, an area in which the various impulses to different kinds of gestures are elaborated into independent emotional states. The wish to possess Albertine—the constant factor throughout Marcel's love for her—is experienced consciously, when he loves her, in a series of "secondary" impulses: the impulse to kiss her, to say disagreeable things, to spy on her. In the reflective mood in which the narrative is written, Marcel transforms these different moments of his love into states of tenderness, anger, jealousy. Sartre has written that only in reflection can we posit affectivity for itself; the psychology of states is a psychology of the inert.[33] The narrator, remembering his love for Albertine, tends to transform the gestures he made or started to make toward the external world into feelings that act on each other rather than on the world, that move among themselves in the now closed spaces of the mind. While the novel records the pursuit of the self in the external world, the pursuit itself, since it is now a memory, becomes a kind of introspective activity. Psychological analysis thus helps to create a strictly mental history of extraordinary density and complexity.

iv. *The monologue of love as a dialogue*

Paradoxically, now that his impulses form an autonomous world of inner states, Marcel, unable to make plans for possessing Albertine, is able to qualify his idea of the subjectivity of love, and he can, perhaps for the first time, think of and see Albertine with leisure. The narrator hesitates between a wholly subjective view of love, in which the lover blindly pursues a woman unable to modify the direction or the intensity of his needs, and a more dramatic view of the exchanges possible in love. The extreme nature of his statements about the subjectivity of love seems both to express a self-consciously literary sense of questioning conventional assumptions about love, and to satisfy certain of the psychological needs I have discussed earlier. The evidence of the same "processus d'émotions, d'angoisses" reappearing each time that he falls in love is, in spite of the pain this causes Marcel, proof of a continuous identity in his life. And the discovery of an underlying repetitiousness in his desires for various women justifies and encourages the writing of a work in which, as I shall show in another chapter, metaphorical connections among apparently dissimilar incidents provide a literary documentation of the unity of personality. The subjectivist theories of love also seem to appease the fear of his personality being invaded, overwhelmed by possibly hostile influences. The idea that we are hopelessly shut up in the needs of our past has been for the narrator, at least partially, a reassuring safeguard against the dangers of new experience. He despairs at not being able to dominate Albertine, but if she cannot reach him either, if he is only acting out an old "processus d'émotions, d'angoisses" with her, then the fragile self is protected, and Albertine's very elusiveness has certain advantages. Each time he feels that love is a monologue, he prepares the way for thinking, finally, that a tranquil possession of the self is possible: a hopeless solitude rules out any unmanageable complications and challenges to the self in new experience.

It is, however, significant that the narrator also emphasizes, from time to time, how his reliving of past needs in each of his loves also re-created those needs, enriched his personality with new and unpredictable elements. It seems that only from the distance of memory can the narrator represent—and perhaps create—a variety in his own responses that suggests his openness to variety in the external world. In the past he felt that the women he loved were perversely keeping their lives a secret from him and depriving him of a reassuring image of himself; now, with the appeasement of these terrifying fantasies, he can show how they gave him personality, so to speak, by contributing to the history that is uniquely his. There is a certain contradiction between Marcel's exasperated sense of constantly projecting the same desires on an elusive reality with which he can never establish an authentic contact, and the narrator's portrayal of his *responsiveness* to particular situations. He does not merely repeat monotonously the same "fundamental notes" with each woman he pursues. With Albertine his various strategies become the causes of new feelings and new behavior; the past "processus d'émotions, d'angoisses" which she has set in motion operate creatively in the present. The narrator analyzes in great detail how both his need of Albertine and his slow detachment from her develop because of what he does to keep her with him. For example, the sadness he pretends at the idea of their separation becomes real; his lies start the process of his getting used to living without her at a time when his anguished need of her presence is actually strongest. Moreover, he affects her life and she affects his. The monologue of love turns out, surprisingly (once the other person is no longer there as a different body on which Marcel cannot "place" himself as Golo takes on the form of the doorknob), to be a dialogue, a relation in which each person is seen to have become what he or she is partly because of the other. In *La Fugitive*, the narrator writes that it is in vain that we try to reduce the mystery of another person "to elements meanly similar to those of our own self." His attempt to imprison Albertine changes her life in ways that then change his own life:

> So that the long plaint of the soul which thinks that it is living shut up within itself is a monologue in appearance only, since the echoes of reality alter its course and such a life is like an essay in subjective psychology spontaneously pursued, but furnishing from a distance its 'action' to the purely realistic novel of another reality, another existence, the vicissitudes of which come in their turn to inflect the curve and change the direction of the psychological essay.

Albertine may not be the original cause of Marcel's anguished need to possess her, but he recognizes that by associating this need with her, he does in fact live as if she were that cause: ". . . habit gives to the mere association of ideas between two phenomena . . . an illusion of the force, the necessity of a law of causation." [34] But what he calls illusion here seems a result of the important truth that he does respond to Albertine, that his "désir premier" does not simply apply itself to anonymous figures, but itself changes in response to a person first used as a pretext but then experienced as a cause of new desires and new patterns in the personality.

Furthermore, Marcel's love for Albertine is not the same as his love for Gilberte or for Madame de Guermantes; he reacts differently to each woman both because his responses are less rigid than he sometimes feels, and also because he is aware of each woman's individuality. What seem to be only the "substitute" situations for a single basic desire become, then, important in themselves, and he insists on the particularities of each of his desires and of each of the women he has desired. It is by no means true that the narrator describes his different loves in "almost exactly similar terms," and the analysis of these loves includes individualizing portraits of the women he has wanted to possess. For in spite of the shadowy areas in the characters of Gilberte and especially of Albertine, the narrator does not merely characterize himself in telling the story of each of his loves. He is fortunately only halfhearted in his pursuit of what he calls "yet another truth" for the novelist, and the women he loves have a life clearly distinct from Marcel's desires. Swann's rich, spoiled daughter is sharply differentiated from the orphaned Albertine Marcel dazzles with his expensive gifts, an Albertine also simpler and at times more directly tender than the capricious girl from the Champs-Elysées who will later be ashamed to admit who her father was in the Duchesse de Guermantes's drawing room. And neither Albertine nor Gilberte could be confused with Oriane, who is individualized even when Marcel is most blinded by his infatuation for her: we see her real elegance with marvelous clarity even when our perspective is that of a frightened young man stalking her on her daily walks.

Marcel's memories of the hopeless self-pursuits of love include, therefore, several distinct images of the women loved, of people he clearly sees and lucidly describes. For, at the distance of memory, and in the security of a literary document that testifies to the contents of the self, the outer world that threatened to break up the patterns of feeling and behavior by which Marcel recognized himself can itself be re-created as part of those patterns. The narrator, when he writes his work, refuses any future experience of love, but he can at least have, at times, a generous view of his loves in the past, even be glad, now that the dangers are gone, of having exposed himself. Living only in his past except for the work that will testify to this past, the isolated narrator, dead to any life outside of his book, can nevertheless, with a curious mixture of melancholy and pride, think gratefully of Albertine and how she drew him out of himself, if only to make him suffer so much that he had to build a new and permanent wall between himself and the world before being able to pay her this moving tribute:

> And if it was necessary that I should lose for her sake years, my fortune—and provided that I can say to myself, which is by no means certain, alas, that she herself lost nothing—I have nothing to regret. No doubt solitude would have been better, more fruitful, less painful. But if I had led the life of a collector which Swann counselled (the joys of which M. de Charlus reproached me with not knowing, when, with a blend of wit, insolence and good taste, he said to me: "How ugly your rooms are!") what statues, what pictures long pursued, at length possessed, or even, to put it in the best light, contemplated with detachment, would, like the little wound which healed quickly enough, but which the unconscious clumsiness of Albertine, of people generally, or of my own thoughts was never long in reopening, have given me access beyond my own boundaries, upon that avenue which, private though it be, debouches upon the high road along which passes what we learn to know only from the day on which it has made us suffer, the life of other people? [35]

It is, moreover, precisely because the narrator has in memory the leisure necessary to portray the women with whom his desire and anxiety became most intense that he is able to underline the distorting fantasies in his images of these women. To come back once again to *La Jalousie,* it could be said that Robbe-Grillet's novel fulfills the narrator's theoretical requirements for a story about love better than *A la Recherche du temps perdu.* A . . . is a dimmer figure than any woman in Proust's world. We see her very often in the novel, and may have an impression of a coldly sensual, narcissistic nature; but there are few scenes in which we hear her, in which she is given the chance to express herself outside the jealous point of view from which she is described. The very refusal to give her a name deprives her of any reality independent of the husband's thoughts about her. It is significant, moreover, that the whole narrative is in the present tense. This naturally upsets one of our traditional certainties in the reading of fiction; since there is no present point of reference, no time that corresponds to the writing of the book, it is impossible to say when scenes are being lived for the first time or when they are being remembered. In a sense, Robbe-Grillet's treatment of time is more radical than Proust's. The narrator in Proust describes moments when the past becomes more immediately present, but he never allows us to confuse the two. In spite of the importance involuntary memory has in *A la Recherche,* the story proceeds in quite regular chronological sequence, and our rational concept of time is hardly disturbed at all as we read the novel. But in *La Jalousie* there is no distinction between present experience and memory, for the jealous husband is too much *in* his jealousy to remember it. Everything from the past that once attracted his anxious attention is not recalled but relived; images from any period nourish the compulsive investigations that alone identify the narrative present. There is no detached, novelistic interest in A . . . in *La Jalousie*—or, to the extent that there is, it must somehow be passed on to us through a point of view interested in trapping A . . . rather than portraying her. And this accounts partially for what seems to me unsatisfying in Robbe-Grillet's novel. Because we know so little about A . . . —what she has done or, indeed, what she is—we cannot really say whether the husband's jealousy is a proper or improper reading of her relationship with Franck. We see the pathological effects of jealousy, but it is quite possible that the cause of jealousy is a good guess the husband makes about something real that the other characters are trying to hide from him. There is no *other* dramatic situation in the novel that would allow us to keep a certain distance from the jealous point of view, a reality which might indicate how this jealousy is related both to the husband's whole personality and to the outer world.

It is true that we can never be completely sure, in *A la Recherche du temps perdu,* whether or not Marcel's suspicions about Albertine's Lesbianism are justified. But the narrator gives a full enough portrait both of himself and of Albertine so that this uncertainty does not reduce Marcel to being merely his jealousy. By writing about his love for Albertine after he has stopped loving her, by recollecting and analyzing the jealous man he no longer is at the time the narrative is written, he has the detachment necessary to portray Albertine, to record not only the things she said and did that set off an anguished curiosity in him, but also things that did not awaken his jealousy, that give us a view of Albertine outside of Marcel's desire and pain. We can thus see how she is used by Marcel to dramatize needs from his own past. Whether or not Albertine desires other women is relatively unimportant; what characterizes Marcel, and leads to his conclusion that the loved one is not the cause of love, is that a suspicion about her Lesbianism is enough to change his feelings for her into the anguished need he calls love. Not only is this contribution from Marcel's past made explicit in the novel; we also see enough of Albertine to realize that something wholly subjective accounts for Marcel's investing her with great glamor and mystery. We may find her evasive, but we certainly find her life less fascinating than Marcel does, and the reader sympathizes with Saint-Loup's astonishment when he sees Albertine's picture and betrays his disappointment that there is so little beauty to account for so much feeling. But the narrator educates the reader out of such a naïve astonishment; he has all along shown a rather common and simple girl to make as clear as possible the subjective nature of Marcel's love for her. We share Marcel's sense of what is ambiguous and obscure in Albertine's character, but the narrator's sense of human reality is never equivalent to that of an obsessed lover. In all the love stories in the novel, the lover's fantasies are accompanied by more or less objective char-

acterizations of the loved one; and there is a considerable distance
between the obsessive images of Marcel in love and the convincingly objective presence of Gilberte, Madame de Guermantes, and Albertine as independent novelistic characters.

v. *The merging of fantasy and realism*

But if the perspective of memory allows the narrator to see the
loved one more distinctly, we recognize a single creative psychology in Marcel's most tortured fantasies and in the narrator's
portraits of the real Albertine or the real Madame de Guermantes.
Certain similarities between Marcel and other characters in the
novel are particularly striking when his indifference toward them
presumably allows him to describe accurately personalities very
different from his own. I shall study this extension of the narrator's psychology into the external world in my chapter on his general social contacts. In one aspect of the portrait of Albertine we
see an intermediate stage, as it were, in the process of a novelistic
objectifying of fantasies. The narrator writes that the image of
Albertine played a very small role in his love for her; while this
seems to have been the case for the moments when he was most
actively pursuing her, it is also true that before knowing her, as
well as when he is jealously in love with her, he elaborates certain picture-fantasies of Albertine's life. In the past these images
do not make for a satisfying possession: the real Albertine cannot
be contained in Marcel's pictures of her. But the memory of these
pictures constitutes part of the portrait of Albertine for the
reader, and we have an interesting example of fantasies which,
while they are presented *as* fantasies, nevertheless tend to merge,
in the novel, with objective characterization. And it seems that
the narrator himself is tempted to reduce Albertine to these pictures, to transform them into a fictional character he, the author,
can ideally possess. From *A l'Ombre des jeunes filles en fleur*
through *La Fugitive,* Marcel fixes Albertine in a series of poses;
in memory she can be as immobile as the violets in Elstir's paintings, and Marcel need no longer envy the artist for the stillness

of his subjects. Albertine has not given up her secrets, but Marcel has given up his interest in them, and there is no longer any obstacle to his making her into an image of his desires.

These portraits of Albertine are highly metaphorical; the narrator connects her with the life of nature, usually with the sea, and she often reminds him of certain birds. A comparison between one of the first tableaux of Albertine and one of the last can be used to show how Marcel uses such pictures to express the progress of his desire and anguish. What strikes him when he first sees Albertine and her friends on the beach is how different they are from the other people at Balbec; they are like "a flight of gulls," and the purpose of their movements is as clear to their "birdish minds" as it is obscure to the other bathers.[36] Later, Albertine attracts his attention more than the others; he notices that they seem to respect her, to stop and wait for her whenever she pauses in their walks. And Marcel has a picture of her at these moments of rest in which, much later, when he is most afraid of losing her, he will always be able to "find" her:

> Thus it is, calling a halt, her eyes sparkling beneath her polo-cap, that I see her again to-day, outlined against the screen which the sea spreads out behind her, and separated from me by a transparent, azure space, the interval of time that has elapsed since then, a first impression, faint and fine in my memory, desired, pursued, then forgotten, then found again, of a face which I have many times since projected upon the cloud of the past to be able to say to myself, of a girl who was actually in my room: 'It is she!' [37]

This first image, free of any real and confusing knowledge of Albertine, becomes, then, the reference by which Marcel identifies her. And the appeal of the image is, of course, that it gives life to a fantasy of glamor in Marcel. The mysterious girl, strong and independent, perhaps able to reveal secrets of nature, in contact with that life of the sea which Marcel came to Balbec to discover: this first of many Albertines is a version of Marcel's early dreams of fulfilling truths in the external world. When he meets Albertine, and especially when she lives with him, it naturally becomes increasingly difficult to connect this actual experience of another person with the image into which he projected so much glamorous mystery. It is interesting, and characteristic, that, looking at Albertine in his room, he feels the need to assure himself that she is the girl whose silhouette by the sea intrigued him at Balbec, that the girl talking to him *is* that secretly admired image. For us, she is indeed partly that image: what is perhaps a distortion of Albertine's character is nevertheless such a clear and impressive image of her physical presence that we cannot entirely detach that fantasy from her real character in the novel.

Other aspects of Albertine's life interfere with the glamor of that image, but its mystery comes back in the more trivial and disturbing form of her possible Lesbianism. Germaine Brée has pointed out this rhythm in Marcel's relationships: before knowing people, he sees them as mysterious, then, after meeting them, as banal, and, finally, mysterious again through the secret life of homosexuality.[38] The image of a birdlike Albertine by the sea becomes sinister; the Albertine Marcel has known, by her evasiveness and ambiguous attitude toward women, has given a painfully specific meaning to the mystery of that image, and what Marcel once found only desirable comes to be threatening. In *La Fugitive,* after Aimé writes to Marcel about a laundress who has told him of sexual adventures she and her friends used to have with Albertine by the sea, Marcel recomposes the Lesbian scene in a complex group of images taken from his memories of Albertine in Balbec and Paris, as well as from memories of works of art:

> I had as it happened seen two paintings by Elstir shewing against a leafy background nude women. In one of them, one of the girls is raising her foot as Albertine must have raised hers when she offered it to the laundress. With her other foot she is pushing into the water the other girl, who gaily resists, her hip bent, her foot barely submerged in the blue water. I remembered now that the raising of the thigh made the same swan's-neck curve with the angle of the knee that was made by the

droop of Albertine's thigh when she was lying by my side on the bed, and I had often meant to tell her that she reminded me of those paintings. But I had refrained from doing so, in order not to awaken in her mind the image of nude female bodies. Now I saw her, side by side with the laundress and her friends, recomposing the group which I had so admired when I was seated among Albertine's friends at Balbec. And if I had been an enthusiast sensitive to absolute beauty, I should have recognised that Albertine recomposed it with a thousand times more beauty, now that its elements were the nude statues of goddesses like those which consummate sculptors scattered about the groves of Versailles or plunged in the fountains to be washed and polished by the caresses of their eddies. Now [by the side of the laundress, I saw her as a girl by the water's edge much more than when I had been at Balbec:] in their twofold nudity of marble maidens in the midst of a grove of vegetation and dipping into the water like bas-reliefs of Naiads. Remembering how Albertine looked as she lay upon my bed, I thought I could see her bent hip, I saw it, it was a swan's neck, it was seeking the lips of the other girl. Then I beheld no longer a leg, but the bold neck of a swan, like that which in a frenzied sketch seeks the lips of a Leda whom we see in all the palpitation peculiar to feminine pleasure, because there is nothing else but a swan, and she seems more alone, just as we discover upon the telephone the inflexions of a voice which we do not distinguish so long as it is not dissociated from a face in which we materialise its expression. In this sketch, the pleasure, instead of going to seek the face which inspires it and which is absent, replaced by a motionless swan, is concentrated in her who feels it.[39]

The specifically Lesbian grouping of women—suggested by Aimé's letter and by the playfulness of the women in Elstir's painting—is a more painful image to Marcel than the now familiar, even familylike group of young girls at Balbec. But, in part because of its strangeness and capacity to cause pain, he finds the new image esthetically more satisfying, although, as is often the case in the novel, it is not clear how many of the artistic associations are made by Marcel at the time of Aimé's letter. The Balbec group is recomposed as nude statues of goddesses merely by the introduction of a sinister sexual meaning into the meetings of women. But it is as if this meaning were already hidden in Marcel's picture of Albertine at Balbec. More than at Balbec, it is now, with the laundress and her friends, that Albertine seems to Marcel the "jeune fille au bord de la mer." The mystery of Lesbianism and the suffering it can cause were already contained in the silhouette of Albertine like a sea gull against the sea and in the excited curiosity Marcel felt in front of that tableau. The peculiar esthetic appeal he finds in his strangely hallucinated vision of Albertine and the laundress seems due, largely, to his desperate sense of this form of sexuality as a kind of fate in his life. It is as if he now recognized the source of mystery and glamor in that first image, as if he were able finally to justify his early sense of mystery and glamor.

The connection between Albertine and nature turns out, characteristically, to be in the uninhibited freedom with which she takes her pleasure. At Balbec Marcel had thought of himself entering Albertine's group "like a cultured pagan or a meticulous Christian going among barbarians," and he had excitedly thought of the effect on his troubled, sickly, overconscious self of "a rejuvenating society in which reigned health, unconsciousness of others, sensual pleasures, cruelty, unintellectuality and joy." [40] And Lesbianism expresses for Marcel, at least partly, such unselfconscious, unsocial freedom; it means not being limited, as animals are not limited, to those pleasures society sanctions. There is a triviality, a comical sordidness in homosexuality as the narrator portrays it: we have only to think of the pathetic Mademoiselle Vinteuil trying desperately to profane the memory of the father she loved, or of Charlus exasperated with the stubborn and transparent goodness of the young man beating him. But if there is a complicity with homosexuality in the novel, it is not exactly because, as has often been said, Marcel is "really" Proust and is therefore "really" homosexual. I would say, rather, that it is because of the great mystery Marcel finds in homosexuality, because one part of him finds it totally inconceivable. It obviously appeals strongly to his imagination, but as something frighteningly exotic, and in the passage from *La Fugitive* it even suggests to Marcel a time in history when pleasures would have been so undifferentiated, the evolution of man at such a primitive stage, that there were only weak sexual barriers between man and the animals. The curve made by Albertine's thigh and the angle of her knee, when she was lying next to Marcel in his family's apartment in Paris, reminded him of the curve of a swan's neck, and, after reading Aimé's letter, Marcel painfully realizes the full potentiality of that image in the idea of Albertine enjoying a kind of primitive sexual freedom.

The civilized man's connection with such freedom is through art and the mythological imagination; Albertine, in the last development of the image, becomes a "motionless swan" stretched toward an anxiously expectant Leda. And with this last transformation, which reminds Marcel of another work of art (and was perhaps suggested by that work), the most incomprehensible form of sexual desire—between a human being and an animal—nevertheless makes possible a view of "the palpitation peculiar to feminine pleasure." With no human object to the woman's desire, Marcel can never hope to identify himself either with the quality of her desire and pleasure or with the object of her desire; but in this tableau he can look at and, in a sense, possess something wholly different from himself. The woman desiring the swan is a bizarre version of Marcel's persistent fantasy—both frightening and exciting—of an external world wholly alien to his own history and desires. In Combray the young boy imagined abstract truths hidden in nature; at Balbec he identified Albertine with the sea and yearned to enter the physically healthy, unselfconscious world in which she seemed to live; but alone in bed in Paris after her death, Marcel's final sense of nature is an image of mysterious, potentially violent sexuality. And outside of art and the legends of mythology, such sexuality is painful and threatening to him. He is able to come to terms with it only by turning his back on the world where such scenes may take place and containing them within his artistic consciousness.

We see Albertine at three different stages of imaginative creation. There are the conjectures inspired by Marcel's jealousy, and
which outline a life full of complicated lies and secretive sexual
pleasures; there are also, throughout the novel, the pictorial representations of Albertine in different poses—pictures in which we
recognize Marcel's obsessions, but which also add to our impressions of her physical and psychological reality apart from Marcel's fantasies; finally, Albertine as a fully distinct character says
and does certain things that make up her unique and separate
existence in Proust's fictional world. Now a gap or discrepancy
in a novel between the narrator's analysis or description of a
character and the language and behavior of that character may
undermine the reader's illusion of reading about a real human
being. It is not that in life such discrepancies between our impressions of other people and their real characters do not exist.
But when we recognize, in actual experience, how much of ourselves we have projected into our picture of someone else, his
existence is never threatened; a life outside of our own impressions and judgments is authenticated, in the simplest sense, by
other people's physical reality, which has had visible effects on
the physical world. It may be impossible to describe external
reality objectively, but we feel the presence of reality outside of
ourselves in the way it constantly impinges on our own presence
in the world. Our knowledge of the outer world is, then,
dramatic rather than conceptual; unable to describe it, we nevertheless spend our lives *meeting* it. But since the characters of a
novel exist for the reader only as verbal description, certain tensions in these verbal portraits can easily "kill" the characters. The
omniscient author, for example, who claims to analyze his characters accurately, but whose characters speak and act in ways
that contradict the narrative analyses, can destroy our belief in
his characters' reality. For unless we naïvely think of them as real
persons with a life beyond the written page, such contradictions
make terribly clear their fragile verbal existence. Since the omniscient author speaks *ex cathedra,* there is no reason for us to
strengthen the illusions he himself is weakly maintaining by

deciding that we will, say, believe only the version of character given in dramatic scenes and ignore the narrator's confusion about his characters. Such discrepancies are, of course, not always fatal to a character's existence: a novelist may be able to represent dramatically parts of himself for which he cannot or does not want to account critically, and the character may be sufficiently strong to escape the destructive effects of his creator's muddled view of him. And it is especially easy to continue believing in certain characters if the author is particularly good at dramatic scenes; it is, after all, at moments when we directly see and hear characters that we tend to give them the physical existence we have experienced in seeing and hearing real people. But if the narrator's point of view and the reader's impressions from dramatic scenes contradict each other and are equally strong or equally weak, we may feel that a character floats, so to speak, between two different identities, and judge the novelistic creation poorly realized.

Such tensions can, however, be profitably used when the narrator is himself a character in the world of the novel. For we may then be asked to accept his impressions of other characters not necessarily as statements designed to give us knowledge of these characters, but as expressions of his dramatic meetings with them within the fictional world. And the scenes of dialogue and physical behavior in a novel allow *us* to meet other characters directly. The impressions we gather from such scenes may differ from the narrator's; part of the experience of reading is, if that is the case, in a certain tension between different ways of meeting other characters in the novel. We thus create the work's meaning as we read the work, for it is then that other relationships are created—between the reader and the narrator, and between the reader and other characters—which make knowledge of character a dramatic process of forming impressions. In *A la Recherche du temps perdu* the narrator himself constantly questions the validity of certain of his impressions; his point of view on Albertine cannot be entirely trusted, and he makes a full critique of that point of view, is a skeptical reader of his own past. He presents his statements about Albertine as characteristic of his fears and desires; he does not claim that they also characterize Albertine as she exists outside of his fantasies. Ambiguity is consistently maintained because we see just enough of Albertine "on her own," in dramatic scenes, to question Marcel's sense of her mystery, and not enough so that we can say with certainty that what he sees in her is entirely a product of a "processus d'émotions, d'angoisses" from his own past. And the fact that much of the characterization of Albertine is done through the physical portraits I have just discussed increases the ambiguity: what may be only Marcel's fantasies are so often given in an image of Albertine that we remember them, to a large extent, as part of our memory of her rather than of Marcel.

Now this ambiguity makes for considerable richness of characterization at the expense of a certain definiteness of character. The narrator, by keeping parts of Albertine's life as obscure in his book as they were in his past, and by giving a large role to fantasies about her life that we cannot entirely dismiss as a distortion of her character, moves freely among several novelistic conjectures about a figure he never allows to "settle" into the fixed outlines of a conventional novelistic character. And this rich indefiniteness in the portrait of Albertine makes her somewhat like a *project* of novelistic invention, a focal point around which several imaginative fantasies are being tried out. It is as if we were seeing a character in those stages of the creative process that usually precede the final version of a novel. The narrator thus encourages us to a special kind of attention as we read his work. It would be even more useless for us to try to discover the "truth" about Albertine than it was for Marcel when he loved her; the narrator himself does not possess that truth, and he is therefore not asking us—as other writers have done—to find the clues that would unravel the mysteries of a psychological detective story. The only way we can miss the point about Albertine is to read the novel as if there were any one, exclusive point to be made about her. It seems to me that we are, instead, expected to enjoy the very multiplicity of perspectives we have on her life, to substitute for Marcel's emotional interest in her an appreciation of the novelistic richness of what he at first experienced as a desperate helplessness. The painful efforts of the imagination to reach an elusive reality in the world thus take on, within the novel, another meaning: they suggest the imaginative experimentation of the artist, the different steps on the way from vaguely outlined images and feelings to a fully realized fictional character.

The ambiguities in Albertine's character are dramatically justified by Marcel's relation to her: his love stimulates his fantasies, and perhaps blinds him to what might be obvious to someone else. This tension between subjective fantasy about character and the objective reality of character is also important with people toward whom Marcel is comparatively indifferent, or toward whom he quickly becomes indifferent after meeting them. With these other characters, however, the tension tends to be expressed not by ambiguities that persist throughout the novel, but rather by two quite different portraits of the same person, one of which is largely intended to correct the other. The narrator gives us first of all his idealizing fantasies about people, and then he presents the usually sharply satirical portrait of their real personalities. And we have more definite ideas—ideas we are not asked to question seriously—about most of the other characters in the novel than we ever do about Albertine. But while the narrator wants us to feel that he can distinguish between fantasy and reality in characterizing most of the people he has known, his realistic portraits have many of the characteristics of a fantasy creation. With certain people Marcel's distortions turn out, surprisingly, to have been shrewd insights into their characters. There are, of course, crucial differences between his images of people before and after he meets them, but the real world also peculiarly reflects subjective images which presumably make any reliable knowledge, any penetration of that world impossible. More generally, there are important psychological parallels between Marcel and the people he is supposedly remembering from his past, parallels which make us feel that the objective report on reality is actually a self-dramatization by means of novelistic character and incident.

The central theme of the barrier of subjectivity between the self and others is both qualified and unintentionally illustrated by these equivalences between the narrator's psychology and the realistic portraits. A closer study of the Proustian social world is necessary in order to define more adequately both the degree of separation in the novel between the narrator and external reality, and the role of the world as an allegorical representation of the narrator's psychology.

CHAPTER FOUR

SOCIAL CONTEXTS:
OBSERVATION AND INVENTION

1. *The aristocracy's glamor*

The first time we see the Duchesse de Guermantes at a party is in *Un Amour de Swann,* when she is still the Princesse des Laumes. By dropping in for a few moments at Madame de Saint-Euverte's, she gives the party its cachet of elegance. The only time we have seen her before has been at a marriage in the church at Combray; but we have imagined her with all the prestige and glamor that the name of Guermantes has for the young Marcel. Of course, even at the marriage ceremony Marcel has difficulty applying his idea of Madame de Guermantes to a particular face with oval-shaped cheeks and a red nose. But his imagination quickly recovers from the shock and he replaces her apart from the rest of humanity by repeating to himself: " 'Great and glorious before the days of Charlemagne, the Guermantes had the right of life and death over their vassals; the Duchesse de Guermantes descends from Geneviève de Brabant. She does not know, nor would she consent to know, any of the people who are here to-day.' " [1] Indeed, until the narrator is invited to the Guermantes *hôtel* in Paris, the glamor persists. Different by nature from the people Marcel knows, the Guermantes appear to him as an amalgam of art and history; he expects them to make visible and concrete both the charm of his own fantasies about the past and the color of their musical name:

> . . . whenever I thought about them I pictured them to myself either in tapestry, as was [the Comtesse de Guermantes in] the 'Coronation of Esther' which hung in our church, or else in

changing, rainbow colours, as was Gilbert the Bad in his window, where he passed from cabbage green, when I was dipping
my fingers in the holy water stoup, to plum blue when I had
reached our row of chairs, or again altogether impalpable, like
the image of Geneviève de Brabant, ancestress of the Guermantes
family, which the magic lantern sent wandering over the curtains of my room or flung aloft upon the ceiling—in short, always
wrapped in the mystery of the Merovingian age, and bathed, as
in a sunset, in the orange light which glowed from the resound-
ing syllable 'antes.' [2]

It is hardly necessary to insist on the extent to which the real
Duchesse de Guermantes falls short of Marcel's dreams about
her. The snobbery implied in her much advertised horror of
snobbery, her vanity and cruelty, the obviousness and question-
able taste of her famous *mots:* in all this we find not the fabulous
descendant of Geneviève de Brabant, but a very ordinary and
very spoiled woman. But there is more in the portrait of the
duchess than this simple contrast between fact and fantasy, and
at Madame de Saint-Euverte's she does have a certain charm. It
is not exactly the kind of charm Marcel imagines her to have,
but it fulfills, in a general way, his requirements for glamor.
There is, first of all, such self-assurance in her vanity that it becomes a physical grace. Like her cousin, the Princesse de Guermantes, the duchess adds to the prestige of her name the appeal
of personal beauty. The features of other aristocratic women, the
narrator notes in *Le Côté de Guermantes,* have only "the conventional value of [written characters,]" they do nothing more
than identify a famous name; but the duchess's face is a justification of the aristocratic claim.[3] The pleasure she takes in her
beauty expresses itself, because the beauty is real, in a heightening of that beauty, and at times we forget the fatuousness and
the inability to think of anyone else, because the vanity seems
almost like a generous wish to give others pleasure. She feels the
attractiveness of her body, sees and arranges it in poses she is the
first to admire. At Madame de Saint-Euverte's, her admiration
for the Chopin piece being played becomes the occasion for one

of these poses: "And she murmured 'How charming it is!' with a stress on the opening consonants of the adjective, a token of her refinement by which she felt her lips so romantically compressed, like the petals of a beautiful, budding flower, that she instinctively brought her eyes into harmony, illuminating them for a moment with a vague and sentimental gaze." [4] It is difficult to feel any pity for Madame de Gallardon when she is mercilessly snubbed by Oriane: she tries gracelessly and with a false self-assurance to force the princess to accept an invitation; while Oriane's insolence, which seems a way to intensify her physical appeal, becomes a positive charm.

It is this confidence in their own value that is the secret of the Guermantes coterie. When the Princesse des Laumes learns that Swann is at Madame de Saint-Euverte's party, she can think only of attracting his attention, and the narrator comments: "She belonged to that one of the two divisions of the human race in which the untiring curiosity which the other half feels about the people whom it does not know is replaced by an unfailing interest in the people whom it does." The special quality of the Guermantes coterie is a limited but real one: it is not so much in what its members talk about among themselves as in the fact that they do have a way of talking to each other. They have found their style. And it is not the superiority of this style but the absence of style in others that makes the rest of this society anxiously wait to be dazzled by Oriane's latest *mot*. She and Swann have little to say to each other, but they can be perfectly happy in each other's company because their meeting is an occasion for self-recognition. The advantages that have made for Oriane's self-assurance are probably a combination of social eminence, physical appeal, and, perhaps more crucially, a certain amount of sensitivity to literature and language. Oriane's puns—however bad—express a playful interest in the sounds and meanings of words. Swann, of course, brings an extremely wide culture into the group, but even Madame de Guermantes, whose cultural references are by no means remarkable, has at least been brought up to be familiar with certain literary conventions, with more or less

interesting efforts to create distinctive styles. The narrator writes
that there are traces in the Guermantes coterie of "the alert mentality, stripped of all commonplace phrases and conventional
sentiments, which dated from Mérimée, and found its final expression in the plays of Meilhac and Halévy."⁵ The literary
value of this tradition is not important here; it has served Oriane
as a familiar example of how language can express and emphasize a particular personality. And in Proust's world such a technique can be a formidable instrument of social power. The spectacle of Swann and Oriane recognizing what they share, laughing
approvingly at each sign of the Guermantes wit, not even caring
to have the dull-minded Madame de Saint-Euverte recognize
their talk *as* wit, is enough to inspire in the dimmer lights of this
society envy and jealousy that are not merely *mondain*. For what
the Guermantes clique advertise with such insolence is their
assurance about, and satisfaction with, their own being.

If Madame de Guermantes has no light to shed on the "mystery" of Merovingian times, she is not entirely without the qualities Marcel has imagined her to have. His imagination comes to
his rescue after his first disappointment in the Combray church
by assuring him: "She does not know, nor would she consent to
know, any of the people who are here to-day." The real Madame
de Guermantes can continue to excite Marcel's interest because
she seems to be indifferent, self-sufficient, without curiosity. She
is for Parisian society what Albertine is for Marcel: an "être de
fuite." Her desires seem as unpredictable and mysterious as Albertine's. She shocks, excites, and mystifies the ordinary run of
Parisian hostesses by doing what they never would have imagined as possible: she takes, for example, a trip to the Norwegian
fjords at the height of the social season, or goes to the theatre
with her husband the evening of a party no one else would have
dared to miss. It is, of course, soon clear that this indifference to
social judgments is essentially a refinement of snobbery, not the
absence of it; Oriane's apparent detachment is calculated to add
new luster to her social prestige. But, unlike Marcel during much
of his life, she does not feel that anything worth knowing or hav-

ing must be completely different from herself. She is a snob in that she expects everyone around her to reflect her own sense of her distinction, and the narrator notes that in the home of this woman so intolerant of snobs, every servant has guessed that she must be addressed in the third person, as "Madame la duchesse." But she is confident of containing all that is valuable within herself; she can impose a favorable image of herself on others, whereas Marcel can only long for such security.[6]

This partial realization, in certain members of the Guermantes family, of Marcel's fantasy of self-sufficiency qualifies the irony of the social portraits in *A la Recherche du temps perdu,* and, in part, explains the long period of the narrator's interest in what he essentially judges as "the realm of nullity," "le royaume du néant."[7] (It is also true, as Howard Moss has said, that we never entirely forget the glamorous impression of the aristocracy we have before seeing the falsity of that impression.[8]) The social scenes in the earlier parts of the novel reflect the extent to which society does fulfill Marcel's fantasies of a special, secretive, valuable world. The moment when the aristocracy seems to come closest to realizing Marcel's dream about it is at the *soirée de gala* at the Opéra, the evening when he hears Berma for the second time (and, free of any preconceived notions about her genius, recognizes and enjoys it). The audience in the orchestra has come as much to see the spectacle of social elegance as to hear an act of *Phèdre,* and no one is more sensitive to the glamorous show in the boxes and balconies than Marcel. Having heard a man he takes to be the Prince de Saxe ask for his "cousin's"— perhaps Madame de Guermantes's—loge, Marcel is sufficiently excited so that the usher has only to say the word "baignoire" for him to feel that the prince then walks down a hall leading "to subaqueous grottoes, to the mythical kingdom of the water-nymphs."[9] And, in the following pages, the narrator exercises his extraordinary virtuosity of style in a description of the boxes occupied by the aristocratic part of the audience as submarine caves, from whose depths the fabulous water-gods and goddesses who rule Parisian society come occasionally to the sea's surface to dazzle the inferior race of orchestra spectators.

The passage is, of course, also an exercise in a double point of view, and if the images of nymphs and Tritons express the prestige this aristocratic gathering has for the young Marcel, the extravagantly rich style the narrator uses to remember the scene is not without ironic effect. He has already had the long and unexhilarating contact with the nobility which he will begin to record soon after the description of the evening at the Opéra. It is with obvious pleasure that he indulges once again, now that he has lost his illusions, in the exciting impressions of that evening. But his enjoyment is now entirely verbal—the element of belief has disappeared—and the humorous effect of the passage can be accounted for by the verbal feast of exaggeration that replaces the lost belief. The narrator occasionally introduces a realistic detail by which he makes Marcel himself look silly; or the comparison with sea deities is pushed so far that it makes comical what was glamorous for Marcel. The latter envies the Marquis de Palancy for "the indifference with which he allowed the Princess to hold out to him her box of sweetmeats"; and the marquis is described more like a fish than a god, with the result that the exaggerations that exalt the Princesse de Guermantes to more than human beauty lower Palancy to less than human gracelessness and mindlessness: "Now and again he paused, a venerable, wheezing monument, and the audience could not have told whether he was in pain, asleep, swimming, about to spawn, or merely taking breath." [10] Finally, the mysterious lives of the sea-gods are perilously close to being reduced to the somewhat less than divine activity of passing around and choosing from a box of candy.

But Marcel's belief is so powerful during this evening that even the trivial talk among the nobles adds to his sense of mystery. The banality of the princess's offering candy to her guests seems to him "a conventional refinement and therefore all the more mysterious and instructive." The very lack of character in what Marcel sees acts as a guarantee of that precious, "real" life which the princess and her friends seem to have agreed not to display publicly. It is the absence of any personality in the scene that keeps Marcel's interest alive. The reason he gives for this brings us back to the ambiguity of his thought about "truth" and "reality." He compares his fascination at the Opéra with the pleasure he has in reading the empty, elegant formulas in a play by Meilhac; he finds a kind of aristocratic disdain in "the absence of poetry, of lofty thoughts," a noble preference for promise and potentiality over realization. For Marcel would recognize the interesting ideas, the poetry—"things so familiar to me"—and once reduced to something like what he has already imagined himself, they would no longer interest him.[11] Behind the longing to be fulfilled by something entirely different from himself, there seems to be a more realistic sense that the lives of other people, even the life of nature, will necessarily turn out to be at least partly familiar to him. In order, then, to keep the illusion of something marvelously new and unexpected in the Guermantes world, he refuses to accept what he sees as characteristic of that world; it is rather a conventional way of suggesting that the aristocracy's real life is elsewhere. And so Marcel's strongest impression of the nobility is a negative one, of something deliberately being withheld. Since he seems to suspect that this other life cannot be absolutely different from his own, he has, in a sense, to work himself into a state of excitement great enough to drown out the voice of his intelligence, to prevent himself from hearing too clearly that the promise he is anxiously pursuing is only a promise of familiarity. He would like to have his own daydreams about the aristocracy revealed to him as an entirely new reality, to be surprised and fulfilled by an external realization of his fantasies. To have himself revealed to himself as an unfamiliar, unexpected reality: this is the paradox which Marcel sustains by avoiding the moment of deflating recognition. By seeming to elude him in the external world, Marcel's fantasies take on an aura of mystery; their mere absence seems to contain the promise of finally appearing to him both as the glamorous reality he has imagined and as different from anything his imagination could create.

Characteristically, the narrator analyzes and judges his past feelings as he remembers them; he gives us not only the story of his past, but also a long reflective essay on his life. In the Opéra passage, his present point of view on this past incident is implied both by the comical aspects of his description and by his account of why he could now appreciate Berma's talent. The first time he saw her his mind was so "steeped in these dreams of perfection on the dramatic art" that he was naturally disappointed both by the difference between Berma's acting and his idea of great actors' talent, and by the similarity between her acting and his sense of the character of Phèdre. But now his mind, free of any "pre-existent, abstract and false idea of dramatic genius," is receptive to the "individual impression" Berma's performance makes on him, and he learns the important truth that the only reality such ideas as beauty and truth have is in a particular style.[12] The words are conventional labels to account for unique impressions; they are not pre-existent realities whose abstract content we can use to judge individual works. And the passage on Berma suggests the disillusionment Marcel will soon feel at Madame de Villeparisis's and Madame de Guermantes's. His expectation that the aristocracy will be the perfect incarnation of some absolute idea of aristocracy makes it inevitable that his contact with the Guermantes world will be disappointing. It is only when he has been forced to give up such expectations that he will find a more solid, if not essentially different, justification for his interest in the aristocracy.

II. *Society as a work of art: the poetry of the past*

There are certain aspects of the aristocratic world that continue to interest Marcel even after it has become familiar to him. Since his childhood at Combray, he has had the anguished feeling of possessing no past, except in the unsatisfactory form of an intellectual memory. Any strong feeling—from his despair as a child at being separated from his mother in the evening to his jealous love for Albertine—seems to cut him off from his past, and he thinks of his life not as a single psychological history, but as a succession of disconnected personalities. Lacking a sense of his own continuity in time, he seeks, in various ways, to fix a permanent image of himself in the external world. Now if the Duchesse de Guermantes does not incarnate Marcel's dreams about the medieval past, he does find in her a living image of his own past at Combray. Unlike her sisters who, less intelligent and less secure socially than she, have tried to abolish all traces of their provincial origin from their voices, Oriane deliberately cultivates the harsh and heavy pronunciation Marcel recognizes as the peasant accent of the Ile de France and of Champagne. She thus gives to herself a larger existence both in time and in space. Her language reminds Marcel of "an old song"; he finds in her voice and her eyes "much of the life of nature round Combray," and ". . . as I looked at, as I listened to Mme. de Guermantes, I could see, a prisoner in the perpetual and quiet afternoon of her eyes, a sky of the Ile de France or of Champagne spread itself, grey-blue, oblique, with the same angle of inclination as in the eyes of Saint-Loup." [13]

We see something similar in the narrator's description of how genealogical discussions restore to the aristocracy some of its "vanished poetry." [14] The name of the Prince d'Agrigente loses all its glamor for Marcel when he meets the colorless man to whom the title belongs, but when he hears that the prince's mother was Damas, the granddaughter of the Duc de Modène, the prince himself "was delivered, as from an unstable chemical alloy, from the face and speech that prevented one from recognising him, and went to form with Damas and Modena, which themselves were only titles, a combination infinitely more seductive." The name of Guermantes also receives "a new sense and purpose, purely poetical," from being attached to names from the past belonging to faces which "were not discoloured for me by any trace of physical experience or fashionable mediocrity." [15] In a sense, the duke's genealogical knowledge, designed to im-

press his guests with the extraordinary value of his person, per-
forms for Marcel the poetically useful service of doing away with
some of his personal existence. The name Guermantes loses its
prosaic familiarity and is poeticized a second time by being joined
to names and faces outside of Marcel's experience. As with the
aristocracy at the Opéra, the Guermantes family becomes once
again promises or possibilities of existence; emptied of any "trace
of physical experience," the name regains the power of exciting
Marcel's imagination.

Except for his mother and grandmother, all the people in the
novel appear intellectually and morally uninteresting to Marcel
as long as they do not direct his attention to something beyond
themselves. His interest is awakened only when he suspects or
clearly sees in objects or people another reality that gives depth
to their individual presence. Without this transcendental reference, the world is either incomprehensible or boring. The discovery of unsuspected links among names in French history
seems to satisfy Marcel's fundamental need to penetrate beyond
the reality his senses perceive. In the church at Combray, Marcel's effort to join himself to the "action" of the hawthorns'
"blossoming" is expressed in the metaphor of a girl's rapid,
coquettish head movement. In the experiences of involuntary
memory, moments from the past suddenly come to life to give
great temporal "depth" to a seemingly isolated present moment.
The sense of mysteries hidden behind physical appearances, the
feeling of possession which metaphorical expression gives, and
the support given to Marcel's present life by the past he relives
when he tastes the *madeleine* or to the Guermantes name by the
history of their family's many branches: these are all forms of
Marcel's habit of defining the possession or value of the present
in terms of a transcendence of present sensory experience. The
amount of "reality" or "truth" in people, places, or things depends
on the persuasiveness of their reference to other people, places,
or things. It is only by the discovery of a second term of reality
that Marcel's needs for possession and unity can be satisfied.
Metaphorical expression is, as I shall later show in more detail, a

means of assimilating the outer world to the accumulated past that makes up Marcel's inner world; and the presence of the past in the aristocracy's names, as well as in the chance experiences that re-create Marcel's own past for him, is a guarantee of permanence and unity in spite of the destructive effects of time.

The narrator writes that when he went into society his "historical curiosity" was weak in comparison to his "aesthetic pleasure." Marcel is capable of enjoying society, even after realizing that at the duchess's door he has landed "not as upon the threshold (as I had supposed) but as at the farthest confines of the enchanted world of names," to the extent that he finds in society the qualities he admires in works of art.[16] The passage on the duchess's voice is full of comparisons to the artistic world. Like the actresses Réjane and Jeanne Granier, Oriane has made of her voice "something admirable and distinctive"; she uses, the narrator writes, the pure vocabulary an old French author might have used; and, in creating her artistic effect, she herself is partly influenced by art: "To all these reasons for displaying her local originality, the favourite writers of Mme. de Guermantes—Mérimée, Meilhac and Halévy—had brought in addition, which the respect for what was natural, a feeling for the prosaic by which she attained to poetry and a spirit purely of society which called up distant landscapes before my eyes." [17] The particular artistic quality Marcel enjoys in listening to the duchess is actually a kind of historical allusiveness, and although his final judgment of society will be almost wholly negative, the aristocracy helps him to become aware of the role history will play in his esthetics. The narrator often uses metaphors taken from art to describe his pleasure when the Guermantes and their guests trace their family trees. Since he lacks the experience of having known Henri IV's father or the Duchesse de Longueville, no single name can fix his attention and, as Oriane's guests evoke their ancestors, his mind can indulge in the esthetically pleasing activity of arranging the names they mention into various colorful patterns. "Each name displaced by the attractions of another, with which I had never suspected it of having any affinity, left the unalterable position which it had occupied in my brain, where familiarity had dulled it, and, speeding to join the Mortemarts, the Stuarts or the Bourbons, traced with them branches of the most graceful design and an ever-changing colour." The Duc de Guermantes is no longer the rich, vain *coureur* Marcel is disappointed to meet, but part of a harmonious set of associations among the names of different regions in France and among different periods in time. And this system of reflections and *renvois,* of multiple connections among various names, this pattern of variety within unity which is the design of the Guermantes family tree, naturally make Marcel think of a work of art. He sees the colorful panes of ancient stained-glass windows as he hears the names which, "at regular intervals, each of a different hue, detached themselves from the genealogical tree of Guermantes, and disturbed with no foreign or opaque matter the buds—pellucid, alternate, many-coloured— which (like, in the old Jesse windows, the ancestors of Jesus) blossomed on either side of the tree of glass." [18]

By reminding Marcel of a work of art, the aristocracy helps him to define value in art. But it is many years before he is able to make explicit the connection between the kind of pleasure he experiences in society and his own potentialities as an artist. Indeed, when, years later, he reads a description by one of the Goncourts of an evening spent at the Verdurins', he naïvely equates Goncourt's idiosyncrasies with "literature," and feels that his own "lack of qualifications for a literary career" is "a less regrettable thing, as if literature did not reveal any profound truth, and at the same time it seemed to me sad that literature was not what I had thought it to be." [19] The narrator's pastiche of the Goncourt style is, in spite of superficial similarities in the abundance of detail and images, in such a strikingly different voice from the one we have been listening to for well over twenty-five hundred pages that, unlike Marcel when he reads the passage, we can easily refute his argument against literature. Goncourt's picture is elaborately flat. Marcel seeks an image of himself in the outer world, but the Goncourt description makes clear how remote this pursuit is from superficial self-involvement. For what

is most striking about Goncourt is the extraordinary self-indul-
gence of his style. And this is perfectly compatible with the
equally extraordinary attention he brings to things outside of himself, with his great curiosity. The disagreeably comic aspect of his
style is due to the fact that his attention to detail makes objects
seem wholly insignificant. There is, so to speak, no transcendental
impulse behind the vision he has of the world, and instead of
giving objects greater depth by going beyond them, he actually
undercuts their physical reality by his verbal excesses *about* their
physical reality. His *écriture artiste* is a way of using the external
world to stimulate in himself the pleasurable activity of deform-
ing ordinary language; his style expresses no personal vision of
that world, but rather a theoretical ingenuity about words. Everything at the Verdurins'—from the design on the dinner plates to
Cottard's medical anecdotes—provides him with the same literary
enjoyment, and the world as he sees it strikes us as meaningless
apart from this enjoyment, and as sickeningly rich.

In his comments on the differences between Goncourt's and
his attitudes in society, the narrator writes that he was able to
"reassure" himself by thinking that he is capable of observing
people and things, but only to note "the point that two human
beings had in common," or "some general characteristic common
to several things." It is his interest in the historical allusions contained in Oriane's voice or in the Prince d'Agrigente's name that
explains the narrator's peculiar claim, often repeated in the novel,
that he is a poor observer of external reality. His many detailed
descriptions would seem to belie this claim, but it is a valid one
insofar as he exhaustively describes things in order to go beyond
the individual object of description to a second reality, which
may be metaphorical, historical, or a general law of human behavior. "It was of no use for me to go out to dinner, I did not
see the guests because, when I thought I was looking at them, I
was looking through them as with an X-ray." [20] Of course, what
makes X-rays useful in medicine would hardly make them recom-
mendable as a device for portraying individual characters in a
novel: they do not record external appearances, and there is

much more uniformity among people's insides than among their looks and manners and uses of language. Now it is clearly not true that the narrator gives us only "general characteristics," but there is in his book a tension between his interest in dramatic particularities and his interest in general laws of behavior. I shall presently attempt to account for this tension and also define the literary values and defects in which it results. The concern about a reality beyond the individual person or place does not, however, always make for the level of abstraction we find in the general laws. In the case of the aristocracy's ties with history, Marcel sees the Guermantes and the Prince d'Agrigente in a temporal perspective that actually enriches the individual portrait. And, given Marcel's moral disappointment with society, it is this other, transcendent reality which feeds his imagination enough to make him continue to observe an otherwise depressing scene. His ability partly to dematerialize the social scene is what saves it from oblivion; it is the psychological condition for our enjoyment of social portraits as part of the narrator's work.

In his remarks after the passage from the Goncourt *Journal,* the narrator refers to certain of his own impressions of the Verdurin drawing room as an example of what he has pursued in society: something which "was located halfway down, below the range of vision, in a zone somewhat recessed." [21] The incident he mentions here is recorded in *La Prisonnière;* it occurs during a visit to the Verdurins' home on the Quai Conti in Paris. Goncourt would have accepted with delight Charlus's offer to show him the Verdurins' silver, but the baron's proposal leaves Marcel indifferent. He is not only preoccupied with his jealous curiosity about Albertine's relationship with Mademoiselle Vinteuil, but, he writes, he is always "far too distracted and agitated" in society "to fasten my attention upon objects that were more or less beautiful." Only "some general element," or a reality corresponding to something he has already desired in his thoughts can fix his attention. This "general element," this appeal to his imagination is furnished, unexpectedly, by Brichot, who tells him that the room they are in can give him an idea of the Verdurin drawing room of twenty-five years ago, in the Rue Montalivet. And the existence of the drawing room of the Quai Conti is, suddenly, threatened by intrusions from the past. Recognizing himself "a certain common air of family life, a permanent identity" between the arrangement of furniture in the present drawing room and the furniture at La Raspelière, Marcel is able to think of physical reality as merely the material extension of an inner history. The drawing room he is now in is the last version of the Verdurin drawing room as it exists in his and Brichot's memories. The passage impressively illustrates the power of memory to spiritualize matter, and to establish a continuity between the internal and external worlds. The room seems to Marcel actually to waver, in almost hallucinatory fashion, between the physically present one and the mental images of former drawing rooms which, so to speak, make it possible to assimilate the masses of furniture, to soften and break up their hard outlines.

> Those pieces of the original furniture that had been transported here, and sometimes arranged in the same groups, and which I myself remembered from la Raspelière, introduced into the new drawing-room fragments of the old which, at certain moments, recalled it so vividly as to create a hallucination and then seemed themselves scarcely real from having evoked in the midst of the surrounding reality fragments of a vanished world [which one had the impression of seeing in another place].[22]

Although Brichot may prefer the remembered drawing room to the present one, the narrator writes that his memories also give a beauty to the drawing room of the Quai Conti that it could not have for a newcomer. For this partial dematerialization of reality does not involve a total suppression of the object. The narrator's description is full of physical details; memory simply gives to things an extension of being, an existence beyond the physical. The narrator lists the objects which,

> for Brichot, an old frequenter of the Verdurin parties, had that patina, that velvety bloom [ce velouté] of things to which, giving them a sort of profundity, [their spiritual counterpart] has

been added; all these things scattered before him, sounded in his
ear like so many resonant keys which awakened cherished like-
nesses in his heart, confused reminiscences which, here in this
drawing-room of the present day that was littered with them, cut
out, defined, as on a fine day a shaft of sunlight cuts a section in
the atmosphere, the furniture and carpets, and pursuing it from
a cushion to a flower-stand, from a footstool to a lingering scent,
from the lighting arrangements to the colour scheme, carved,
evoked, spiritualised, called to life a form which might be called
the ideal aspect, immanent in each of their successive homes, of
the Verdurin drawing-room.[23]

There is no explicit statement in the passage that this "double
spirituel" bridges the gap between the self and the outer world,
but Marcel's impressions here clearly suggest the role of memory
in creating a continuity of being between the two. In the same
way that a metaphor internalizes an external object by expressing
a trait common to the object and to an image the mind already
possesses, the "patine" or "velouté" which memories project on
things is, precisely, the presence of the self, of a personal past, in
a world now revealed partly *as* an inner possession.

The aristocracy's names have a gloss similar to that of the Verdurin drawing room. Just behind the ordinary physical presence
of the Prince d'Agrigente or the Duc de Guermantes, there are
the "spiritual counterparts" of the Duc de Modène or the illustrious Guermantes history. It is not in this case a question of
Marcel's personal memories, but of a past beyond any individual
memory which can, however, become a personal memory through
the mediation of the people Marcel meets at the Duchesse de
Guermantes's. Much of the history of France is literally alive in
these guests who, like the drawing room of the Quai Conti, are
the present links in a historical chain which is otherwise wholly
spiritual. Furthermore, the history of these aristocratic families
appeals to Marcel's imagination in more ways than the history of
the Verdurin drawing room. The genealogical discussions give a
new perspective on great historical events. The latter are enclosed
in and made subsidiary to domestic concerns; a king of France

appears in the name of a certain property, or as the grandparent who left an inheritance to one of Oriane's ancestors. Their illustrious names make it possible for the aristocracy to feel in possession not only of their families' past, but also of the national past of France, with which these names are so closely connected. The names provide, then, a continuity between past and present which Marcel has found impossible to establish in the psychological history of a single individual.

It is, therefore, the experience of depth in time that awakens Marcel's greatest interest when he goes into society, and the artistic metaphors he uses to describe this experience suggest how it will be useful to him when he writes his own book. The way in which the aristocracy contains and encloses the past reminds him of the round and powerful masses of Romanesque architecture: "Similarly the aristocracy, in its heavy structure, pierced with rare windows, admitting a scanty daylight, shewing the same incapacity to soar but also the same massive and blind force as the architecture of the romanesque age, embodies all our history, immures it, beetles over it [la renfrogne]." [24] The artistic metaphor can be developed further. For in the history of a name there are numerous, complex patterns and connections; no one name is isolated, and each one refers to others which explain it as it explains them. And so it is his experience in this disappointing society that helps Marcel to develop the idea of a work of art in which each part alludes to other parts, in which the meaning of each passage cannot be exhausted by that passage alone, but must be completed by the reader's memory of what he has already experienced of the work as well as by what the work has yet to offer. The names of the aristocracy fill the "spaces" of Marcel's memory with just this kind of complex artistic organization. And it will be when he realizes that these inner spaces are already covered by his own past that Marcel will give a future to the contents of memory; the artistic metaphors that best express an inner possession of the past become the model for a literary expression of his past.

III. *Reflections of Marcel's psychology in the social world*

The connections among the nobility's names are familial; several names branch out from a single family tree. Marcel's experience in society reveals other similarities among apparently unrelated individuals. And instead of demonstrating the continuity in time of certain families, these similarities establish a continuity of being among all men. We soon realize that every person we meet in the novel has a psychological allusiveness to other persons, and to the extent that the reader remembers much of the characters' behavior at the same time that he is presumably seeing it for the first time, his reading experience vindicates the general laws. Moreover, the latter only partially describe a psychological uniformity of which the narrator himself, for reasons that will presently be clear, is not completely aware. For Marcel, this generality is a source of profound discouragement, in spite of his apparent pleasure at formulating it when he writes his book. His contacts with other people (and here it is a question of all his social experience, not merely his experience of aristocratic society) reveal extraordinary parallelisms both among these people and between them and himself, parallelisms that permanently destroy his dream of finding in the social world a fulfilling, precious "truth." The man who formulates general laws of behavior has changed very much from the man who believed that certain people lead special, unique lives, governed by rites and laws inconceivable to the rest of humanity. The foundation on which the general laws are built is Marcel's discovery that the gods and goddesses whose marvelous life he has both dreamed and despaired of penetrating have desires and fears similar to his own. Now the image of himself Marcel sees in his mother's eyes does not necessarily indicate a similarity of nature between her and him. There remains something mysterious and fascinating about the life she leads when she is not with him—when she is, for example, downstairs having dinner with Swann—and she seems to have the strength and self-sufficiency he lacks. The great value of her possessing, in her maternal love, a permanent

image of her son is that, because of her anguishing but also com-
forting difference from him, Marcel feels confident that she can
contain and preserve his identity as he cannot. He finds himself
in someone stronger than he; with his mother, the two sides of
his wish to find both himself and total otherness in the external
world thus appear to be satisfied. In the rest of the social world,
however, Marcel finds, so to speak, neither a reliable container
for the self nor a complete realization of his idealizing fantasies,
but mainly duplications of his own anxieties. Other people provide, as Georges Piroué has said, a historical reflection of his
own solitude, of his personal drama.[25] And the universality of
these anxieties, as well as the grotesque forms they can take, explain Marcel's final sense that other people cannot give him the
security he needs.

At the beginning of "Combray" the narrator recalls a story his
grandfather used to tell about Swann's father. He describes the
latter as "an excellent but an eccentric man in whom the least
little thing would, it seemed, often check the flow of his spirits
and divert the current of his thoughts." Unable to console himself after the loss of his wife, he dies two years after her; but
immediately after her death, during a walk Marcel's grandfather
makes him take to prevent him from seeing the body being
placed in the coffin, he suddenly exclaims how happy the fine
weather makes him feel, and says enthusiastically: " 'Ah! whatever you may say, it's good to be alive all the same, my dear
Amédée!' " The narrator writes that he was inclined to think of
Swann's father as "a monster," but the reader will soon be able
to recollect this anecdote as a first example of the important law
of emotional discontinuity.[26] Marcel's first direct experience of
this law is during his childhood at Combray: the happy, energetic
boy he feels himself to be during the day seems a completely
different person from the anguished child terrified at being separated from his mother at night. And the long period during
which his grandmother's death seems to cause him no deep pain,
broken by the sudden eruption of suffering during his second stay
at Balbec, inspires the famous statement about "the heart's inter-

missions." [27] The anecdote about Swann's father is the first example of these discontinuities of feeling, but it is a bizarre and humorous example: the different feelings occur in such a short space of time, the moment of change is so abrupt and so precisely located, that we may consider the incident as a caricatural illustration of a psychological law Marcel will later formulate in a wholly serious, solemn tone.

Other variations of psychological patterns characteristic of Marcel account for much of the dramatic variety in the novel. I have mentioned his ambivalent attitude toward habit. On the one hand, anything new terrifies him; unfamiliar surroundings —such as the hotel bedroom at Balbec—do not contain any recognizable image of himself, and their total otherness seems menacing to his fragile sense of self. But habit also deadens our receptiveness to life; we live within a narrow range of predictable experiences, avoiding any event for which we do not have a ready-made response, repeating mechanically the same behavior in different situations. Marcel wants so deeply both to be protected by habit and to allow himself the occasions for self-discovery and self-creation that a rebellion against habit makes possible, that he speaks of it as if it were a god, half god and half evil, making the world safe for the self but creating a world in which the self cannot grow. The example of Elstir, as I shall demonstrate more fully in another chapter, suggests that the artist is above all free of habitual responses to experience; he dares to meet the world without giving in to the need to identify it at once in order to make it familiar. But, except for the artist, people prefer the safety of habit. Marcel sympathizes with Françoise, who is brought "positively to the verge of dissolution" when the family moves to a new house in Paris; there is nothing "friendly" in the new place and, like Marcel in the Balbec hotel, Françoise "faced even silence with a strained attention." [28] She also illustrates the tenacity of linguistic habits. She calls a York ham a Nev'-York ham, simply replacing the word she has heard more recently with one that is—her mispronunciation notwithstanding —more familiar to her.[29] The elevator boy at the Balbec hotel also assimilates new words into the vocabulary he already possesses: he stubbornly calls the Marquise de Cambremer the Marquise de Camembert, and, the narrator remarks, ". . . it was quite natural that he should have heard her say a name which he already knew." [30] These are, of course, humorous examples of the power of habit. The linguistic mistakes of Françoise, the elevator boy, and the manager of the Balbec hotel bring out sharply the mechanical aspect of rigid responses to experience. The habits they cannot give up are merely habits of sound, and their inability to adapt to the most elementary kind of novelty gives them the verbal obstinacy of parrots. As extreme examples of absorption in fixed behavior, one thinks of the "marquise's" customer at the Champs-Elysées public toilet, who in eight years has failed only once—the day of his wife's death—to come at exactly 3 p.m. to spend, as the "marquise" says proudly, more than a half-hour "to read his newspapers [while relieving himself]." He seemed, she adds, happy to come back after having missed a day: " 'You could see,' " she notes with sympathetic perceptiveness, " 'that all his little habits had been quite upset.' " [31] Or there is "the famous Professor E . . . , almost a friend of my father and grandfather," more interested in manipulating the elevator buttons—"this being a mania with him"—than listening to Marcel's pleas to look at his grandmother, who has just had an attack.[32] The most trivial gesture or act becomes a necessary ritual; it then demands absolute devotion, and what we think of as superior human duties seem only annoying obstacles to a performance that has actually become a guarantee of security and perhaps even of identity.

Habitual responses can, of course, involve a wide range of commitments and consequences. Brichot corrects the etymological mistakes the former curé of Combray makes in his work on the origins of place names in Brittany. The mistakes are due to the curé's Christian point of view: he comes to each name determined to trace it back to events in Christian history, thereby often ignoring the name's particular history.[33] Habit also determines social behavior. The "force" of habit is greater than the shock of war; the postponement of a Verdurin dinner party would be a worse catastrophe for the "patronne" than thousands of deaths at the front. And Madame Verdurin's satisfaction is greater than her horror the morning she both is able to resume her habit of dunking a *croissant* in her coffee and reads about the sinking of the *Lusitania*.[34] We see still another version of Marcel's ambivalent feelings about habit in people's tendency to move in closed coteries, at the same time that their often malevolent gossip about people outside of the coterie reveals an uneasy curiosity about other forms of social life. Madame de Villeparisis arrives at the Balbec hotel surrounded by "the barrier of her [habits]" that effectively protects her from possibly painful new contacts. The other guests act in the same way, convince themselves that the few people they speak to are the only ones to whom they want to speak, thus "sacrificing, if not to self-importance, at any rate to certain inculcated principles and mental habits the thrilling delight of mixing in a strange kind of life." [35] Fixed ideas prevent the narrator's family from believing that Swann is part of the most exclusive aristocratic circles; a similar attachment to a favorite idea makes Madame de Varambon insist that Marcel is the Admiral Jurien de la Gravière's nephew, and leads Madame de Chaussegros to think that she has known Marcel for a long time. Such errors illustrate the mechanical inflexibility of the "social personality" that others give us; Madame de Varambon's mistake is "a crowning instance of all the other mistakes, less serious, more elaborate, unconscious or deliberate, which accompany one's name on the label which society writes out and attaches to one." [36]

Social behavior in the novel includes numerous variations on Marcel's psychology. He notes a peculiar reluctance in Oriane and Charlus to let their guests leave; he speaks of "that reluctance common to all the Guermantes to bring anything to an end, which kept them plunged in a sort of anxious inertia." [37] Marcel visits Charlus after his first dinner at the Guermantes'; the baron hurls insults at him, claiming that some treachery on Marcel's part has permanently destroyed his, Charlus's, protective interest

in him, but he seems unable to let Marcel go, as if he were afraid
of being alone again.[38] His anxiety reminds us of Marcel's panic
as a child when he kisses his mother good-night. With Charlus
and Oriane, a similar need not to be separated from someone else
is played out in other contexts, and we see not only the reflection
of Marcel's fear, but also the "adaptability" of this fear to a
variety of dramatic situations. With Charlus, his insistence that
Marcel stay, that he listen to music and have a drink, makes a
comic contrast with his half-furious, half-melancholy claim that
he wishes never to see him again. It emphasizes the wildly eccentric, unpredictable aspect of Charlus's character. Both his arrogant demand for absolute obedience from everyone and his sentimental dream of perfect trust between himself and another man
make for an extreme, mock version of Marcel's anguished curiosity about what others think of him and his wish for oneness
between himself and the outer world. And while the parallel
to Marcel's psychology is clear, we do not have an impression of
monotonous repetition. A certain combination of violence, senti-
mentality, and vanity is particular to Charlus, and he re-creates an
anguish characteristic of other people in the novel in his individual style.

In the case of the Duchesse de Guermantes, her somewhat
anxious reluctance to be separated from her guests is expressed
in a charming and flattering display of affection, which, although
it "does not outlive the exaltation that has dictated it," makes of
the final moment of an evening spent with her "a compelling
masterpiece of grace and goodness." Marcel suffers at being
separated from his mother because he feels empty without her.
When she leaves him alone at the hotel in Venice, he feels that
she has taken his self with her, that he is nothing more than a
beating heart. And, in a sense, the anxiety typical of the Guermantes when they see their guests prepare to leave is also due to
a fear of emptiness in themselves. Marcel notes that, unlike the
Courvoisiers, their social generosity is both material and moral;
they offer their guests "a lavish display of charming words, of
courteous actions, a whole system of verbal elegance supplied

from a positive treasure-house within." But, because of their idle lives, this inner richness is ordinarily "unemployed"; it seeks an outlet "in a sort of fugitive effusion, all the more [nervously excited,]" which, while it is part of the Guermantes charm, also expresses the sterility of their lives.[39] It is, then, in the aristocracy that Marcel naturally finds a social version of his personal doubts about the strength and content of the self. Their inner richness is only potential except during brief moments of gracious hospitality. And in these moments they express no reliable affection for their guests, but only the anxious need to realize, to give specific content to a vague sense of their inner resources. Its history cannot give to the aristocracy a personal enough image of itself; these people produce nothing in their daily lives in which they could continuously recognize themselves. The same thing is true of Marcel until he writes his book. Through his narrator's portrait of the aristocracy, Proust emphasizes the social context of unproductivity in which anguish about self-identity is the most probable form of spiritual sickness.

Madame Verdurin's "feeling of hatred" toward Charlus the evening he invites his aristocratic friends to her home to hear Morel play is, the narrator remarks, only "a special, social form of jealousy." [40] The "patronne" is the most extreme example of the Proustian psychology of love in the service of a ruthless social ambition. Her portrait is one of unrelieved falseness and nastiness, but there is a kind of esthetic appeal in the very exaggeration of the picture the narrator gives us. She is hypocritical and cruel and vain so energetically and so unashamedly, and the narrator is so ruthlessly generous in giving her space in which to express and expose herself, that she becomes almost an abstract force, marvelously comical and marvelously improbable. We recognize in her behavior a caricatural version of some of Marcel's desires and fears. Like everyone else in the novel, she dreams of penetrating into the circles that exclude her; her life is a patient and unavowed ascent from a *salon* dominated by a Sorbonne professor, a bourgeois doctor, and a demimondaine to the *salon* of the Prince de Guermantes, where she enjoys the perfect triumph of receiving rather than being received, of being the princess herself. But while quietly dreaming of more glorious evenings, she is fiercely possessive with the members of the "petit clan." They are her "fidèles," and indeed she demands of them a faithfulness even more unqualified than what Swann and Marcel jealously demand from Odette and Albertine. She willingly protects Swann's love for Odette and Charlus's love for Morel provided that they love within the group; but she makes Brichot give up his mistresses and discourages visits to a sick mother's bedside because love and sickness become intolerable when they mean an absence from one of her "Wednesdays." Charlus seals his own doom when he fails even to present his aristocratic friends and relatives to her the evening of Morel's concert: it is as if he had excluded her from her own circle. Madame Verdurin praises only what reminds her of herself. Somewhat like the Duc and Duchesse de Guermantes, who admire only those pictures by Elstir that they own, but more extreme than they, she admits Elstir's talent only insofar as she can claim to have directed it and to have inspired him. Madame Verdurin's social ambition is a ferocious desire to control and assimilate the world around her; she expands the circle of the "petit clan" until the most elusive groups of Parisian society become her "fidèles," admiringly sending her back a flattering image of herself.

Snobbery is the social vice that corresponds to Marcel's anxious curiosity about what Albertine and her friends think of him when he first sees them on the beach at Balbec. The worst snobs in the novel are not the people of royal blood, such as the Princesse de Parme or the Reine de Naples; they are the bourgeois Legrandin and his sister, or nobles snubbed by the Duchesse de Guermantes, such as Madame de Gallardon and Madame de Saint-Euverte. Snobbery in Proust is not merely an admiration of wealth and social prestige. It is an active pursuit of the attention and interest of those who, because of their wealth and position, can afford to play a role of indifference, that is, to play the role of the pursued. Social prestige, like sexual desirability, depends on indifference, on an apparent lack of social ambition; the best way to attract the attention of an indifferent social group—or of an indifferent woman one desires—is to appear indifferent oneself. Success may also depend on guessing the desire of the pursued so that an exchange of satisfactions may take place. The Prince de Faffenheim gets Norpois's support for his candidacy at the *Institut* when he finally realizes that what Norpois wants is an introduction for Madame de Villeparisis to the prince's wife and to the Grande-duchesse Jean. Social life, like the life of the lover, is essentially hypocritical and strategic. The ambitious man and the lover play a political game: the person with a desire to be satisfied must guess the strategy that will induce someone else to satisfy that desire.

It is because of their experience as diplomats that the prince and Norpois are able to maneuver effectively in the area of individual social ambitions. The diplomat's life develops his sense of the indirect, symbolic ways in which language expresses intentions. It is a training in what the narrator calls a "method of reading beneath superimposed symbols." Threats of war or a real desire for peace are not necessarily expressed directly in notes between countries; in each case a superficially banal phrase or action can more effectively both translate an intention and safeguard a certain freedom of maneuvering. International politics involves the same testing of how far one can go in demanding further satisfactions without losing advantages already enjoyed as that between two lovers. The fallacious view of the balance of power, the narrator writes, is to suppose that "good feeling, sounding speeches, earnest entreaties" count for a great deal; ". . . the heavy weight, the true determinant consists in something else, in the possibility which the adversary does (if he is strong enough) or does not enjoy of satisfying, in exchange for what one oneself wants, a desire." [41] The interest of this remark is not so much in the "rightness" or "wrongness" of the narrator's ideas about love or politics, but is rather in his refusal to admit any break of continuity between his personal experience and his views of social life, war, and international diplomacy. In refusing to be opti-

mistic about the moral capacities of nations, he implicitly rejects
the idea that what he himself has not encountered can somehow
become an effective reality when large groups of people are involved. The rightness of assuming that generous feelings do or
should operate in relations among countries perhaps depends
simply on one's having seen them operate in personal experience.
It is a fact that in Marcel's life such feelings have been—except
with his mother and grandmother—almost entirely inoperative,
and however limited we may find his moral imagination in certain respects, it is characteristic of his particular form of intellectual rigor that he should refuse to admit that international relations magically give birth to virtues absent from personal
relations.

In Proust, to have wide experience means to be in a position to
realize the fundamental sameness in what appear to be the most
diverse experiences. What Marcel discovers, during the period
that he is particularly attentive to social life, is that his most personal memories help him to understand aristocratic society and
international politics, and, conversely, that the vocabularies of
snobbery, diplomacy, and military tactics give him a deeper understanding of, for example, his own behavior when he has been
in love. Charlus can ridicule what is stupid and illogical in the
French position during World War I because of his detachment
from the "corps-France"; he lacks the passion which in war is
called patriotism, and which effectively blinds us to what may be
the other side's chances for victory, or the partial justness of its
cause. And for the man without passion, the logic of passion is
never irrefutable. Marcel, "one of the body cells of France," is
as incapable of judging the German adversary objectively as he
was of being detached in his quarrels with Albertine.[42] But it is
the memory of his jealous love which nevertheless helps him to
see why he is himself incapable of judgment during the war.
Conversely, when Albertine is still living with him, the possibility
of a bluff in one of Germany's threats to France helps him to
clarify some of the alternatives in his trying to figure out if his

"adversary," Albertine, "is really determined upon war," that is, is about to leave him.[43]

These parallels support the analogical density of *A la Recherche du temps perdu.* They also make necessary the novelistic form of dramatic scene and narrative comment. Because behavior is essentially strategic, it requires an interpreter. Language is a code that needs to be deciphered, and in the long analyses that interrupt the conversations in the novel the narrator unravels the intentions masked by what characters say to each other. He is attentive to "the evidence that is not a rational and analytical expression of the truth; the words themselves did not enlighten me unless they could be interpreted in the same way as a sudden rush of blood to the cheeks of a person who is embarrassed, or, what is even more telling, a sudden silence." [44] The narrator writes that the words he said to Albertine in no way reflected his feelings; but because today he knows the truth of those feelings, he explains them to the reader at the same time that he repeats his words. "But if I concealed the former and he were acquainted only with the latter, my actions, so little in keeping with my speech, would so often give him the impression of strange [changes of feeling] that he would think me almost mad." [45] In society, the narrator deduces feelings from this very incongruity between language and the rest of behavior, an incongruity that makes people behave like puppets pulled in opposite directions by an inattentive puppeteer. Jealousy trains Marcel to be particularly sensitive to those revelations that escape the camouflage of deliberate language: a verbal slip, an intonation, an uncontrollable facial expression, or the beginning of a certain gesture. Narrative comment fills in the gaps, and adds to the social comedy a clinical investigation into the psychological machinery of subterfuge.

IV. *"Le royaume du néant"*

The psychological parallels Marcel discovers between his own experience and more general forms of social behavior prove to be

both fruitful and discouraging. They are discouraging because
they destroy his illusions about social life. Society offers no
"truth" or "reality" that can help him to escape from his uncertainties and anguish, but only mirror images of his own behavior.
And as if the mirror were cracked, it sends back a distorted image,
a parody of what Marcel discovers to be true of himself. He
writes in *Le Temps retrouvé* that the love we feel for people is
something of an "aberration," since we are really pursuing a certain inner "dream." "It was my faith in Bergotte and Swann
which had made me love Gilberte, just as it was my belief in
Gilbert the Bad which had made me love Mme. de Guermantes.
And what a wide expanse of unfathomable ocean was set apart
in my love for Albertine, painful, jealous and individual though
that love was!" The paradox is by now a familiar one: Marcel
pursues a reality he imagines wholly different from himself, but
his image of that reality expresses what is most individual in his
own imagination. Behind the physical brutality that Charlus requires for his sexual pleasure, there is also a "dream": his "dream
of a virility proven by brutal tests, if need be, and all the rich
store of medieval scenes, crucifixions and feudal tortures which
his imagination treasured, invisible to us, but reflecting themselves in his acts, as we have seen." [46] But the behavior is grotesque without the dream. And Marcel's disillusionment with
other people as a source of fulfillment is largely due to his perspective: from the outside, he necessarily sees only the aberra-
tions, the self-defeating pursuit of unsatisfying goals. Given this
point of view, it is natural that, as Ramon Fernandez remarked,
depth and intensity are always in the narrator rather than in
other characters in *A la Recherche*.[47] Others reflect not the content of Marcel's dreams, but his mistaken choices of trying to
possess those dreams in the Guermantes salon or by imprisoning
Albertine. He can trace in himself the steps by which his adolescent idealism becomes an obsessed curiosity about the pleasures
Lesbians enjoy with each other, but in others he sees only the
most debased forms of what is essentially an attempt to possess
the self in the external world as something different from the

self. Such dreams are undoubtedly self-defeating in any form, but the "royaume du néant" is where a profound need for self-identification and self-possession is expressed only as a desperate wish to have the Duchesse de Guermantes attend an annual garden party.

The spectacle society offers Marcel is one of frantic agitation. He is unique in that he is the only person in the novel in whom the discrepancy between the inner dream and social satisfactions is fully realized and therefore profoundly affects his attitudes. The other characters illustrate perfectly the absurdity of the social *divertissement*: they continue to plot ways to increase their social prestige, although social prestige cannot really quiet their restlessness. Indeed, those who are at the top of the social ladder cannot rest any more than those who are still climbing, and, having reached the highest rungs, they begin to go down: Charlus with Morel and the Verdurin *salon,* the duchess in her friendships with actresses, and Swann in his pursuit of working-class women. And because there is almost no satisfaction possible in society, the demand for satisfaction is all the more exacerbated. In a sense, the picture of society in the novel is extremely simple: everyone acts out of the same ruthless determination not to miss a single occasion of possible pleasure. The peculiar weakness we first see in Marcel's inability to give up his mother's kiss a single evening before going to bed is shared, in various forms, by almost everyone in the Proustian world. In this world the postponement of pleasure is an impossible sacrifice; Odette can no more give up a party to spend a few hours with Swann than Jupien's clients can be concerned about losing their positions in society because of their compulsive pursuit of sexual pleasure.

This single-minded hunt for pleasure can take on fantastic proportions. It is naturally the pursuit of sexual pleasure that is painted in the most lurid colors. When, in Le Temps retrouvé, Marcel walks home from Charlus's male brothel during an air raid, he thinks of the freedom Jupien's customers must enjoy during such moments of catastrophe. The police will not bother them for a few hours; above all, there is no catastrophe great enough to distract us from the immediate satisfaction of a physical desire: "The tempest rages at sea, the ship rolls in every direction, torrents of rain, whipped by the wind, pour down from the sky; we give heed for just an instant—and then only to protect ourselves against some inconvenience it is causing us—to the immense scene in which we and the beloved body we are clasping close are but insignificant atoms." It is partly this overwhelming urgency of an impersonal sexual need that makes love between two people impossible in *A la Recherche du temps perdu*. Sexual anarchy is the ultimate release into action of the need to possess, to force something different from the self into a momentarily total service of the self. And if the narrator is detached and often sarcastic when he describes snobbery, his imagination responds melodramatically to the image of sexual chaos. His guilty fascination makes him wonder if a bomb has fallen on Charlus's hotel, "that building on which M. de Charlus might well have placed the prophetic inscription *Sodoma*, as did some unknown inhabitant of Pompeii with no less foresight, or perhaps after the eruption had begun and when the catastrophe was already under way." [48]

The urgency of this pursuit of pleasure and power gives to the later volumes of *A la Recherche* their Balzacian flavor. Balzac is, of course, more naïve than Proust in his portrait of a society in which those who survive act most ruthlessly on their will to be at the top. He makes theoretical moral condemnations of his selfish characters, but it is clear that he shares their feeling that social power is exhilarating. Nothing could be more distant from the kind of stylistic excitement we often find in Balzac than the dispassionate, ironic analyses Proust's narrator makes of social behavior. But the worlds they portray are essentially the same. Balzac gives more emphasis to political ambition and power, while Proust's social picture is almost exclusively of a world of garden parties and dinners; but in both writers the great majority of characters are unable to resist trying to force others into satisfying a desire—and thus to affirm personal power. And both Balzac and Proust heighten the morally shocking aspect of this psychology of egoism with scenes in which an apparently trivial pleasure has a greater claim on characters' attention than the death of a relative or friend. Proust's scenes are less melodramatic than the contrast between Goriot's agony and his daughters' preparations for Madame de Beauséant's ball. But he presents several examples of a similar refusal to allow death to spoil an evening of pleasure: the Verdurins give parties the days of Deschambre's and the Princesse Sherbatoff's deaths, and, by insisting that his cousin Amanien d'Osmond is recovering from an illness when he has actually just died, the Duc de Guermantes manages not to miss the costume ball "with a view to which a costume of Louis XI for himself, and one of Isabel of Bavaria for his wife were waiting in readiness." [49] Marcel and Swann are present at this last scene— one of the most extraordinary in the novel—and it is just before leaving for her evening of three parties that the duchess learns from Swann that he will probably die within a year. But the aristocratic society of which she is the finest example can imagine death only as an occasion of choice among wholly conventional- ized expressions of feeling, and she knows exactly when it is right to attend a funeral, or send an empty carriage, or have her name on the list of those who have written to the bereaved family. Swann's news demands a personal response, some expression of feeling for a man she really does enjoy more than anyone else in her coterie. But aristocratic society, by brilliantly providing appro- priate responses to all situations, has eliminated the pain of creat- ing, facing, and testing personal responses, and has therefore made impossible the process by which an individual moral per- sonality develops. "Placed for the first time in her life between two duties as incompatible as getting into her carriage to go out to dinner and shewing pity for a man who was about to die," she solves her conflict by denying it exists, and she suggests to Swann what the duke will cry out in more vulgarly direct fashion as their carriage pulls away: " 'You'll live to bury us all!' " It is Swann who, a man of the world himself, has the most pathet- ically refined manners in the scene. He knows, the narrator writes, that invitations come before a friend's death, and, rather than embarrass Madame de Guermantes, he encourages her to leave, for he "put himself in her place by dint of his instinctive politeness." [50]

The portrait of society is, in a way, similar to the one we have of Albertine. At first, to possess Albertine means possessing certain poetic aspects of nature, to embrace the life and rhythm of the sea; but in La Fugitive, Albertine's hidden life contains nothing more glamorous than a possible sexual secret. In the second half of A la Recherche du temps perdu, we find a parallel degeneration of the aristocracy's mysterious real life into a secretive sexual freemasonry. The parties of Le Côté de Guermantes destroy any idea of mystery in the aristocracy's private life, but in Sodome et Gomorrhe we begin to see what is a secret life within society, and the reasons for the secrecy. Charlus reveals to the dazzled Monsieur de Vaugoubert the existence of an immense fraternity of homosexuals, whose members often do not know each other, but who may—as in the case of the Embassy staff who greet Charlus at the Princesse de Guermantes's party—occasionally lead an organized social life within the larger unsuspecting or tolerant society. In Le Temps retrouvé we see one of the "salons" of this secret society: Charlus's male brothel. If the aristocracy's indifference is a parody of real indifference, the homosexual's exclusiveness is a caricature even of the Guermantes exclusiveness. Their existence as a secret society has no meaning except in terms of their fear of and curiosity about the rest of the world. The homosexual shares, but in a more exacerbated form, what is the main concern of the snob: a dependence on the image of himself he finds in other people's attitudes and behavior toward him. The Duchesse de Guermantes goes to the Norwegian fjords at the height of the social season in order to attract the attention of the hostesses whose invitations she thereby refuses, but she has so completely transformed her need of other people into successful strategies of control that her arrogant independence is comparatively convincing. The homosexuals, on the other hand, are forced into a closed society; they exclude others because they are afraid of being discovered by others.

The closed society's interest is nonetheless in people outside of this society. The nobles who do not belong to the Guermantes coterie spend their lives thinking about the group that excludes them; Oriane's latest *mots* are the social refreshment served by all the Parisian hostesses Oriane does not invite. And, more generally, almost all the conversations at the parties in the novel are about people who are not at the parties. Actually, it is not even necessary that the latter snub people in order to be talked about: when the Duc and Duchesse de Guermantes discuss their royal relatives, they are speaking of people who are pleased to invite and be received by the Guermantes. For the psychological mechanism that makes an envious Madame d'Epinay repeat Oriane's puns to her guests is the most obvious form of a more basic law in Proust's world: what is interesting is what is absent. This law operates so powerfully in the novel that the absence need only consist of the few feet that separate one group from another in the same drawing room. Even Swann and Oriane speak, during at least half of their conversation at Madame de Saint-Euverte's, of Madame de Cambremer and Madame de Rampillon. This universal need obviously determines the content of social talk; every social gathering in the book is a feast of either snobbish name-dropping or nasty gossip, or both, as in the case of the Duchesse de Guermantes, whose references to royalty usually begin with pride at knowing them so well and end with vicious anecdotes about them. There is a psychological continuity between Oriane's puns on Madame de Cambremer's name in *Un Amour de Swann* and her almost exclusive interest in actresses by the time of the Princesse de Guermantes's *matinée* in *Le Temps retrouvé*. Toward the end of her life she is interested principally in people outside her own social class; the witty gossip about absent royalty—the source of shocked admiration in the dull-witted Princesse de Parme—has developed into a curiosity that leads, finally, to her own social *déclassement*.

The homosexual's interest in people outside his group is an extreme and often dangerous expression of this law. The narrator writes, in the long essay on homosexuality that begins

Sodome et Gomorrhe, that the sexual invert cannot possibly find fulfillment: since he pursues a wholly masculine ideal, he can be satisfied only by men who, by definition, would not be interested in him, since, if they were, they would share the feminine desires that make him desire them.[51] This paradox makes of the homosexual's life neither an exclusive pursuit of other easily recognizable homosexuals nor, obviously, successful seductions of heterosexuals, but rather a kind of continuous tension of interest in the *possibility* of homosexuality in apparently heterosexual men. Their talk is often a guessing game; or—as in the case of Charlus when, knowing it is a lie, he cannot resist suggesting that there may have been homosexual incidents in Swann's life —it is a series of titillating exposures that create ideal, brief moments during which supposed heterosexuals are suddenly moved into the homosexual world without having yet lost, through constant confirmation of their homosexuality, the prestige of their heterosexual nature. Charlus's homosexual talk in the novel implies one obsessively repeated question: "Est-ce qu'il en est?" The outside world is an immense promise of pleasures, as well as a possible source of great danger: the thrilling new contact may lead to physical humiliation (as with the man who accosts Saint-Loup in the street) or to the police station and social disgrace (as with Charlus and Monsieur d'Argencourt, who are betrayed by Morel). It is for thousands of envious, excluded readers that Madame de Saint-Euverte sends her party lists to the *Gaulois* and Madame de Villeparisis writes her memoirs; a similar wish to attract the attention of people outside his ordinary social life— to attract their sexual attention, to awaken not merely social but sexual desires—leads Charlus into the risky pursuit of butchers and trolley conductors.

The increasingly larger role that homosexuality plays in the novel from *Sodome et Gomorrhe* on corresponds to a more general social decadence. The portrait of homosexual secrecy and promiscuity does not represent a narrowing of the narrator's sense of society (or an obsession in Proust with a limited, "abnormal" kind of behavior); it allusively describes the breaking up of the

brilliant society Marcel glimpses in its moment of perfection at
the Opéra. The picture of Charlus's brothel in *Le Temps retrouvé* prefigures the social promiscuity Marcel will find at the
Princesse de Guermantes's *matinée*. The narrator speaks of a
group of men from the highest society who come to the same
place every evening in search of physical pleasure:

> In Jupien's hotel, a number of men who did not wish to flee had
> all come together in the same room. They were not mutually
> acquainted, but still they were all of about the same social stand-
> ing, wealthy and aristocratic. There was something repugnant in
> the appearance of each of them, probably due to indulgence in
> degrading forms of enjoyment. . . . It is probable that, if you
> had asked these men for their calling cards, you would have
> been surprised to find that they were all of high social position.
> But one vice or another—and that greatest vice of all, lack of
> will power, which makes it impossible to resist any of the others
> —brought them together there, in separate rooms, it is true, but
> every single evening, I am told, so that, although society women
> knew their names, they had gradually lost sight of them and
> never had an opportunity to entertain them at their homes any
> more. The men still received social invitations, but habit always
> brought them back to their common rendezvous of vice.[52]

The pursuit of pleasure is no longer connected with an admiration for healthy physical vitality, as it was when Marcel enviously
watched Albertine and her friends run along the beach at Balbec. It is associated now with sickness and decay, and two of the
men who come every evening to the brothel Marcel describes
are an enormously fat alcoholic and a distinguished young noble-
man who has mysteriously lost the ability to coordinate his facial
expressions with what he is saying.

Finally, when, several years later, Marcel goes to a *matinée* at
the Princesse de Guermantes's, the spectacle he describes seems
to reflect not only the destruction in, and by, time of the people
he used to know, but also the objective breakdown of society
and his own inability to project any glamor at all into the social
world. He describes the guests in extraordinarily grotesque

images. When he enters the drawing room, he has the impression of being at a "masquerade fête": the signs of age on his friends' faces seem to him to be part of a deliberate disguise, a disguise so successful and so thorough that it transforms personality itself. The decrepitude of the guests makes, first of all, for a visually ugly scene, in contrast to the real physical beauty Marcel admired at the Opéra. The world of nymphs and Tritons has become a museum of natural history; the narrator compares people at the party to insects rather than to sea gods. He breaks out laughing in front of the "remarkable old dotard" that his former enemy d'Argencourt has become; once hostile and dangerous, d'Argencourt is now so comically inoffensive that Marcel feels he is seeing the proof that human beings can undergo metamorphoses as complete as those of certain insects: "I felt as if I were looking into the instructive show case of a natural history museum at [what can happen to the swiftest insect, having the surest sting,] and, before this soft chrysalis, which did not move so much as it vibrated, I could not experience the feelings which M. d'Argencourt had always inspired in me." [53] The section is full of such exaggerations. We are, for example, somewhat surprised by the description of Bloch: "Over his face I saw [superimposed] that sickly and garrulous expression, that feeble nodding of the head which so quickly comes to a stop and in which I would have recognised the erudite weariness of amiable old men if I had not, after all, recognised my friend standing before me. . . ." [54] You would think that Bloch were closer to eighty than to forty. He cannot, in fact, be much older than forty, since he and Marcel were in school together, and it is difficult to think of a senile narrator tottering at his grave's edge and also starting to write his book. But it occasionally seems as if this party is being given in 1940 or 1950 . . . It is, at any rate, the image of people with, as the narrator says, "one foot in the grave" that dominates the passage. The bent figures of some of the women at the party make him think that their dresses are caught in their tombs, making it impossible for them, in spite of their feeble efforts, to stand up straight once more before giving in completely and letting themselves be pulled down into death.[55]

If the title Princesse de Guermantes survives the many women who, through the centuries, have held the title, this suggestion of permanence in the aristocratic world does little to cheer Marcel, for he naturally compares with sadness the beauty of the former princess with the vulgarity and ugliness of the ex-Madame Verdurin. Her eminence in this society is only the most striking example of what the narrator calls its chief characteristic: "its prodigious aptitude at wiping out social classifications." Those whose social eminence seemed permanent have lost much of their prestige: Monsieur de Charlus because of his love for Morel, which had tied him to the Verdurin *salon,* and also because of his senility; Madame de Guermantes, because of her almost exclusive interest in artists; and the Duc de Guermantes, who has become Odette's last jealous lover. Dozens of people are now received by the Guermantes whose names Oriane and her cousin would never even have mentioned in Marcel's youth; ". . . a certain aggregate of aristocratic prejudices and snobbishness, which had served automatically to keep away from the Guermantes name everything that did not harmonize with it, had ceased to function." [56] It is, of course, by no means the narrator's own snobbery that explains his regret for the closed aristocratic world of the past. Bloch's and Legrandin's presence in the highest society does not mean that this society has been liberalized or humanized; the same stupidity and snobbery prevail at this last party as at the first dinner we see at the Duchesse de Guermantes's. The guests, like Oriane and her husband, talk mainly about genealogy. But whereas the Duc de Guermantes made no mistakes in tracing the history of family names, and would have considered such mistakes as grave moral errors, in the new society false information about more or less noble families is the rule rather than the exception. There is almost no one left to be outraged by the ignorance and pretensions of the American wife of the Comte de Farcy, an obscure relative of the Forchevilles. The narrator calls these social transformations a phenomenon of memory, but it would perhaps be more accurate to say that they illustrate a loss of memory: the aristocracy has forgotten its past.[57] All traces of the godlike self-sufficiency and exclusiveness Marcel admired in the church at Combray and at the Opéra have disappeared from this society. It has gained no moral value by opening its doors to hundreds of people excluded in the past, and it has lost those values which, even in the days of Marcel's growing disillusionment, made him continue to go into society. Certainly he never found in the aristocracy those "truths" of history and art he imagined embodied in the person of the Duchesse de Guermantes when he watched the evil Golo pursue Geneviève de Brabant on the walls of his Combray bedroom, or when he admired the stained-glass windows of the church in Combray. But, in spite of the monumental vanity in the Duc de Guermantes's snobbery, Marcel also found in his genealogical mania proof of the reality of the past. In the aristocracy's names, in their old-fashioned manners, in their furniture, in certain archaic turns of speech, there was a rare example of continuity between past and present. At the last Guermantes *matinée* this continuity no longer exists; the day that Marcel enters fully into the possession of his own past also reveals a loss of memory in the aristocracy. Much of their past now lives only in Marcel's memory, and it is in writing about his past that he will give back to the aristocracy values they once suggested to him and have now lost.

v. *Variety of characterization and the general laws*

Marcel continues to go into society long after he has lost his illusions about the people whose invitations he accepts, but he plays a role of almost total passivity and uninvolvement in his social life. The long period during which he goes out is, at the time, an apparently sterile one for him. The enthusiasms of Combray have almost entirely disappeared, and he seems to give himself to a life of mild social pleasures mainly because he can think of nothing else for which he has any desire or talent. He is the one person in this society who has no social ambition. There is a striking difference between Marcel's behavior with Albertine and his behavior in the *salons* of Odette, the Verdurins, and the Guermantes. In love, his desire to possess the other person is painfully strong, but the social portrait Marcel gives us of himself is one of total indifference. And, according to the implacable laws of the Proustian world, he has, because of this very indifference, the most astounding social success. As the one person without desires for social eminence in this society, Marcel plays a catalytic role. The urgent projects with which other characters go into society make them easy targets of everyone's mockery, but Marcel risks very little self-exposure; he is peculiarly self-effaced. He invites others to expose themselves; he is a kind of "straight man" who skillfully helps others to say the lines that "clinch" their characters. Even when he is most talkative, we feel that what he is saying is designed to bring out something characteristic in someone else. Occasionally he does this with conscious calculation. When Legrandin's sister, Madame de Cambremer, visits him at Balbec, he amusedly disturbs her silly excitement about only the most recent art by assuring her that Degas admires the Poussin paintings in the Louvre which she is then somewhat embarrassed to have called "appalling." [58] At other times, Marcel is unbelievably naïve. He impolitely tells the Verdurins what disappoints him in the view from La Raspelière, and in their annoyance we see their unwillingness to admit that anything they offer to their guests can be less than perfect. On the other hand, his extravagant praise of other aspects of the view brings out the Verdurins' indifference to nature except insofar as it can be used as a social asset.[59] Marcel's role in society makes possible an extraordinary but double-edged freedom of self-characterization for the other characters. And, although his detachment is psychologically justified, his habit of provoking the revealing response does make for some rather improbable scenes. His lack of anxious desire sharpens his image of other people, but we sometimes feel that Proust uses him, as a character, as an awkward device for dramatically justifying other characters' talk.

Because of his indifference, Marcel is able, when he goes into society, to see other people in a way he is never able to see Albertine. He can appreciate Berma's acting only when he no longer expects to appreciate it; in the same way, ". . . when the Guermantes had ceased to impress me and the tiny drop of their originality was no longer vaporised by my imagination, I was able to distil and analyse it, imponderable as it was." [60] It is, to a large extent, the discovery of parallels with himself that discourages Marcel when he goes into society, but his detachment then enables him to see clearly what is different from himself in other people. Paradoxically, his intuition of sameness, which is the basis for the general laws, checks the distorting tendencies of his imagination and helps to make him aware of human variety. When Swann, wholly absorbed by his love for Odette, goes to Madame de Saint-Euverte's party, he is "in a state of melancholy indifference to everything that did not involve Odette, and in particular to the details of fashionable life, a state which invested them with the charm that is to be found in anything which, being no longer an object of our desire, appears to us in its own guise." [61] The passage suggests the typically Proustian dichotomy between interest and knowledge; whatever engages our feelings thereby becomes unknowable. Knowledge is not thought of as part of the experience of involvement with someone else; it is an intellectual possession made possible by the absence of desire. Other people's personalities therefore tend to seem most sharply individual outside of relationships. The social snobs, like the lover, because of their wish to force the admiration of other people, do not have time to pay attention to others. Involvement with someone else increases isolation; it even prevents characters from seeing and hearing each other. At the parties in A la Recherche, characters seem to take turns coming forward to say their piece; there is much talk, but little conversation. A question, as Léon Pierre-Quint pointed out, does not lead to an answer, but rather "sets in motion, in the other person, a kind of mechanism that functions for a variable amount of time. Then, like a compressed spring that unwinds, the next person takes his turn." [62] Anxious to dominate others, characters

are aware only of themselves; it is by putting the distance of indifference between themselves and others that Marcel and
Swann have a clear image of the differences between themselves
and others.

From this perspective of detached interest, other people may
appear static, or take on pictorial qualities. The narrator mentions
Swann's tendency to compare living people with portraits he has
seen in museums; because of his love for Odette, ". . . it was
society as a whole, now that he was detached from it, which presented itself to him in a series of pictures." [63] I have shown that
the pictures of Albertine, while they include Marcel's feelings
about her, objectify these feelings in physical images distinct
from Marcel. With characters with whom he is less involved, his
emotional distance makes for even sharper individual outlines.
However great the psychological sameness he discovers between
himself and others, Marcel finds enormous variety in the world
of appearances, and he gives us a gallery of widely diversified
portraits. There are some particularly striking "apparitions" in
the novel. The narrator remembers Odette, for example, on winter mornings in the Bois de Boulogne,

> in an otterskin coat, with a woollen cap from which stuck out
> two blade-like partridge-feathers, but enveloped also in the de-
> liberate, artificial warmth of her own house, which was sug-
> gested by nothing more than the bunch of violets crushed into
> her bosom, whose flowering, vivid and blue against the grey
> sky, the freezing air, the naked boughs, had the same charming
> effect of using the season and the weather merely as a setting,
> and of living actually in a human atmosphere, in the atmosphere
> of this woman, as had in the vases and beaupots of her drawing-
> room, beside the blazing fire, in front of the silk-covered sofa,
> the flowers that looked out through closed windows at the falling
> snow.[64]

Or there is the first time Marcel sees Saint-Loup at Balbec, standing out in a crowd "like a precious vein of opal, azure-shot and
luminous":

. . . I saw, tall, slender, his head held proudly erect upon a springing neck, a young man go past with searching eyes, whose skin was as fair and whose hair as golden as if they had absorbed all the rays of the sun. Dressed in a clinging, almost white material such as I could never have believed that any man would have the audacity to wear, the thinness of which suggested no less vividly than the coolness of the dining-room the heat and brightness of the glorious day outside, he was walking fast. His eyes, from one of which a monocle kept dropping, were of the colour of the sea.[65]

Finally, the narrator describes the Duc de Guermantes, superbly considering the whole *quartier* as "an extension of his courtyard, a longer track for his horses":

After seeing how a new acquisition trotted by itself he would have it harnessed and taken through all the neighbouring streets, the groom running beside the carriage holding the reins, making it pass to and fro before the Duke who stood on the pavement, erect, gigantic, enormous in his vivid clothes, a cigar between his teeth, his head in the air, his eyeglass scrutinous, until the moment when he sprang on the box, drove the horse up and down for a little to try it, then set off with his new turn-out to pick up his mistress in the Champs-Elysées.[66]

Each character in the novel thus has a physical presence that successfully resists the total assimilation of which Marcel dreams, but which would have made of his work a monotonous succession of self-repetitions.

Variety of characterization in *A la Recherche du temps perdu* is, of course, not limited to variety in physical appearances. Even in my examples of conduct which reveals important psychological parallels between Marcel and other characters, I have provided much evidence of an impressive range of novelistic invention. In reading the novel, we realize on reflection that from character to character we are rediscovering a single and very special psychology, but our immediate impressions are usually of strongly individualized portraits. It is not surprising that Henri Peyre grants Proust "the primary privilege of the great novelist: he

could, and did, create a variegated and haunting gallery of characters, the richest in French literature next to Balzac's." [67] And
Jean-François Revel, implicitly rejecting much that has been
written on *A la Recherche*, insists that Proust is a great writer
not when he is metaphorical, but rather "when he is direct, and
it is not when he is a poet that he is original and has something
to teach us, it is when he is writing a realistic narrative of social
history." [68] In a sense, the variety of characterization in Proust
seems more impressive after we have noticed the repetitiousness.
Given the significant areas of human experience that are closed to
his characters (there is, for example, no picture of a generous or
fulfilling love between a man and a woman), the diversity among
these characters suggests an almost miraculously open imagination in their creator. And through his narrator Proust dramatizes,
as I have already partly shown, the differences between art and
the rest of life that seem to have made it possible for Proust himself to be freer in his work than in his life, or than his characters
are in their relationships with one another. The psychological
pressures that make Marcel try to suppress Albertine's individuality are absent when he is with Saint-Loup or the Duc de
Guermantes; he can observe them without feeling threatened by
the differences between them and himself. From the perspective
of memory from which the work is written, this security is permanent; a wholly internalized world is now described as a richly
diversified world outside of the self.

I have shown, in discussing the similarities between Marcel's
inability to separate from his mother at night and Oriane's and
Charlus's anxiety at the moment of leaving people with whom
they have spent an evening, how a general characteristic is par-
ticularized with different characters. Each personality repeats a
basic pattern in its own style. This combination of sameness and
variety is particularly striking if we compare Marcel to the two
other characters who seem most obviously to be extensions of
Proust's personality, and who are also the most successful creations in the novel: Charlus and Swann. Charlus's fantastic pride,
his wildly changeable moods, and his stature as a kind of mock-

epic homosexual hero are the main elements in a masterfully distinct portrait. Marcel is, on the whole, "saved" from certain aspects of Proust's personality—his homosexuality, his almost hysterical sensitivity to being slighted—which are wholly concentrated in the baron. Charlus's voice is generally unmistakable, except at rare moments when the intellectual quality and style of some of his monologues remind us too strongly of the narrator's particular intellectual strength.[69] The subtlety with which Swann is differentiated from Marcel is perhaps even more impressive. The parallels between Swann's intelligence and Marcel's, between their artistic interests, and especially between the former's love for Odette and the latter's love for Albertine are clear enough. And yet Swann is admirably unique. The most obvious difference between him and the narrator has often been pointed out: he remains a superior dilettante of artistic sensations, incapable of the effort and concentration that enable the narrator to write his work. A distinction is at least implied in the novel between the intellectual lethargy and doubts that prevent Marcel, for many years, from looking closely at the reasons for his intense joy at certain moments in his life, and a kind of incurable mental heaviness in Swann which makes it impossible for him to think for a long time about one thing. He wonders, for example, if the words "kept woman" can be applied to Odette, but "he could not explore the idea further, for a sudden access of that mental lethargy which was, with him, congenital, intermittent and providential, happened, at that moment, to extinguish every particle of light in his brain. . . ."[70] Now Marcel comes to enjoy a position in society similar to Swann's, but his self-effacement and the clinical attention he brings to the *salons* of the aristocracy contrast with Swann's elegant participation in the social game, his self-conscious wittiness as he exchanges puns with Oriane. Finally, Swann's Dreyfusism toward the end of his life, and his sense of a moral solidarity with other Jews, "a solidarity which Swann seemed to have forgotten throughout his life," place him almost at the same psychological distance from the narrator as other, less important characters whose lives present fewer paral-

lels to Marcel's.[71] The half-Jewish Proust once passionately involved in the Dreyfus Affair has been absorbed into Swann's
life (and, insofar as Proust looks on that part of himself as almost
wholly distasteful, into Bloch's life); [72] and, at the distance from
which Proust remembers himself through his narrator's remembering Swann, the latter becomes an object of a rather unsympa-
thetic intelligence. The narrator has an easy time of it exposing
the silly intellectual gyrations by which Swann explains both
why the aristocracy has to be anti-Dreyfusist and how Saint-Loup
or the Prince de Guermantes can escape this fate; but it is possible for the reader to find that Swann's commitment to Dreyfus
gives to his character a new dignity and seriousness. The narrator's critical point of view exposes Swann's double talk, but it
also makes him less appealing than Swann, especially since we
sense a slight but nonetheless real and disagreeable revulsion at
Swann's belated and blatant "Jewishness." One feels, certainly,
that Proust's point of view here is his narrator's, yet the very fact
that we can think differently from him about Swann's Dreyfusism suggests the extent to which Swann has an independent
dramatic existence in the novel. As a character, he has, so to
speak, escaped his creator's control, and while it is undoubtedly a
weakness that Proust only inadequately accounts for his behavior
through his narrator's comments, it is part of Proust's creative
strength to have convincingly put in the life of this character—
who at times seems Marcel's double—certain interests and traits
that Marcel's temperament makes him incapable of viewing with
more than the critical curiosity of a stranger.

But in spite of the individual distinctness of characters in
A la Recherche, there is a persistent tension between elements
that make for dramatic variety and others that threaten our sense
of that variety. If, for example, the behavior and physical appearances of most of the characters give us an impression of diversity
as we read the novel, the narrator often seems determined to
undermine that impression by insisting on the most general
aspects of different people's behavior. Picon has spoken of the
movement in the book away from the shock of individual appear-

ances to the flattening perspectives of the general laws.[73] Especially in *La Prisonnière* and *La Fugitive*, the laws almost smother
the dramatic circumstances; it is clear that the narrator takes
pleasure and pride in them, and his tone when he formulates
them tends to be solemn, pontifical. He even suggests that it is
"superfluous to make a study of manners, since we can deduce
them all from psychological laws." [74] Justin O'Brien has made a
collection of the Proustian maxims; there is an extraordinary
number of them, and every aspect of Marcel's life seems to have
nourished this appetite for generalization.[75] They are often aph-
oristic abstractions reminiscent of classical moralists, especially
of La Rochefoucauld. Leafing through the later volumes, one
comes upon such typical formulas as:

> As soon as jealousy is discovered, it is regarded by her who is its
> object as a challenge which authorises deception.[76]
> The bonds that unite another person to ourselves exist only in
> our mind. Memory as it grows fainter relaxes them, and notwith-
> standing the illusion by which we would fain be cheated and
> with which, out of love, friendship, politeness, deference, duty,
> we cheat other people, we exist alone. Man is the creature that
> cannot emerge from himself, that knows his fellows only in him-
> self; when he asserts the contrary, he is lying.[77]
> Every woman feels that, if her power over a man is great, the
> only way to leave him is sudden flight. A fugitive because a
> queen, precisely.[78]
> We consider innocent to desire a thing and atrocious that the
> other person should desire it.[79]

This passage from *je* to *on* is, as I have shown, justified to a large
extent by Marcel's experience. All the other love stories in the
novel, for example, support the conclusions Marcel has come to as
a result of his experience in love. Everyone loves when love is
not returned, and in every love affair in *A la Recherche du temps
perdu* the lover is tortured by the idea of deliberately withheld
sexual secrets. Swann wonders if Forcheville is Odette's lover,
and if she makes love with other women. Charlus tries to find
out whom Morel meets in the house of prostitution at Maineville.

Saint-Loup, furious, tries in vain to decipher Rachel's jokes with
the mime. Different individual histories provide the basis for a
set of theoretical, universal statements.

Novelistically, the general laws seem to me to be one of the
less satisfying aspects of Proust's work. But if they provide little
more than an abstract and leveling commentary on Marcel's
experience, they take on a certain interest when we look at them
in the context of the painful tensions they partially resolve. The
narrator's attachment to these general statements makes even
more ambiguous the role of individuality in the novel: not only
is it both desirable and dangerous, wished for and feared; its very
existence is both affirmed and denied. But the laws are important
to Marcel: in spite of his discouragement when he finds in society
so much that is already familiar to him, the psychological parallels he discovers create bonds between himself and others. Communication among people is impossible, but there is a kind of
harmony and continuity between the self and the world. The
general laws draw other characters into the patterns of Marcel's
personality; they are an intellectual strategy by which he possesses a world no longer irremediably different from the self. And
this possession seems to me to take place as the narrator writes
his work; the formulation of the general laws is part of the act of
writing, and it is *now* that Marcel absorbs into a familiar system
of reference things he was unable to absorb in the past. The general laws are, furthermore, by no means the only sign of this
process of assimilation; they legislate an identity between the narrator and the world which he tries in various ways to create. The
effort to remember the past seems to become, in the process of
writing, an attempt to suppress, retrospectively, the duality between himself and external reality.

VI. *Marcel the character and Proust the author*

Not only does the narrator insist more and more on universal psychological mechanisms; in several respects, the society he portrays
strikes us as a self-projection. It develops, for example, in ways

parallel to Marcel's psychological development. The disintegration of aristocratic society which we witness in the later volumes reflects Marcel's disillusionment with that society. There are, in fact, such precise analogies between social behavior and the direction which Marcel's life is taking that we are tempted to feel that Marcel's development is the *cause* of other characters' behavior. A curious parody of what will be an extremely fruitful movement toward isolation for Marcel takes places in society. The aristocracy is at first held together by its exclusiveness and its genealogical pride. Its memories are shared memories, and in addition to the solitude of each snob trying to impose a flattering image of himself on the social world, there is also some sort of aristocratic community. At the Princesse de Guermantes's *matinée* in *Le Temps retrouvé*, only the snobbery remains; the aristocracy has lost its memory, and everyone is alone in his private version of the past of society. The "spread" of homosexuality in this world as the novel goes on is a more grotesque version of this movement toward an anti-social absorption in self-created images. Marcel's love for Albertine repeats many of the aspects of his early love for Gilberte, or of Swann's love for Odette, but the atmosphere has become heavier and more somber; almost every page of analysis in *La Prisonnière* and *La Fugitive* demonstrates that jealousy of another person is really self-jealousy. In homosexuality the very choice of an object of desire testifies to this truth. The homosexual looks for a body that reminds him of his own, and the virile men that awaken Charlus's desire provide images of what he himself would like to be. Homosexuality is the next-to-last step in a turning away from the world of others and toward a world in which there are only mirrors. The final step is literally a total self-involvement; it is, in fact, the step taken by Marcel himself when he becomes his own prisoner and peers for the time it takes him to write his work into the past his mind both contains and creates.

But this ultimate choice in Marcel's life holds the promise of a future more valuable than the past that has thrown him back on himself. The work he writes will justify his choosing to die to everything that he cannot possess as part of himself. The kinds of social disintegration he records seem almost to be a "throwing-off" of unfruitful forms of self-absorption into dramatic images he can then confront as distinct from himself. One feels that for Proust, too, the creation of his novel's social world, while it undoubtedly includes intelligent observation of the society he knew, was a way of discharging and controlling alternatives such as snobbery and obsessive homosexuality that might have prevented the writing of this book. The society he reports on seems partly the creative strategy by which he projects out of himself those impulses most hostile to his becoming an artist; he makes them into a dramatic moment of social history. And in creating Marcel as a character living in this society, he increases the distance between his narrative "I" and the frightening roles that absorb other characters' lives; not even Marcel's imagination can be held responsible for Charlus's degrading pleasures or Madame Verdurin's ruthless vanity, for he is the witness of their destructive impulses and not their source. But society offers so many parallels with Marcel's psychology that it becomes difficult for us to believe that he is merely an observer of the external world: he seems rather to be recording a *dream* of nature and society. The dream, however, is presumably Proust's and not Marcel's: the memories belong to the character Marcel, but the novel is Proust's invention. But to the extent that the world the narrator remembers objectively reflects his personality, we have the impression that he has created that world, and our belief in the distinction between Proust the author and Marcel the main character is necessarily weakened. It is, after all, this separation that safeguards the novel's dramatic structure and makes plausible a distinction between Marcel's fantasies and the "real" world.

Marcel's experience in love and in society dramatizes the gap between versions of life he nourishes in his imagination and an external reality he is forced to recognize as independent of his private images. Now the ways in which imagination can distort reality was, of course, no new subject in European and American fiction. The dangers of reading personal desires or fears into the world is treated in novels as different as *Emma*, *Madame Bovary*, and *Moby Dick*. We can indeed imagine this subject to be a novelist's natural, spontaneous choice. The pleasures of dramatic fantasies can lead to a more or less dangerous refusal to accept life on terms different from those of one's desires, or to the successful creation, in art, of another world that does realize these fantasies. Having himself chosen to remake the world through language, the novelist may choose a hero who attempts, in a direct "attack" on the world, to force reality to conform to his images of reality. The novelist thus plays with risks he himself has prudently avoided. And his work can reflect either a fascination with ambitions he has apparently renounced, or an interest in the educative process through which we come to recognize and accept our limited power over the world. In novels such as *Emma*, *Portrait of a Lady*, and *Middlemarch*, the principal characters are educated to distinguish between their private, imaginary worlds and an external social world that refuses to provide docile actors for a prepared script. The maturity thus reached is not necessarily a guarantee of happiness (as the example of Isabel Archer makes clear), but these works seem to stress the rightness of accommodating an ambitious imagination to the world outside of the self. But there are novels in which, even while the hero may be destroyed, it seems that the dream of making the world resemble a personal dream of the world continues to appeal strongly to the novelist himself. Balzac and Melville, for example, are fascinated by the energy and daring quality of Balthazar Claes's and Ahab's pride, at the same time that they show the tragedy of that pride and label it a kind of madness. It is as if they felt that a strictly literary re-creation of life were merely a *pis aller* in comparison to their heroes' excitingly direct defiance of nature. The novelist contains and reshapes the world as linguistic images, but the very "adjustment" which literature implies may be accompanied by a more or less intense dissatisfaction with literature.

It may, however, appear to the writer that his verbal creation is equivalent to a more than verbal creation. Aware that language

does, in a sense, create the world for each of us, and make it possible for us to possess what is different from ourselves, he may
confuse the power that words have to organize life into a personal
"system" with the power actually to confer objective existence
on a world different from ourselves. It is, however, significant
that we think mainly of poets, such as Rimbaud and Mallarmé,
and not of novelists, in connection with attempts to give language
such extraordinary power. For the novel—until the twentieth
century, at any rate—has generally dramatized the resistances of
nature and society to any attempt to force them to conform to an
individual version or vision of the world. Novelistic drama has
tended to consist in the tension between such ambitious visions
and a more or less antagonistic social context. The resistance of
the social and natural environments is, especially in the nineteenth-century realistic novel, generally strong; the hero may be
destroyed if he does not learn to adjust to realities over which he
has very limited power. Because of this, and seen as a social phenomenon, the novel has tended to be a conservative social force.
A hero's vision of a new world is subject to ironies provided by
the mere existence of an already established world. The profound
links between the novel and comedy also seem clear: the bounc-
ing-off of the hero's fantasies from a wall of immovable reality is
an essentially comic fate for demiurgic aspirations. And comedy,
as Ortega y Gasset has remarked, ". . . is the literary genre of
the conservative parties." [80] Because much of the novelist's language thus portrays realities that check individual extravagances,
he can never be as committed as his hero to illusions about what
individual imagination and will can do. The novelist surrounds
his hero with the weight of other reality, and *his* imagination
takes into account what the hero's imagination excludes. It is, I
think, in this sense that Stendhal's irony with a hero such as
Fabrice can best be understood. He is not only protecting himself
from the mockery of hostile readers; by maintaining a certain distance from what is most lovable in Fabrice—his simplicity and
his enthusiasms—Stendhal expresses his own sophisticated awareness that a man like Fabrice can only be tragically defeated by

the sort of society in which he lives. Although all Stendhal's sympathies are with Fabrice, he separates himself from his hero by a sophistication which is much less appealing than the latter's naïveté, but which enables him to keep sight of the dangers of naïveté.

As readers we realize, of course, that the fictional world in which the hero lives is as imaginary as the hero's visions of that world may be, and that they both reflect the author's vision of life. He creates both his hero's illusions and the external world that challenges them. But he commits himself to a statement about what *is* an illusory view of the world. He does this by asking us to accept what is actually an arbitrary distinction between, say, Emma Bovary's "unrealistic" fantasies about the possibilities of romance in life and a world that is "really" profoundly dull and prosaic. In a certain sense, there is no reason for us to find Yonville a more convincing view of social life than Emma's fantasies of glamor. But we accept the convention that the novelist *can* be "realistic," that he can portray objective resistances to individual dream-worlds. Harry Levin has emphasized how much the novelist's ability to convince us of this depends on a certain deprecation of the novelistic medium itself: each writer's "real" world is made up, to a large extent, of objections and exceptions to the artificial worlds of earlier fiction. The novelist himself thus shares the responsibility for the peculiar fact that ". . . our highest recommendation for a work of fiction is that it be as unlike fiction as possible." [81] Indeed, we must accept the novelist's claim of being a good observer of the world outside of himself in order to begin to discuss the particular vision he has of that world. And we recognize this vision in the way he distributes values of illusion and reality to different parts of his creation.

Some modern novelists have been unwilling to make such clear-cut commitments about the nature of reality. It is characteristic of much fiction since James and Proust that the separation between author and hero can no longer be taken for granted. The much discussed ambiguity of twentieth-century fiction is due in large part to novelists' refusal to distinguish explicitly between "right" and "wrong" points of view of characters and events in their fictional worlds. The favorite technical device that expresses this refusal is, of course, narration from the point of view of a character involved in the action of the novel. The novelist himself stays behind the scenes, and it is often difficult to judge how trustworthy the narrative report is. But, as I have said earlier, this becomes an irrelevant question, and what we have, in examples of this kind of fiction from *The Turn of the Screw* to *La Jalousie,* is a change in novelistic conventions that requires a change in critical approach. It is as if the novelist were hesitating to betray his own illusions by a definite statement about the illusions of his characters. His work thus dramatizes, by its very ambiguity, the necessary uncertainties and tentativeness in all efforts to possess the world and make of it a familiar home for the self. The limiting of the narrative point of view to characters' awareness does not, however, necessarily make for serious doubts about the author's point of view in novels that follow the traditional pattern of a protagonist's education. It can rather be mainly a device for bringing the reader closer to the processes of that education; he is, simply, not provided from the very start with a judgment of the main character's point of view. In *La Symphonie pastorale* and *The Ambassadors,* the possible ambiguities due to the story's being told from a character's point of view are lessened since the reader is clearly meant to see how and to what extent the pastor and Strether are attached to certain illusions about themselves and other people in the novel. While James refrains from directly approving Strether's final point of view, an identification between the two seems probable partly because we do have a final point of view. The distance between the author and his main character, while not explicitly spelled out, is what keeps the novel going; it is the space the novel occupies, and when the gap is closed, the story is over. In spite of obvious differences, then, James and Gide have, through Strether's mature awareness at the end of *The Ambassadors* and through Gertrude's suicide in *La Symphonie pastorale,* made as clear a statement of their own points of view as, say, Jane Austen and Dickens in *Pride and Prejudice* and *Great Expectations.*

Ambiguity is greatest in works such as *The Turn of the Screw* or *La Jalousie,* in which little is done to supplement a narrative point of view limited to the awareness of a character who never feels a need to modify his attitudes, and who at the end of the story may be as uncertain or confused about what is happening around him as at the beginning. And, if there is no physical crisis that forces the drama to a conclusion, such novels are theoretically endless. *La Jalousie* records no gradual adjustment of the jealous husband's fantasies to the "real" behavior of A . . . and Franck, and, in a sense, the novel could stop anywhere. It records different intensities in a jealous point of view, but the novel does not move from one point of view to another; its only *possible* progress is from compulsive curiosity to an outbreak of violence, not in any progressive lighting up of the world in which the husband is jealous.

Proust's narrator develops in a much more traditional way. He begins with certain illusions about the external world and the novel is largely the story of how his experience in the world educates him out of these illusions. Moreover, from the very beginning of *A la Recherche du temps perdu* until the Guermantes *matinée* in *Le Temps retrouvé,* we have a narrative point of view that can never be completely identified with Marcel's point of view in the past, and it is one that we are encouraged to trust. The narrator's *je* has the full authority of the author's *je.* We are constantly tempted to confuse the two; it is as if Proust were trying to make us forget the differences between Marcel and himself. The extent to which Proust transformed the facts of his own life in order to create Marcel's life suggests that these differences were important to him. But at the same time he tends to deny them. We discover, in *La Prisonnière,* that he has given the narrator his own first name, but he never gives him a family name; it is as if he could not commit himself either to a total identification with, or a clear-cut distinction from, his main character.[82] The narrator nonetheless tends to take the role of an omniscient and critical author with regard to his own past experience; he is, so to speak, half Marcel and half Proust, and his analyses of characters and events clearly have the full sanction of his creator. He re-creates his past as he writes about it, but he re-creates it definitively; the point of view he develops during his work gives to his life its permanent character. There is no suggestion that he can learn any more than he now knows, and even his uncertainties seem final. His awareness is complex, but it never has the kind of tentativeness that would suggest his own existence beyond the time of the work's composition. With the possible exception of Albertine's Lesbianism, Marcel now seems to know everything important there is to know about the other characters, and his use of multiple motivations to explain a piece of behavior shows less the hopelessness of trying to understand other people than it reveals his subtle sense of all that can go into a single act.

But a narrator who is a character in the story he tells must convince us that his writing about the other characters does not exhaust their existence, and that he, for example, may continue to wonder about them when he has finished portraying them. The peculiar exclusion of the future from Proust's narrator's point of view on the past gives him an authorial control over his past. He can speak of people he has known as a novelist speaks of his characters. The latter creates people whose existence is over when he stops writing; they cannot be anything outside of the book or after the book, unless the writer comes back to them as a reader, and then he is as bound to respect their given literary character as any other reader. Because Marcel describes people from his past as if their existence were entirely circumscribed by his analyses, we easily take his point of view on himself and on other characters as Proust's point of view. Early in "Combray," he writes, apropos of his family's ignorance of Swann's social connections: ". . . our social personality is created by the thoughts of other people," [83] but nothing in the narrator's subsequent portraits suggests that *his* social impressions are either incomplete or arbitrary. When he speaks of most of the people he has known, the narrator's importance as a character in the novel diminishes, and he records conversations and analyzes motives with all the assurance of an omniscient and infallible author. In fact, in *Le Temps retrouvé* he suggests that, like Proust, he too has given us a fictionalized version of his past:

> Moreover, since in this book the individual entities, human or otherwise, would be constructed from numerous impressions which, derived from many young girls, many churches, many sonatas, would go to make up a single sonata, a single church, a single young girl, would I not be making my book the way Françoise made her *boeuf à la mode* so liked by M. de Norpois, the jelly of which was enriched by so many carefully selected pieces of meat? [84]

This statement has peculiar consequences for our retrospective sense of Marcel's relationship to the other characters: his very uncertainties about some of them seem somewhat unconvincing, since, it turns out, they are his novelistic creations. His inability to say something final about Albertine is convincing as long as we feel that he is *remembering* his doubts about her personality. But if she is not only Proust's imaginary creation but also Marcel's, the mysteries in her character seem as arbitrary a literary decision for the narrator as they obviously are for Proust. The dramatic justification of Marcel's confusion about *Albertine* is thereby weakened; the fictional world is exposed as deliberately fictional, our illusion of reality is undermined, and Marcel's love for Albertine is merely an invented story meant to illustrate his experience of love outside of his work for some other "real" girl. The narrator's remark sets up a singularly complicated situation: the novel we have been reading is a novel written by a character whose "real" life, which is presumably not to be confused with Proust's, exists only by implication.

I am, it could be said, taking the distinction between the narrator and Proust too seriously. In reading the passage from *Le Temps retrouvé,* one instinctively feels that Proust himself is expressing what *he* has done in creating both Marcel and the other characters of *A la Recherche du temps perdu.* But the sentence is nonetheless symptomatic of persistent ambiguities in the novel. On the one hand, it is important for us to feel that while

Proust has written a novel, his narrator is remembering real incidents from his past. It is easy to imagine why Proust preferred a first-person narration from a character's point of view to the third-person voice of the author as he used it in *Jean Santeuil*. By refusing himself any possibility of explicitly supplementing Marcel's point of view, he could best show how personal needs imprison an individual in a private vision of the world. When Marcel writes, in a passage already quoted, that the novelist should give only a vaguely outlined portrait of the woman his hero loves, he is pointing to the kind of novel Proust seems to have had in mind when he created Marcel. And, in part, he does write this novel, especially in *La Prisonnière* and *La Fugitive*, where the narrator's recollections of his anguished ignorance about Albertine's desires take on a special intensity from our sense that, limited as we are to Marcel's awareness, there is no chance of our having any answers to certain questions about Albertine. In these volumes, Proust as the creator of Albertine is, as it were, absent, and we see all the consequences of the story's being told not by him, but by a character who is remembering his love for Albertine. But in much of the novel Proust's authorial privilege of omniscience is given to Marcel. We are told that indifference, or the lack of desire, makes accurate observation of others possible, and this claim—which is, of course, really quite arbitrary—is never questioned. It could be argued that since indifference toward others is a state in which we are unresponsive to what is lovable in others, but sharply aware of what is pretentious and ridiculous in their lack of indifference, it is no more reliable a disposition than desire. But Proust nowhere suggests any such comment on Marcel's analyses of others, and the "silence" which in the case of Albertine reinforces our sense of Marcel's limitations is, in much of the novel, clearly equivalent to an approval of Marcel's point of view, even a kind of broadening of that point of view so that it may include an author's thorough and definitive statements. It is as if the passage from character to author were brought about by growth: Marcel develops from a fallible person within the world of the novel to someone having an author's control over novelistic material.

This is, of course, more or less true of all novels of education. But ordinarily we have main characters—such as Emma Woodhouse or Isabel Archer—who make mistakes about other people because of some tendency in themselves—for example, their desire to control the lives of others—of which they are largely cured once they have suffered the consequences of their mistakes. But in *A la Recherche* Marcel's incomplete or distorting impressions of other people are not presented as a sign of some particular aspect in his character, but rather as an example of the universal unreliability of the statements men make about the external world. In *Emma* and *Portrait of a Lady,* Mr. Knightley and Ralph Touchett see people as they really are; but Proust insists that no point of view can be trusted. The fault is not in Marcel, but in the very nature of perception. *A la Recherche du temps perdu* is a novel about character in the sense that Marcel's fantasies express his individuality, but in a larger sense Proust's work purports to be about the mental processes that make knowledge impossible. The only kind of "knowledge" possible is imaginative creation. Marcel cannot know others, but he can dramatize his own needs in fantasies in which other people play various roles. But he is, it appears, also capable of accurate reporting on others. The advantages of his perspicacity are clear. The full extent of his illusions about Madame de Guermantes is, for example, obvious only because we have such a clear image of a woman different from his ideas about her. And the novel gains enormously in dramatic variety from the narrator's being so little limited by what he insists are universal limitations. The freedom Marcel enjoys is nonetheless curious, and it emphasizes, finally, the limitations of his creator's freedom. The range of *Proust's* inventiveness is, of course, defined by the whole novel; it includes both Marcel's expectations and the "real" world that generally disappoints these expectations. But Marcel himself seems to contain this world within his imagination; he describes accurately a world that sends back his own image. The narrator's claim that we cannot escape from self-images is curiously supported by Proust's own inability to get beyond the limitations which experience and indifference are supposed to overcome in his narrator. The tendency toward identification between the narrator and Proust, as well as the psychological repetitiousness codified in the general laws, seriously qualify the dramatic and realistic aspects of the novel. From a certain point of view, the whole work seems to be an exploration of the main character's resources. But this is precisely the view of art which we see the narrator develop in the novel. His interest in literature is an interest in a reliable form of profound self-exploration, one in which the self has the objective clarity of the world at the same time that it has absorbed the world into its own history.

CHAPTER FIVE

MARCEL'S VOCATION

1. *The artist and the "résidu réel" of personality*

The narrator deliberately organizes the story of his life so that we may see it as he himself has come to see it: as the story of his "invisible vocation." [1] He gives us the various stages of his doubts and enthusiasms about literature, and he ends his work with a long essay on why he gave up everything else in his life in order to write. The language the narrator uses to recall his doubts about the value of art strikes us at first as rather vague: he wonders if the pleasure certain works give him corresponds to something "real" or is simply a response to shrewdly calculated effects, if the work of art is "necessary," if it expresses essential "truths." But these questions are rephrased from the point of view of the answers the narrator has found when he writes his work, and the essays on Bergotte's literary style, on Elstir's painting, and on Vinteuil's music include the definitive views on art which, in his life, Marcel seems to have formulated confidently for the first time at the Guermantes *matinée* described in *Le Temps retrouvé*. From his childhood days at Combray, he has looked in art for the same extraordinary revelations about "truth" and "reality" that he has expected to find in nature, love, and society; only art, he discovers, is able to fulfill these expectations. The narrator's views on literature are therefore anything but "literary" in a narrow sense; when he turns his back on life in order to be only a writer, it is because literature alone can satisfy his demands on life.

As a boy at Combray, Marcel dreams of having Bergotte's opinion about everything, so that he himself may know what to

think about life. But in the same way that he gives up expecting
nature and society to reveal valuable truths to him and turns to
his impressions of nature and society for truths about himself, he
learns to look, in the work of artists like Bergotte, for the signs of
their peculiar visions of things rather than for keys to the nature
of reality. Marcel's greatest joy in reading Bergotte at Combray—
"a joy which I felt myself to have experienced in some inner-
most chamber of my soul, deep, undivided, vast, from which all
obstructions and partitions seemed to have been swept away"—
is one of recognition: he finds in the third or fourth passage he
isolates from the rest of the novel he is reading "the same taste
for uncommon phrases, the same bursts of music, the same idealist philosophy" which have already given him a pleasure he now
understands. These are the signs of Bergotte's uniqueness, and
the sentences he has just read are not merely a specific passage in
one of Bergotte's books, but an " 'ideal passage' of Bergotte, common to every one of his books, and to which all the earlier, similar passages, now becoming merged in it, had added a kind of
density and volume, by which my own understanding seemed to
be enlarged." [2] What Marcel has discovered—and what he now
possesses—is, as he writes in another passage, "the little drop of
Bergotte buried in the heart of a thing and which he had distilled
from it." [3] And esthetic pleasure is essentially a function of memory: it accompanies the moment when Marcel identifies Bergotte
by locating his most significant self-repetitions.

The discussions of art in *A la Recherche du temps perdu* are,
it seems to me, of rather uneven quality; the kind of satisfaction
Marcel looks for in art accounts, to a considerable degree, for
what is uninteresting or vague in his thought. There are also
special problems connected with the portrayal of artists as characters in the novel. Bergotte, for example, remains a rather
shadowy figure—both as a writer and in the rest of his life—and
the few details we have on his style make him sound dull and
affected, an unfortunate blend of Anatole France and Maurice
Barrès. The narrator seems more interested in trying to give us an
idea of Vinteuil's music, but the very nature of his effort dooms

it to failure. With what is often an irritating literary virtuosity, Marcel and Swann translate into nonmusical terms the particular world expressed in Vinteuil's music. Through a dubious process of equating phrases and movements in Vinteuil's sonata and septet with emotions such as sadness and joy, with Platonic notions of love and happiness, with colors, and with the rising of the sun, the narrator attempts, by following the chain of associations the music awakens in him and Swann, to arrive at a kind of formula for Vinteuil's individuality.[4] The essence of Vinteuil's work is finally seen as "a prayer, a hope," a prayer found in all his music and only in his music, and whose uniqueness seems to Marcel to prove that, "notwithstanding the conclusions to which science seems to point, the individual did really exist."[5] As the examples of Bergotte and Vinteuil show, remarks about individual artists in *A la Recherche du temps perdu* are disappointing compared to Proust's notes in *Contre Sainte-Beuve* on Balzac and Baudelaire, or the *Nouvelle revue française* piece on Flaubert. A problem in the novel is, of course, that we read Marcel's appreciations of Bergotte, Vinteuil, and Elstir without any knowledge or independent sense of their work. When Proust writes about *Les Fleurs du mal,* we can use our own readings of Baudelaire to corroborate or qualify his remarks. But with his fictitious artists, we have an appreciation in a void, and Marcel's impressions often seem abstract and unconvincing with no recognizable work to support them. This is somewhat less true of Elstir, who is the most successful of these creations, and whom we see not only as the great painter Marcel meets at Balbec, but also as the clownish Biche of Madame Verdurin's *salon.* His personality has a certain interest, and his paintings are described with the detail necessary to attach Marcel's thoughts to an actual experience of specific works of art.

But our sense of the reality of such works is by no means always sufficient in itself to make the narrator's critical remarks interesting. In the passage in *La Prisonnière* where we see him talking to Albertine about literature, for example, the idea of finding a writer's most personal accent leads to generally disappointing comments on the writers he mentions. His apparently casual remarks can be thought of as another attempt to fix Albertine's attention, this time by dazzling her intellectually; their talk about literature alternates with Marcel's falsely calm questions about relations Albertine may have had with Gilberte. But the narrator never suggests that he was speaking inattentively here, and he seems at the time of writing fully to approve of what he remembers having said. He is a little too fascinated with the idea of being able to find *phrases-types* in all artists, and his remarks on Stendhal (he gives examples of the connection in Stendhal's novels between spiritual life and "a certain sense of altitude") and on Dostoevski (he speaks of a characteristically Dostoevskian house, and of his women's ["vivid faces, with their dual expressions and sudden bursts of pride which make the woman seem different from what she is"]) are a disappointing, overly clever reduction of these writers to a few facile formulas.[6] These passages indicate the limitations of Marcel's—and Proust's —approach to art. It is inevitable that this attempt to reduce a body of work to a kind of central pattern discernible along a wide range of inventiveness (the Proustian approach prefigures "thematic" criticism . . .) should make for rather meager views of writers such as Stendhal and Dostoevski. The narrator's comparative indifference to other angles from which a novel can be approached—for example, the social contexts of characters' lives, the psychological complexities of their relationships with one another, the writer's use of conventions peculiar to the form he is using—gives a thinness to some of his critical remarks and, when they are not particularly striking, they seem merely to be evidence of a limiting and too "special" point of view. There are traces in this approach of Marcel's old desire to find the key that will give him access to the mysteries of nature, of history, of personality. And his extraordinary concentration on the mystery of individuality undoubtedly makes it inevitable that he should equate truth in art with the expression of the artist's uniqueness. Each time that he finds the typical image or phrase or pattern of sounds, it is as if he had made a fresh penetration into the double mystery of art and personality. But Marcel's psychological satisfaction is not necessarily a guarantee of esthetic value in the work he is considering, and it by no means adequately validates his critical judgments. A combination of "uncommon phrases," "bursts of music," and "idealist philosophy" may, for example, characterize Bergotte, but it hardly gives us an idea of the supposedly high quality of Bergotte's novels. We are obviously expected to take for granted that in Bergotte's "ideal" passages there is—as the narrator implies there is for all artists—a necessary equivalence between the most authentic self-expression and literary quality.

For Marcel, the artist is first of all a man who allows himself to be *seen*, and in his enjoyment of a work of art the narrator most fully satisfies his need to look at and absorb another individuality. He compares the completeness and generosity with which the artist exposes himself to the hypocrisy and elusiveness of the people it is our misfortune to love and thus hopelessly pursue in life. "As the spectrum makes visible to us the composition of light, so the harmony of a Wagner, the colour of an Elstir enable us to know that essential quality of another person's sensations into which love for another person does not allow us to penetrate." [7] Marcel can look at the work of art, examine it from different points of view; the artist has given up the possibilities of escaping in time and space from which Albertine profits to make Marcel suffer. But the notion of possessing the artist through his work leads to an extremely peculiar use of the work of art. During the time that he lives with Albertine, Marcel often listens to music in his room; he plays the same piece several times, until his intelligence finally dissipates its mystery, after which ". . . often there was for me a piece of music less in the world, perhaps, but a truth the more." [8] In its most extreme form, Marcel's compulsive need to possess something different from himself makes him consider the work of art almost as something to devour; when he has fully digested the truth it contains, the pleasure of assimilation and with it his esthetic pleasure disappear.

One could, of course, wonder why the fact that the work of art can be examined at leisure is a guarantee that the individuality it expresses can be apprehended. It is not, after all, merely Albertine's willful elusiveness that makes her unknowable; the narrator continually emphasizes that the greatest obstacle to knowledge is our inability to separate our self-projections from the "real" nature of the external world. Even if Albertine were to "pose" for Marcel with the same docility that models pose for Elstir, there is no logical reason to believe that he could either possess what makes her different from him or transform her into a calming reflection of himself. Why, then, does he feel so confident of being able to penetrate, through art, "that essential quality of another person's sensations" which eludes us in love? Indeed, the highly impressionistic nature of his remarks on Vinteuil's music strengthens our doubts. It is true that a piece of music, being an irreversible succession of sounds in time, is more elusive than a painting. It cannot be possessed all at once: "Since I was able only in successive moments to enjoy all the pleasures that this sonata [by Vinteuil] gave me, I never possessed it in its entirety: it was like life itself." [9] But at least the notes that make up a piece of music stay the same, and in the passage quoted in the previous paragraph, the narrator speaks of having fully assimilated certain musical works by listening attentively to them several times. Knowledge of another individuality is, then, presumably as possible through music as through the other arts. This contention may strike us as quite arbitrary. It is, however, understandable in terms of the extraordinary value Marcel gives superstitiously to the act of attention. It is as if exhaustive description were the equivalent of possession, and since, in a work of art, another personality offers itself to Marcel's tireless scrutiny, it naturally seems to him that in art the barriers to knowledge of others disappear. If someone else gives up his resources of flight, he also gives up the secrets of his individuality.

If art makes it possible to know another personality, it should also contain answers to Marcel's questions about the nature of personality. What *is* individuality, how does the artist find and express what is unique in his vision of things, and how can this uniqueness be recognized in specific works? These questions are partially answered in the narrator's long and impressive discussion of Elstir's painting in *A l'Ombre des jeunes filles en fleur*. Now his analysis is rich in implications about the nature of perception, and about the relation of ordinary perception to artistic vision. I can perhaps best explain Elstir's achievement and the reasons for Marcel's great interest in his painting by first of all developing some of these implications. The narrator suggests that Elstir's genius depends on his marvelous aptitude for forgetting. More precisely, he so completely forgets what he knows when, for example, he looks at the sea that he can remember—and express in his paintings—a past impression analogous to his present impression. He seems almost to have, as Cézanne said of himself, a faulty vision.[10] When most of us look at the sea, we immediately recognize it *as* the sea. But there seem to be three stages in perception, although we are generally aware only of the last one; the first two would be an absence of any identification at all, and then an incorrect identification. When our eye falls on something there is a fraction of a second in which we make a mistake. From a certain distance and in certain atmospheric conditions, for example, we may confuse part of the sea with the sky or the land, or we may see, in a group of trees on a mountain slope, only geometric patterns of colors. "Our mistake [is to present things] as they are in reality, names as they are written, people as photography and psychology give an unalterable idea of them. As a matter of fact this is not at all what we ordinarily perceive. We see, we hear, we conceive the world quite topsy-turvy." The artist should render "this perpetual error which is precisely 'life.' . . ."[11] The profound link the narrator finds among artists as different as Dostoevski, Madame de Sévigné, and Elstir is that all three give us these errors of perception which are our first impressions of people and things. Comparing the last two, he writes: "I realised at Balbec that it was in the same way as he that she presented things to her readers, in the order of our perception of them, instead of first having to ex-

plain them in relation to their several causes." [12] Elstir has tried
to paint things "not as he knew them to be but according to the
optical illusions of which our first sight of them is composed." [13]

The analogies we find between what we see in the present
and images of things we have seen in the past give to the world
a look of familiarity; by establishing a continuity in our contacts
with the world, they help us to deal with new objects of perception. But from the point of view of an effective physical control
over the world, they could be considered confusing and even
potentially dangerous. It is necessary to perceive the differences
between an external object and an inner term of comparison if
we wish to exploit the object's specific potentialities for serving
us. It may therefore seem risky, so to speak, to linger over the
analogical stage of perception; a "precise," nonmetaphorical
identification perhaps provides more reliably the information we
need to act with maximum efficiency on external reality. But in
the process of learning to identify objects immediately, we collect
groups of identifying labels that apply to general categories of
objects or sensory perceptions. In the strictest sense, no two
objects and no two impressions ever resemble each other exactly,
and the names we apply to them can quickly become like worn-
out metaphors that hide from us the specificity of *this* object or
this impression. Names give us a false epistemological security;
we need them in order to organize, communicate, and act on
our experience in the world, but they encourage us to take what
are really approximative analogies for exact knowledge of particular things. In a sense, then, it can be argued that the frankly
mistaken identification of an object serves an extremely useful
purpose: by failing to use the conventionally proper name to
describe our experience, we may use an analogy that increases
our knowledge about this class of objects in general, or reveals
how one object differs from apparently similar objects, or at
least expresses something specific to the conditions in which we
are now experiencing it. In analogies, and especially in metaphors in which the literal term of the comparison is not even
expressed, one thing tends to be reduced to what makes it similar

to another; but the trait they have in common may be a part of the specificity of an object or a feeling which we would never have noticed if we had successfully identified it with the impoverished analogy we call its correct name. To "forget" the names of objects, while it threatens the coarsest kind of immediate control over the world, therefore makes possible a rare openness to the world, a freshness of impressions that finally give us a more complex control over a world whose variety and particularity defy the names we use to describe it.

Elstir gives us an image of things different from the images habit has trained us to find, "some unusual picture of a familiar object, a picture different from those that we are accustomed to see, unusual and yet true to nature, and for that reason doubly impressive to us because it startles us, makes us emerge from our habits and at the same time brings us back to ourselves by recalling to us an earlier impression." The narrator seems to be claiming both an objective and a subjective value for the "unusual picture of a familiar object" which he finds in Elstir's paintings. But he insists less on its truthfulness to nature than on the way in which it expresses the artist's direct contact with a past impression. Our habitual responses to things not only make us insensitive to the particularities of things in the world; they also block our most profoundly individual responses to the world. The analogies Elstir makes when he looks at nature come from his memories of things already seen, but they are no longer limited to the learned analogies of habit; they are determined by *his* past perceptions. In general, the arrangements of past images in our minds, their relative strength and weakness, the various connections among them are the unanalyzable conditions that explain why one person's "optical illusions" cannot consistently be the same as someone else's. These errors of perception are, then, a spontaneous and concentrated expression of an individual history; they reveal the existence of a particular point of view on the world. They are also metaphors: we identify one thing with an image of something else. Elstir's paintings, in which the sea is painted in terms of the land and the land in terms of the sea, are

essentially visual metaphors; the narrator remembers feeling that
". . . the charm of each of them [of Elstir's seascapes] lay in a
sort of metamorphosis of the things represented in it, analogous
to what in poetry we call metaphor, and that, if God the Father
had created things by naming them, it was by taking away their
names or giving them other names that Elstir created them
anew." Elstir sees nature "with poetic vision," which means for
the narrator (at least partly: the ambiguities in his discussion
will be considered later) that he paints external reality in terms
of metaphors that express an individual perspective on the world;
he re-creates nature as a reflection of his own inner world.[14]

Elstir's re-creation of the world is, therefore, a tapping of resources in himself that habit ordinarily prevents us from exploiting, and the narrator's discussions of art are almost always an
attempt to define the nature of the self the artist reveals in his
work. In *A l'Ombre des jeunes filles en fleur* there is an attempt
to explain the contrast between the extreme moral sensitivity
Bergotte shows in his work and the selfishness and snobbery he
displays in his life. To expect an exact reflection in the writer's
life of the feelings he expresses in his books is, the narrator suggests, to assume that an individual is nothing more than his social
behavior. It is in fact in the most vicious lives, he argues, that
moral problems may be felt with the greatest anxiety. The writer,
unable to control his destructive impulses with the people he
knows, creates in his books a world in which his generous nature
can affirm itself. To moral issues ". . . the artist finds a solution
in the terms not of his own personal life but of what is for him
the true life, a general, a literary solution." [15] The view that personality is not entirely expressed in social behavior seems accept-
able enough, and yet certain of the narrator's remarks—especially
the rather highhanded one about the "general solution" the
artist gives to what are, after all, his own specific vices—sound
like an unpleasant use of art to silence the reproaches of those
who might have cause to complain. And when we think of the
guilt Proust felt for the suffering he knew or guessed that his
apparently frivolous life and his neurosis caused his parents, the

passage may strike us as an attempt at self-justification. Indeed, it is probable that Proust could not help but think partly of his book both as a penance and as a vindication of the good intentions and the moral strength his mother must have been forced seriously to doubt. And it is, of course, ironic and characteristic that his very obedience to his mother's wishes is, on a certain level, only a mocking fulfillment of them: parts of his book would have made her suffer more, and, at any rate, he "offers" his work to her when she is no longer alive to see him work.

It is, however, not necessary (nor is it really possible) to establish with certainty the biographical origins in Proust's life of the narrator's ideas. Furthermore, in the novel Marcel's life sufficiently accounts for these ideas. It seems clear that the narrator's distinction between the artist in his work and the artist in the rest of his life, and his experience of the self as a succession of discontinuous personalities are variations on a single psychological pattern. The first experience of unrelated selves is, as I have shown, at Combray: the happy, energetic boy of the daytime hours seems to be an entirely different person from the frightened child who cannot bear to be separated from his mother at night. Maturity confirms as a profound truth of personality what we might at first have been inclined to see as the melodramatic experience of an overwrought, excessively sensitive child. What relation can there be between the man who feels only irritated when, due to a mistaken signature on a telegram, he thinks for a moment that Albertine is still alive long after he has at last become indifferent to her death, and the desperately jealous lover who had kept her—and himself—a prisoner in his family's Paris apartment? These experiences of psychological discontinuity surely account in part for the conviction with which the narrator affirms the separation of the artist's personality into a self that is expressed only in his work and a more superficial self that operates in the other activities of his life. But while Marcel experiences these discontinuities in his life as a source of anguish before he writes, he comes to feel that in that other self which the artist reveals in his work there are the durable accents of an individuality that survives the many deaths of our more fragile social personalities. Paradoxically, the narrator's sense of the split between art and life enables him to assert the existence of a permanent self—which art expresses—unaffected by the fragmented history of the self in time.

Marcel comes to consider artistic genius as the ability to transcribe the "residuum" of individuality that we are ordinarily forced to leave unexpressed when we use a language designed to emphasize what men share, and thus to strengthen our belief in a human community. The artist, like Bergotte, may have led a mediocre or morally objectionable life; he may be socially and even intellectually uninteresting. For the narrator his gift is the mysterious availability of himself to himself, and his morality is in an uncompromising devotion to the reflection, in his work, of his uniqueness. Art is an escape from the language of friendship and love, of society and intellectual talk, in short from the language in which we sacrifice our most personal accent in order to be recognized by others as belonging to a life already familiar to them.

> But is it not the fact then that from those elements [that compose the soul] all the real residuum which we are obliged to keep to ourselves, which cannot be transmitted in talk, even by friend to friend, by master to disciple, by lover to mistress, that ineffable something which makes a difference in quality between what each of us has felt and what he is obliged to leave behind at the threshold of the phrases in which he can communicate with his fellows only by limiting himself to external points common to us all and of no interest, art, the art of a Vinteuil like that of an Elstir, makes the man himself apparent, rendering externally visible in the colours of the spectrum that intimate composition of those worlds which we call individual persons and which, without the aid of art, we should never know? [16]

An artist like Elstir is a man whose consciousness, at certain privileged moments, enters into possession of his whole being. He can fully *have* his impressions before he distorts them; he can express a whole reaction before limiting himself to a partial one. It would, therefore, seem that depth of response is associated with immediacy of response, and reality and truth appear to be on the side of the unreflective first impression. "Only the subjective impression, however inferior the material may seem to be and however improbable the outline, is a criterion of truth . . . ," for it is an immediate individual response to the world.[17]

II. *Involuntary memory and the work of art*

In front of his work the artist can be his own audience; he can enjoy what Marcel pursues painfully and in vain in his love for Albertine: knowledge of himself as an object outside of himself. For many years Marcel anxiously wonders whether or not he has the talent to be a writer, for he obscurely realizes that only in art will he be able to hold firmly in his grasp the image of himself he desperately pursues in his excessive attachment to his mother, in his jealous love of Albertine, and in his superficially snobbish need to be accepted by aristocratic society. It is therefore inevitable that he consider his own vocation as an artist as a miracle of salvation. In danger of losing his sense of himself both in a succession of discontinuous personalities and in a hostile, unfamiliar external world, Marcel comes to see the work of art as his only chance of saving himself from the deaths that make up life. When he speaks of the immortality the artist achieves, he is not merely repeating the commonplace notion of the artist's work being read after his death; indeed, in *Le Temps retrouvé* he seems indifferent enough to this idea to suggest that even the greatest works are finally forgotten.[18] What might have been a cliché takes on specific meaning in the context of a life which, on a certain level of Marcel's mind, has actually been experienced as a series of deaths. The work of art can give to the artist's life a permanence *during* his life, and, from the point of view of Marcel's anguish about the self, this fixed image of his individuality is felt as a kind of immortality of the self.

But Marcel's vocation as an artist depends, first of all, on his being able to exploit the depths of being in himself which he recognizes in the works of other artists. Elstir's painting and Vinteuil's music suggest to him the connections between art and individuality; certain other experiences—apparently unrelated to art—testify to the existence of a profound and permanent individuality in his own life. Now it is only in terms of Marcel's inability to find continuity in the history of his personality that we can understand (and, in fact, be tolerant of) the extraordinary importance he gives to a few experiences of involuntary memory. The passages that describe these experiences have been subjected to so many complicated exegeses that it is only too easy, as Proust might say, to forget our original impression of them and to find the narrator's language perfectly natural. It does, after all, seem eccentric to describe these banal events as metaphysical illuminations that bring a sort of religious felicity: "An exquisite pleasure," he writes about the *madeleine* experience, "had invaded my senses, but individual, detached, with no suggestion of its origin. And at once the vicissitudes of life had become indifferent to me, its disasters innocuous, its brevity illusory—this new sensation having had on me the effect which love has of filling me with a precious essence; or rather this essence was not in me, it was myself. I had ceased now to feel mediocre, accidental, mortal." [19] And toward the end of *Le Temps retrouvé*, where the narrator describes a rather humorously rapid succession of these revivals of the past, he writes that only at such moments does he enjoy "the essence of things, that is to say, entirely outside of time," at the same time that they make available to him "a fragment of time in its pure state." [20] Some critics have treated such statements as detachable insights about personality, time, and memory, apparently finding it unnecessary to account psychologically for the description of the *madeleine* incident as an experience of immortality and eternity. Proust himself was inclined to speak of such passages in a mystifying way. He told Elie-Joseph Bois, in an interview published in *Le Temps* on November 12, 1913, that he had written "a series of 'novels of the Unconscious' "; he emphasized the "extratemporal essence" of the sensations that accompany involuntary memory, and insisted that his work "is in no sense built upon reasoning." [21] In the most abstract and theoretical part of his work, Proust's narrator expresses a warning to which he himself is strangely deaf: "A book in which there are theories is like an article from which the price mark has not been removed." [22] The price tag does, indeed, give a poor idea of the article's value. The narrator's theorizing about his own work often seems inadequate to describe what he has done; his intellectual claims seem both pretentious and thin, as he himself might have realized, in comparison to passages written from deeper levels of his mind than the one at which the would-be metaphysician operates.

The passages on involuntary memory have, however, considerable dramatic interest if we look at them in the context of Marcel's particular psychology. I have spoken of the panic he feels in new places when he is unable to find saving analogies between them and familiar places from his past. He is, in a certain sense, peculiarly unimaginative; and because he has great difficulty assimilating what he does not immediately recognize, he longs to suppress all differences between the self and the world. In involuntary memory, recognition is immediate and total; what he is now experiencing is felt almost entirely as something he has already experienced. Such moments abolish the usual duality between past and present, between the imagination and the senses. And this is made possible by a momentary effacement of the external world. Marcel has painfully learned that he cannot make the world contain only self-images. When he is in love with Gilberte, he suffers the consequences of what he calls in *Le Temps retrouvé* "the inexorable law which decrees that only that which is absent can be imagined." Each time he meets her on the Champs-Elysées, he notices things about her that do not correspond to the way he has imagined her; but when he is alone, his imagination functions abstractly, his only experience of Gilberte is mental. But the sensation felt at the moment of involuntary memory is "both in the past (which made it possible for my imagination to take pleasure in it) and in

the present, the physical stimulus of the sound or the contact
with the stones adding to the dreams of the imagination that
which they usually lack, the idea of existence"; there is a momentarily perfect equivalence between imagination and sensation.
The external world is, as it were, used for its own destruction; instead of modifying the contents of imagination, it provides the stimulus that allows imagination to substitute itself for
the outer world as the object of sensory experience. Marcel thus
experiences present external reality as a memory. And if, as he
notes, these resurrections of the past can never succeed in wholly
breaking down the resistance of the world to the self, they can
at least make the world seem less real for a split second, and the
hardest and heaviest objects seem to waver between existence
and nonexistence.[23] It is through the life of our senses that we
are constantly aware of the external world; the paradoxical fea-
ture of an involuntary memory is that it is a sensation that
dematerializes the world.

For Marcel, such experiences are overwhelming evidence of
the persistence in time, and therefore of the reality of the self.
They are a necessary preliminary to his literary activity, for they
prove the existence of exactly those levels of the self that must
enter into the artist's style if his style is to include his most
personal accent. There is, then, a profound connection—which
at first may seem tenuous or artificial—between the moments of
involuntary memory and the work of art as the narrator conceives it. The source of inspiration for his own book is the evidence of self given by the involuntary memories of the Guermantes *matinée,* and "Combray" quite naturally begins as an
essai of self-analysis. The novel will, of course, be more than
that, but for the narrator it is first of all a process of self-discovery.
"[Literature is] life as it really is, life disclosed at last and made
clear, consequently the only life that is really lived, that life
which in one sense is to be found at every moment in every
man, as well as in the artist." It is, however, important to see the
limited value of Marcel's involuntary memories for the form and
style of the work he writes. First of all, this work is obviously

written from the perspective of voluntary memory, which is as inadequate for recapturing moments of involuntary memory as it is for bringing back the full experience of the past. The narrator's book cannot be written in the ecstatic trance induced by the taste of the *madeleine* or the sound of a spoon hitting a plate. And by making his hero and his narrator the same person in *A la Recherche,* Proust draws our attention to the difficulties of being faithful to the moments of involuntary memory in writing about the past. For we are constantly reminded that the man who has the voluntary memories has lost them at the moment we read of his having them; it is *his* voice that is now making the effort to remember moments in which remembering required no effort. The chance experience must be transformed into a deliberate investigation, a conscious *recherche.* The title of the work indicates how unimportant the experiences of involuntary memory are for the actual writing of the work: Marcel was certainly not *in search of* his past when he tasted the *madeleine* or stumbled on the flagstone. But now, in writing, he must use his intelligence to undo retrospectively the distorting of his intelligence in the past: ". . . all the work of our pride, our passion, our imitative spirit, our abstract intelligence, [our habits,] art will undo and will make us retrace our steps and return to the depths of our own selves, where what has really existed lies unknown to us." [24]

This "return to the depths" might have been attempted in a style of impressionistic notation. To be as faithful as possible to the moments of involuntary memory, for example, the narrator might have described his past in terms of fleeting and even incoherent impressions, denying himself any analytic perspective on the people and places evoked. Indeed, the wish to render such moments by freely distorting ordinary language would not have been surprising in a late nineteenth-century writer. But in spite of a persistent theoretical interest in an impressionistic use of language, in practice Proust had gone far beyond such notions by the time he was steadily writing *A la Recherche.* It is, furthermore, obvious that language itself and therefore the literary work are necessarily a fall from the paradise of involuntary memory. The narrator reluctantly admits the difference between his style and the sensations that accompany a total recall of the past. After speaking at length of the work he will write as made up of the extratemporal sensations of involuntary memory, the narrator finally, if somewhat cautiously, explains that before beginning his book he saw that he would have to do more—although he still suggests that it means doing less—than re-create these impressions:

> And yet I felt that these truths which the intelligence draws directly from reality are not entirely to be scorned, for it may be that they enchase, in a grosser substance, it is true, but nevertheless pierce with understanding those impressions which are brought to us, outside of all considerations of time, by the essential qualities common to sensations of the past and the present, but which, being more precious, are too rare for the work of art to be composed wholly of them. I felt surging within me a multitude of truths concerning passions, characters and customs which might well serve in that manner.

It is, in fact, these superficially less valuable truths—some of which, the narrator writes, he had discovered "through suffering and others in the midst of very commonplace pleasures"—that help him to realize that

> . . . all these materials for literary work were nothing else than my past life and that they had come to me in the midst of frivolous pleasures, in idleness, through tender affection and through sorrow, and that I had stored them up without foreseeing their final purpose or even their survival, any more than does the seed when it lays by all the sustenance that is going to nourish the seedling.[25]

Maurice Blanchot has pointed out that in *Jean Santeuil* Proust attempts to be more faithful to the rare moments of involuntary memory than in *A la Recherche*. Blanchot finds what he calls the "exergue" of Proust's early work in the passage describing Jean's happiness when, long after his stay in Brittany, a view of the Lake of Geneva suddenly reminds him of the sea

near Begmeil. "And all at once, finding it once again in front
of him, he sees the sea as it was and feels its charm. And suddenly all that life by the sea which he had thought of as futile
and wasted seems charming and beautiful to him, and his heart
swells at the thought of those walks back from Begmeil as the
sun was setting and with the sea spread out before him." The
narrator of *Jean Santeuil* adds that he himself has enough faith
in the intense pleasure accompanying such moments ". . . to
describe in writing not what I might see, or think, or reason
about, or remember, and to write only when a moment from the
past—with imagination hovering above it—would suddenly come
to life again by bursting through an odor or a view, and when
this joy would provide me with inspiration." As Blanchot remarks, a goal of fidelity to pure impressions is thus proposed, and
he suggests that Proust's aim in *Jean Santeuil* is to avoid "im-
pure" novelistic discourse, to portray his hero's life as a series of
separate and immobile hours. Neither *Jean Santeuil* nor *A la
Recherche* realizes these intentions, although some of the theoretical passages in the latter work indicate that Proust continued
to be interested intellectually in them. Blanchot points out how
far even *Jean Santeuil* is from a work of impressionistic notation:
we have psychological analyses of characters as well as pictures of
their physical appearances, and the different moments of Jean's
life are largely treated in conventional novelistic scenes.[26] Yet we
do have an impression of discontinuity in reading the book; each
section has something of the self-contained distinctness of an
isolated period from one's past evoked by an involuntary memory. Proust was clearly more concerned, in writing these thousand pages, with the fullness of individual parts rather than with
a single, continuous narrative.

But Proust abandoned *Jean Santeuil* and began a work of
extraordinary narrative continuity and tightness of construction.
The title and the appearance of *Jean Santeuil* as a separate and
apparently complete work are the editorial decisions of Bernard
de Fallois. It is composed of passages Proust wrote in notebooks
over a period of several years; he evidently had no intention of

publishing them in their original state, and both their fragmentary nature and the parallels between them and Proust's later
work indicate that they are the abortive first version of *A la
Recherche du temps perdu.* The beginning of *A la Recherche*
superficially suggests that involuntary memory is going to play a
larger role in the later work than in *Jean Santeuil,* that Proust
now wants to put together a whole novel according to the principles set forth in the passage I have quoted from *Jean Santeuil.*
We are led to expect that each section will, as it were, be authenticated by a total recall of a part of Marcel's past: the *drame du
coucher* follows the account of momentary confusion of time
and place when, years later, the narrator awakens in the middle
of the night; and the rest of life at Combray is described only
after we have read how the *madeleine* evoked more of Marcel's
childhood than the anguish of being alone at night in his bedroom. But this procedure is soon abandoned, and it does not really
account for what is interesting in the organization of any part
of the novel, even of "Combray." It seems clear that what Proust
found unsatisfactory in the *Jean Santeuil* notebooks could not
be remedied by tightening the connections between experiences
of involuntary memory and various sections of his novel. There
seems to have been no equivalent of *Jean Santeuil* in the narrator's life, but his self-analysis undoubtedly throws some light on
Proust's reasons for abandoning the early work. An involuntary
memory testifies to the presence of a past Marcel has mistakenly
thought of as dead; but it does not create an unbroken continuity
between the past and the present. These rare memories make of
Marcel's past what Georges Poulet has called a "néant étoilé";
they light up certain moments of the past, but there are large
areas of darkness separating the relived moments from one another.[27] Involuntary memory can therefore provide Marcel with
the guarantee that his past is not completely lost, but it cannot
supply evidence of a permanent individuality, of the unbroken
history of a single personality. In a book whose organization
would be completely determined by these rare resurrections of
isolated past moments, there would be even greater discontinuity

from one part to another than in *Jean Santeuil*. The narrator of
A la Recherche wants to be able to affirm, in his work, the unity
of his personality, the "fundamental notes" that reappear in
apparently different desires of different periods. In the same way,
Proust seems to have been mainly concerned with the one literary problem which the organization of *Jean Santeuil* could
not help him to solve: the convincing presentation of a mass of
diversified material as a single, tightly unified work. *Jean Santeuil* would have perhaps lent itself to a greater emphasis on narrative discontinuity; but in order to give unity to the hundreds of
passages he had written, Proust had, significantly, to write an
impressively different work.

III. *The "accent" of individuality in literary style*

Marcel's involuntary memories nevertheless suggest the depth
and completeness of response which must enter into his work if
it is to express his most individual response to life. But our experience of the artist's deepest self is an experience of literary
language, or of the visual and spatial images of painting and
sculpture, or of the organized sounds of music. How do instruments of expression translate a depth of being? And how, in describing a period from his past which he may have relived in an
involuntary memory, can the narrator not only describe a certain
period of time, but also communicate the "fundamental notes"
of his own personality? Now the nature of the narrator's view of
art makes it particularly difficult for him to define the qualities
of literary style that interest him most in other writers and in the
composition of his own work. In a sense, his profound attachment to art is an attachment to certain accents. "And even," he
writes while speaking of the difference between Vinteuil and
other musicians, "when I bore in mind the acquired originality
which had struck me that afternoon, that kinship which musical
critics might discover among them, it is indeed a unique accent
to which rise, and return in spite of themselves those great
singers that original composers are, which is a proof of the irre-

ducibly individual existence of the soul." [28] This accent is necessarily nonintellectual; it would seem, by nature, to be also non-
verbal, since language commits the artist to social definitions of
reality, and therefore to a dilution of his individuality. There is
a time in Marcel's life when music seems to him "something
truer" than literature.

> Sometimes I thought that this was due to the fact that what we
> feel in life, not being felt in the form of ideas, its literary (that
> is to say an intellectual) translation in giving an account of it,
> explains it, analyses it, but does not recompose it as does music,
> in which the sounds seem to assume the inflexion of the thing
> itself, to reproduce that interior and extreme point of our sensa-
> tion which is the part that gives us that peculiar exhilaration
> which we recapture from time to time and which when we say:
> "What a fine day! What glorious sunshine!" we do not in the
> least communicate to our neighbor, in whom the same sun and
> the same weather arouse wholly different vibrations.[29]

Language is an intellectual "translation" of what we feel; its
function is essentially social, and it is consequently bound to
betray the most personal part of the artist's impressions.

In a strict sense the kind of pure individuality the narrator
seems to have in mind in the passages on art simply has no meaning. Our personal vision of the world is not merely compromised
by other visions; our very ability to have impressions of life depends on our having learned from sources outside of ourselves
how to recognize impressions and how to organize and articulate
them. All expression necessarily gives the lie to the abstract idea
of total fidelity to a self untouched by external ideas of the nature
and processes of the self. Proust is, however, less concerned than,
for example, Mallarmé with the inherent limitations of language;
he is not tormented by the idea of a "purely poetic" language, of
an absolute *Oeuvre*. He comes therefore to feel that style and
novelistic organization can express the writer's most profound
individuality; rather than engage in a Joycean experimentation
with the very composition of words, he is concerned with finding

how language can be used in literature in a more expressive and personal way than it is used outside of literature.

Both in *A la Recherche* and in his other writing, Proust speaks with assurance of the signs by which the writer's failure to achieve depth in his vision can be recognized. He consistently separates the notion of truth in art from the notion of intellectual truth. "The ideas formed by pure intellect have only a logical truth, a potential truth; the selection of them is an arbitrary act. . . . Not that the ideas we form ourselves may not be logically correct, but we do not know whether they are true." [30] The authenticity of impressions can be gauged by the extent to which "the ideas formed by pure intellect" have been absorbed into a continuously distinctive, profoundly individual style. When Proust writes, in *Contre Sainte-Beuve,* that there is no style in Balzac, he is objecting to the direct entry into the novelist's work of every thought that comes to his mind: "Balzac uses all the ideas that occur to him and does not attempt to melt them down and make them part of a style [et ne cherche pas à les faire entrer, dissoutes, dans un style] in which they would be in harmony with one another and suggest what he wants to say." [31] There are several passages in which Proust tries to define the qualities of style he has in mind here. In a letter written to the Comtesse de Noailles in 1904, he writes that the "absolute beauty" of certain works of art is "a kind of blending [une espèce de fondu,] of transparent unity in which all things, having lost their original appearance as things, are now lined up alongside of one another and penetrated with the same light; everything can be seen through everything else, and not a single word resists or escapes from this assimilation." Proust excuses himself for his awkward language, saying that ". . . this is the first time that this idea has occurred to me and I don't know how to express it." [32] His later formulations will not, however, add much precision to the idea; he will elaborate it mainly by concrete examples. The crucial words, whenever the idea is restated, are unity, harmony, and the not easily translated "fondu." In Balzac things are insufficiently converted into style. "Since he does not think of a sentence as made of a special substance in which everything that was once an object of conversation, of knowledge, etc., must be eliminated and unrecognizable, he adds to each word the idea he has about it, the reflection it suggests to him." Balzac uses "the most striking images," but—and we find the word again—they are not "fondues avec le reste"; there is no difference between the way he uses images in his novels and the way an inspired conversationalist might use them. In Flaubert, on the other hand,

> . . . all the different parts of reality are converted into a single substance made of vast, uniformly shimmering surfaces [une même substance, aux vastes surfaces, d'un miroitement monotone]. No impurity has remained. Surfaces have become like mirrors, in which everything can be portrayed, but by reflection, without changing their homogeneous substance. Everything that was once different has been transformed and absorbed.[33]

Now Proust's criteria for a successful style are interestingly different from Flaubert's. Theoretically, the latter's notion of objectivity would rule out those qualities for which Proust praises him. Flaubert's ambition was to eliminate style in exactly the sense that most interests Proust. "To paint nature as it is," he wrote to Louise Colet: [34] every subject has its style, and the writer is a kind of catalyst in whom subjects become language without their nature being changed by the nature of the catalyst. A catalyst or a god, for Flaubert's ideal writer is a man without a point of view, whose work expresses not a vision of the world but perfect knowledge of it. It is, then, an ironic commentary on Flaubert's "objectivity" that we immediately feel the rightness of Proust's remarks on the "subjectivism" of Flaubert's novels. He speaks of the "grammatical beauty" of Flaubert's style; he quotes passages in which the place of an adverb in a sentence, the special, nonconnective use of "et," and especially a preference for the imperfect tense over the preterite help to create a world in which there are few distinct actions, and which the reader experiences as an oppressive series of intermingling pictures. For

Proust, Flaubert is most interesting because of what Flaubert was, theoretically, most anxious to avoid. He tends to undramatize experience, to focus our attentions on characters' reactions rather than on objective events. It is this pervading subjectivity that Proust defines as the special quality that Flaubert brings to the novel: ". . . what was, until Flaubert, action becomes an impression." [35] Flaubert has, in fact, a surprisingly superficial view of what constitutes the novelist's presence in his work. Because he avoids Balzac's sociological and philosophical digressions, and the dear-reader chattiness that irritates him in earlier fiction, he naïvely feels that he has "disappeared" from his work. But when Fielding, Balzac, and Thackeray move from narrative passages to dramatic scenes, their characters do speak, they often have the stage all to themselves, and so we see a great deal of them as well as of their intrusive creators. Flaubert's supposed objectivity, on the other hand, does not guarantee his characters a larger dramatic life on their own. They have little existence outside of the narrative voice that describes them; our strongest sense of Emma Bovary is not in passages where she herself speaks, but rather in analytic passages in which her dreams and frustrations are completely assimilated into a partly sympathetic, partly ironic point of view on them. What has been called the impassivity or impersonality of Flaubert is really, as Proust saw, a peculiar way of devaluating the external world.

Whereas Flaubert admires writers capable of renouncing their most personal accent in order to give their imaginary worlds the variety and distinctness of the real world, Proust considers the kind of "miroitement monotone" he finds in Flaubert's prose the sign of literary genius. They are, however, both describing different aspects of the esthetic mediation of personal experience. Especially in dramatic literature, this mediation consists largely of an objectification of feelings in a convincingly distinct and independent world of imaginary characters and events. Both the literary mediocrity and the popular success of dramatists such as Tennessee Williams and Edward Albee can perhaps be explained by an incomplete transformation of certain emotions and attitudes into dramatic situations. Their plays seem excitingly daring to audiences; there is indeed something astonishing in an expensive and solemn public display of psychiatric wish fantasies. The spectator does not have to bring to their plays much more than the indulgence he naturally has for his own fantasies. We all invent situations in which our desires and fears are played out in story form, and the urgency of the needs such fantasies express inclines us to be tolerant of esthetic imperfections in them, for they have fulfilled their purpose once they satisfy the needs. But these fantasies are hardly satisfying literature either at home or in the theatre; the story elements may be elaborate, but they generally have little life of their own apart from the obvious wishes from which they are born. With Williams and Albee, a certain emotional excitement is necessary in the spectator, some participation in the wishes *behind* the story. And because of this equivocal collaboration with the dramatist, the audience tends to see the work as merely instrumental. It seems, on the other hand, that a detachment in the writer from some of his desires, and a less urgent and more complex need for satisfaction are necessary in order to give dramatic fantasies esthetic autonomy. It is perhaps only at a certain emotional distance from a wish to make the world satisfy his desires that the writer can project himself into fantasies that have a look of independence, fantasies in which, considering them as "objects," both he and his public can be attentive to artistic values to which we remain indifferent in our narrower fantasies.

Proust is as aware as Flaubert of the necessity for the writer not merely to insert in his work ideas and feelings as they come to him. But he insists less on the process of dramatizing and objectifying feelings than on the assimilating of conscious thought into a uniform "substance"—or accent, or tone—in which the writer's deepest subjectivity continuously expresses itself. In a novel, variety of characterization clearly interests Proust less than a consistency, even a monotony in the writer's voice that indicates a firm grasp on what is most characteristically *his* way of seeing in his most diverse impressions of life. As he writes in one of the passages I have quoted, things should be portrayed by reflection; the vastly different subjects of *L'Education senti-mentale* and *Salammbô* are absorbed into the "homogeneous" surface of Flaubert's consistently recognizable style. For Proust, all the elements of a novel have, in the broadest sense, a meta-phorical function. Things should be seen, as he writes in the letter to the Comtesse de Noailles, "les unes dans les autres"; each character and each incident could then refer to other char-acters and incidents in the novel, and, ideally, every passage could evoke every other passage, for the accent that informs the novel's first sentence and that is its profound subject would be heard in all of them.

iv. *Metaphor: "les surfaces sont devenues réfléchissantes"*

It is the discovery of metaphor that confirms Marcel's sense of his literary vocation in *A la Recherche du temps perdu*. Robert Brasillach points out that involuntary memory is a sort of meta-phor; Marcel's temporal illusion when he tastes the *madeleine* is somewhat like the optical illusions which Elstir paints.[36] In both cases something is identified with the help of something else, is, actually, first of all experienced *as* something else. From a certain angle of vision, Elstir imagines he is seeing part of the land when he is really looking at the sea; in involuntary memory the meta-phor is temporal, and Marcel's impressions of the present mo-ment are, very briefly, impressions that belong to a moment from his past. The verbal translation of an involuntary memory is necessarily metaphorical. To describe his sensations after stum-bling on the flagstones outside the Guermantes *hôtel*, the narra-tor writes: "A deep azure blue intoxicated my sight, impressions of coolness and dazzling light hovered near me. . . ." When, a few minutes later, he hears a servant strike a spoon against a plate, ". . . the sensations were again those of great heat, but entirely different, mingled with the odour of smoke, tempered by the cool fragrance of a forest setting. . . ."[37] The memories of Venice and of his recent train ride to Paris thus provide a metaphorical language in which the narrator describes one group of sensations in terms of sensations from other times and other places.

But, perhaps because of the narrator's tendency to make a literal identification between memory and imagination, he fails, it seems to me, to distinguish between the analogies of involuntary memory and other kinds of metaphors that are actually more important for his literary work. The central passage on metaphorical activity in *Le Temps retrouvé* illustrates a certain confusion of strictly temporal analogies with descriptive metaphors in general:

> An hour is not merely an hour. It is a vase filled with perfumes, sounds, plans and climates. What we call reality is a certain relationship between these sensations and the memories which surround us at the same time (a relationship that is destroyed by a bare cinematographic presentation, which gets further away from the truth the more closely it claims to adhere to it) the only true relationship, which the writer must recapture so that he may forever link together in his phrase its two distinct elements. One may list in an interminable description the objects that figured in the place described, the truth will begin only when the writer takes two different objects, establishes their relationship—analogous in the world of art to the [unique relationship established by the law of causality in the world of science]—and encloses them in the necessary rings of a beautiful style, or even when, like life itself, [comparing qualities shared by two sensations, he makes the essential nature common to both sensations stand out clearly] by joining them in a metaphor, in order to remove them from the contingencies of time. . . .[38]

The narrator seems to take for granted that the basis for analogy —the "essence commune" in the two terms of the comparison— is the same when the analogy is between a present sensation and a moment from the past, and when the relation between two different objects is *created* by the metaphor. There are, in both cases, similar qualities in two sensations or impressions, but the reasons for these similarities are comparatively uninteresting in involuntary memories, which are really little more than confused perceptions. A present experience accidentally awakens past sensations; there is no imaginative perception of what is present, only an involuntary and arbitrary revival of a specific past. Everyone has involuntary memories, and we would hardly measure someone's imaginative capacities by the frequency with which they occur. The language the narrator uses to describe his impression of the spoon hitting the plate reveals no convincing similarities between the sound he hears and the atmosphere he describes, nor does it suggest anything like the "fundamental notes" of his imagination; his images are justified by nothing more than the historical fact that in the train he heard a similar sound. The metaphors he uses to describe the hawthorns or his jealousy of Albertine, on the other hand, reveal the quality of his imagination, the range of his responsiveness to the world. Marcel can successfully re-create the world of his past as self-characterizing impressions only when he has discovered metaphorical capacities that are not dependent on involuntary memories.

Such capacities are revealed to Marcel at certain privileged moments in his life which he does not connect to specific memories. Very strong impressions, always "associated with some material object devoid of any intellectual value, and suggesting no abstract truth," give him a sense of things "teeming, ready to open, to yield up to me the secret treasure of which they were themselves no more than the outer coverings." [39] In front of the hawthorns on the Méséglise way or the Martinville steeples, he feels a joy as intense as the joy that accompanies his involuntary memories, but whose secret seems to be "not a sensation of bygone days, but a new truth." [40] Jean-Yves Tadié calls these moments "instants profonds." [41] As in his involuntary memories, for a few seconds Marcel has the sensation of ordinarily dormant parts of himself in his response to the external world. Both types of experiences are sudden expansions of consciousness; its limits are momentarily pushed back, and Marcel is naturally exhilarated by a brief sense of the greater range of being that is now "taking in" the world. And because the sensations that accompany the "instants profonds" are not connected to specific past moments, Marcel's impressions seem to involve a more creative use of his past than in the *madeleine*-type experience. In front of the three steeples or the three trees on the road to Hudimesnil, memory acts as imagination. Elements from Marcel's past combine in a new way as his personal response to the present moment; his impression is therefore a self-expression adequate to an external scene. This does not necessarily mean that he seizes the objective nature of the scene, but in feeling so intensely and so deeply his response to the scene, he is fully experiencing his particular way of looking at things, that is, his most individual style.

The narrator notes that he failed to realize fully, in Dr. Percepied's carriage, that ". . . what lay buried within the steeples of Martinville must be something analogous to a charming phrase, since it was in the form of words which gave me pleasure that it had appeared to me. . . ." [42] It would seem, then, that his pleasure is caused by an unexpected discovery of literary language. Tadié's claim is a development of this idea: "The reality which is revealed in the instants of profundity is the reality of the world in the work of art, it is the world already transformed into a work of art." [43] But the world becomes art only when Marcel writes down a description of his different views of the three steeples. The passage is, in fact, not very impressive, but it clearly suggests that the "new truth" which brings Marcel such intense pleasure consists of metaphorical equivalents of the external scene. The steeples are compared to "three birds perched upon the plain, motionless and conspicuous in the sunlight"; to "three golden pivots"; to "three flowers painted upon the sky above the low line of fields"; to "three maidens in a legend, abandoned in a solitary place over which night had begun to fall." [44] These images are what was hidden behind the steeples; they give depth to objects by internalizing them. Marcel's verbal metaphors are, like the visual metaphors of Elstir's paintings, a concentrated expression of individual style. They are not determined by the sensations of a specific past moment; instead, Marcel discovers the kind of imagination his past has created through the metaphorical resources he uses to identify the present.

In re-creating an external scene metaphorically, Marcel does not, however, do away with the scene itself. He traces in detail the different positions of the steeples: his images describe objects but are never substituted for them. In these privileged moments the world mediates the self, and the condition of self-possession is self-forgetfulness. Now this aspect of the Martinville-steeples passage is repeated in the narrator's literary treatment of his whole past. I have spoken of Marcel's inability, at certain moments of his life, to project an air of familiarity on the world. His fantasy of a perfect identification between the self and the world seems intended as a remedy for this failure of his imagination to provide analogies between the new and the familiar. In the past the discovery of metaphor often involves an almost painful attentiveness to the object he attempts to assimilate—as, for example, when he looks at the hawthorns in the Combray church or along the Méséglise way—and the extraordinary activity of his metaphorical imagination seems partly a way of protecting himself from those moments when his imagination fails him. He would like, ideally, to do away with the first term of the metaphor, to substitute the image for the object and thus to transform the latter entirely into a mirror for the self. But even when he successfully finds the image which he at first thinks of as hidden in something outside of himself, he cannot completely suppress the object. More precisely, the object is always present *for us* in the narrator's literary account of his past, and we cannot separate "what actually happened" from the book he is writing, which *is* his past now. It is significant that the narrator usually keeps the two terms of a metaphor; he has, in fact, a marked preference for similes, in which both terms, while brought together in the comparison, retain their individual distinctness. The passage in which the "action" of the hawthorns' "blossoming" is compared to the movement of a young girl's head includes several details that describe the flowers nonmetaphorically; the hawthorns remain hawthorns, and it seems to me misleading to suggest, as Tadié does, that Marcel "frees himself from the visible world, brings about its absence (most probably in the same manner as Mallarmé)," by articulating his impressions.[45] Marcel possesses the flowers in the sense that he has used them to create something for which only his imagination can account: his metaphor. Tadié defines what seems to be Marcel's deepest intention, but this intention is never fully realized in his work. The object can, of course, now be posited without anguish, for from the perspective of memory it, too, is an image; the world of Marcel's past now exists only in his mind. He does, however, seem to relive, as he writes, his old struggle against the resistances, the otherness of the external world. Certain images are remembered as external objects, and he repeats his efforts to assimilate them. The duality between the self and the world is re-created internally, and from the "real" hawthorns to the "real" Albertine, the narrator must be conscious, as he writes, of the inability of his language to do away with his sense of otherness even though otherness is now only a memory. His tactics are now devices of literary style, and it is principally through metaphor that he shows the world in the process of being absorbed into his particular imaginative resources.

The confrontation between Marcel and the world is thus re-created in the details of the narrator's style; the dramatic tensions of the Proustian sentence repeat stylistically the conflicts between the self and the world. It is easy to see the significance of certain characteristics of the narrator's style—for example, the seemingly endless proliferations around any starting point of description. It is as if this could do away with the memory of the word as distinct from the self, as if, under the melting pressure of analysis and comparison, objects could be thoroughly de-objectified and everything made to appear as a metaphor for everything else. The galleys of *A la Recherche du temps perdu* came back to Gallimard covered with additions, and Proust's publishers understandably felt some panic when they saw how a job of correction inevitably became the occasion for uncontrollable elaboration. In looking over his text, Proust apparently never found things sufficiently "digested"; the way to conquer their resistance, their opaqueness, was not to revise or cut out passages, but to inflate them, to "cover" every aspect of the elusive world with a continuously dense reflection on the world.

Various stylistic resources serve this purpose in *A la Recherche*. There is, first of all, the accumulation of images around certain objects. During a walk toward Méséglise the day Marcel first sees Gilberte, he stops in front of a hedge of hawthorns, unable to penetrate the special charm they have for him. He stares at them in order to find out what it is in himself that they have aroused: ". . . but in vain did I shape my fingers into a frame, so as to have nothing but the hawthorns before my eyes; the sentiment which they aroused in me remained obscure and vague, struggling and failing to free itself, to float across and become one with the flowers." But, characteristically, the recollection of Marcel's failure is his belated success. He remembers feeling a "festal intention" in the flowers, they remind him of religious feasts, as well as of good things to eat; and a poppy seems to announce the fields of corn in the same way that the sight of a boat being repaired on some low-lying ground tells a traveler that the sea is nearby. The charm of nature, as the narrator describes it in retrospect, is really the charm of his remembered feelings, of his youthful enthusiasms and, on that particular day, of his excitement at being near Gilberte's home. The images he uses to describe the flowers indirectly describe his own sense of promise, his anticipation of a rare happiness. The hawthorns and the poppies and the cornflowers are thus the occasion for a more adequate expression of Marcel's energies than the inarticulate "Zut, zut, zut, zut" he finds when he tries to express these energies directly. We see in these few pages from "Combray" how the narrator uses metaphorical description to change the apparent object of description into a metaphor for an inner state. The object itself becomes the focal point for a chain of associations, the single metaphor that unifies and contains all the others, and is therefore the most appropriate image of Marcel's feelings at that moment. In the following passage the movement from a description of a flower to the description of an inner state is typical:

> My eyes followed up the slope which, outside the hedge, rose steeply to the fields, a poppy that had strayed and been lost by its fellows, or a few cornflowers that had fallen lazily behind, and decorated the ground here and there with their flowers like the border of a tapestry, in which may be seen at intervals hints of the rustic theme which appears triumphant in the panel itself; infrequent still, spaced apart as the scattered houses which warn us that we are approaching a village, they betokened to me the vast expanse of waving corn beneath the fleecy clouds, and the sight of a single poppy hoisting upon its slender rigging and holding against the breeze its scarlet ensign, over the buoy of rich black earth from which it sprang, made my heart beat as does a wayfarer's when he perceives, upon some low-lying ground, an old and broken boat which is being caulked and made seaworthy, and cries out, although he has not yet caught sight of it, "The Sea!" [46]

The final comparison describes the poppy's effect on Marcel rather than the poppy itself. But the flowers have this particular effect because of the excitement he brings to them; and rather than a detailed description of the flowers themselves, we have the two images of the flowers announcing the fields of corn and the boat announcing the sea as metaphors for Marcel's sense of the ecstatic new life he would lead if only he could participate in the secret rites of Gilberte's life. The profusion of metaphors in this and other passages is thus a way of concentrating in a single image the various aspects of an inner disposition; certain objects become representations of Marcel's feelings.

In the most elaborate of the narrator's metaphorical descriptions, each image becomes the point of departure for a new comparison, and we are often led back to new aspects of the original object by accessory aspects of the images used to describe it. In the church at Combray, Marcel enjoys the "bitter-sweet fragrance of almonds" of the hawthorns around the altar:

Despite the heavy, motionless silence of the hawthorns, these gusts of fragrance came to me like the murmuring of an intense vitality, with which the whole altar was quivering like a roadside hedge explored by living antennae, of which I was reminded by seeing some stamens, almost red in colour, which seemed to have kept the springtime virulence, the irritant power of stinging insects now transmuted into flowers.[47]

The odor is like the sound of the flowers' life; the altar then seems to vibrate with this imagined sound like a hedge surrounded by "living antennae"; and the insects evoked in this second comparison draw Marcel's attention away from the hawthorns' odor to the stamens in whose violent color he finds a visual image of insects' "springtime virulence." Such, at any rate, is the sequence of associations suggested by the way the narrator verbally organizes his impressions in memory. In spite of certain large distinctions he keeps between his present point of view and his past point of view, we are seldom able to separate associations that come to the narrator at the moment of writing from his impressions as he had them in the past. He sometimes suggests that certain analogies occurred to him at the moment being described (he was reminded of living antennae in seeing the red stamens), but more generally he is less interested in tracing the growth of his metaphorical imagination than in using both his memories and his present resources of language to give to his past its definitive shape. The few poppies and cornflowers on the slope simply *were* like the rustic scene on a tapestry's border, or like the scattered houses outside a village, which is to say that they also *are* like that now: these comparisons are Marcel's final decision about their appearance. For the work he is writing is less a literal record of what he felt in Combray, Balbec, or Paris than it is a fresh confrontation with those places in which he has another chance to project himself on them. Each scene can now be fixed once and for all as a reflection of a particular moment in the history of his desires and anxieties. The charm of the hawthorns becomes the charm of his own adolescent feelings by virtue of stylistic choices made at the time of writing. It is useless to wonder if thinking of the insects on a hedge of flowers made Marcel notice the red stamens, or if his attention to the stamens suggested the insects: the sequence of impressions is now wholly a syntactical sequence, and the latter tends to equalize both objects and images as mutually reflecting mirrors on an inner landscape.

The primacy of impressions over objects is often rendered by sentence structure. The reader may, for example, be forced to experience the errors of perception before the rectifying but subjectively less interesting truths. In the following passage the narrator describes the sensation of hearing rain fall before the mind identifies the sound as rain: "A little tap at the window, as though some missile had struck it, followed by a plentiful, falling sound, as light, though, as if a shower of sand were being sprinkled from a window overhead; then the fall spread, took on an order, a rhythm, became liquid, loud, drumming, musical, innumerable, universal. It was the rain." [48] More prevalent than such rather precious writing, however, are certain syntactical habits that express more subtly Marcel's most profound intentions. There are numerous sentences in the novel in which pronouns, adjectives, or subordinate clauses precede their antecedents, or the words or clauses which they modify. We follow what is often a long development around an object of description before we know what the object is. Speaking in La Fugitive of the way in which impressions connected with Albertine's life bring back the suffering of jealousy even when Albertine no longer constantly occupies his thoughts, the narrator writes: "Transported then to a forgotten moment, the force of which my habit of thinking of it had not dulled, and in which Albertine was still alive, her misdeeds became more immediate, more painful, more agonising." [49] Or, when he tries to make Andrée admit that she and Albertine had sexual relations together, he notices a disturbed look in Andrée's eyes, which he describes in the following way: "Before I had completed my sentence, I saw in Andrée's eyes, which it sharpened to a pin-point like those stones which for that reason jewellers find it difficult to use, a fleeting, worried stare, like the heads of persons privileged to go behind the scenes who draw back the edge of the curtain before the play has begun and at once retire in order not to be seen." [50] Finally, writing that if physical suffering is the condition for spiritual knowledge, the writer should accept the former in order that the latter may nourish his work, Marcel describes the qualities that suffering may add to his work before referring directly to the work itself: ". . . let us accept the physical injury it [sorrow] inflicts because of the spiritual wisdom that it brings; let us allow our body to disintegrate, since each fresh particle that breaks off, now luminous and decipherable, comes [—to complete it at the cost of suffering superfluous to others more gifted and to make it more and more substantial as emotions gradually chip away our life—and adds itself to our work.]" [51]

These passages taken at random from *A la Recherche* show very well that complete absorption of conscious intention into style which Proust admired in Flaubert and found wanting in Balzac. The lines from "Combray" describing the rain strike us as too deliberate a working out of a theory. They are a kind of set piece of impressionistic writing, and we are more aware of the narrator's decision to disorient us by withholding the word "rain" until the end of the sentence than we are of the nature of his impressions. The passage is insufficiently "fondu" into a continuous style. But in the other examples a theoretical intention seems to have become a spontaneous habit of expression. And this habit is so generalized that even when the narrator is examining a thought or a feeling rather than an external object, the inner stimulus is treated as an object to be assimilated, and, rather than identify it immediately, he first of all develops his reaction to it. The narrator thus involves us in his complex responses to the world before giving us a clear image of the situation to which he is responding; there is a coherent expression of thought and feeling, but without its initial impetus. Because of this syntactical habit, for a good part of many sentences we see Marcel's mind functioning, as it were, without the aid of the world; by refusing to define at once the *relation* between the two, the narrator is using memories of the world to draw our attention away from the world, and he appears self-sufficient and self-stimulating.

Finally, and most importantly, there is the reduction of character and dramatic incident to the metaphorical resources of the narrator's imagination. The form of the novel is most profoundly affected by his tendency to undramatize his relation to the world, to re-create the people and situations from his past as aspects of his own individuality. By making the various incidents in his work metaphors for one another, the narrator makes them all metaphors for his particular perspective on reality. Poulet speaks of this "reciprocal intelligibility" among originally distinct episodes; analogies establish patterns that bring together apparently isolated moments.[52] Each aspect of life Marcel has encountered becomes an inner resource for understanding other aspects of life; images that are first used to describe certain incidents may become later on real incidents in Marcel's life. Military tactics, for example, are used metaphorically to describe Marcel's servants' shrewd strategies for dealing with his character before we see Marcel at Doncières; but with Saint-Loup and his friends at Doncières, it is military strategy itself that Marcel has to understand with the aid of other analogies (provided, for example, by painting and surgery); finally, the art with which Marcel becomes familiar at Doncières will be useful later on in helping him to understand the psychology of his pursuit of Albertine. Works of art help him to appreciate aristocratic genealogy; certain observations of nature provide a language in which to describe both Madame de Guermantes's beauty and the chance meeting between Jupien and Charlus; and the discontinuities in Marcel's own memory make intelligible the forgetfulness of those people who, at the last Guermantes *matinée,* think that Bloch has always been received in the highest society or praise a man they detested twenty years before during the Dreyfus Affair. These analogies both evoke what has already been written and point to what is yet to be written. As Georges Piroué has said, the memory of the work tends to be substituted for direct experi-

ence of the world; the narrator's book provides him with the
comparisons he needs to finish the book.[53] Metaphor is also used
to anticipate certain events; for the reader, metaphorical description often prefigures what is yet to come in the novel, it points
to a future within the record of the narrator's past. The profound
similarities among apparently different phenomena are, finally,
the basis for the general laws, but the latter are mainly the laws
of Marcel's responses to life. They are a way of forcing various
experiences into the single pattern of his continuous perception.
Each experience is seen from the angle of other experiences, and
in the comparisons he makes the narrator reduces the world to
illustrations and repetitions of his own needs. Dramatic incidents
and other people resemble aspects of a dream; they are shapes on
which the self can glide almost as easily as Golo on a doorknob.
To describe Franco-German relations in terms of his relation with
Albertine, and vice versa, is essentially to reveal the persistent
concerns he brings to both types of experience. What is general
in the general laws—the narrator's claims to universal truths notwithstanding—is Marcel's unique point of view on the world.

This is, of course, overstating the case, and as I have tried to
show in other contexts, our impression of a world that reflects
Marcel's individuality is balanced by our sense of a convincing
variety in the world he describes. Characteristically, this tension
between a work that seems almost entirely a projection of the
narrator's psychology and a work of realistic description of the
world is expressed, but in an incomplete and sometimes confused way, in the narrator's theoretical statements. He has not
lost the desire to possess a reality different from himself, to penetrate the secrets of nature, of other people, of history and art.
Occasionally he proposes the view that the artist not only fixes
his own vision of the world in his work, but also gives us a picture of the world "as it is." He writes that Elstir's work is taken
from "the rare moments in which we see nature as she is, with
poetic vision"; the "as she is" adds to his discussion a claim that
his main definition of "poetic vision" clearly contradicts. Similarly, he speaks of Elstir's having revealed certain "laws of per-

spective," and the relationship between these universal laws and the unique vision of things expressed through metaphors is never clear.[54] J. M. Cocking has spoken of this passage as an example of Proust's trying to unite his irrational transcendentalism and his intellectualism into a single conception: Elstir's work both registers individual impressions and shows us what we would see if we took the same point of vantage.[55] It could be argued that what is universal is only the stages of perception —the fact that, however little we may be aware of them, our fleeting "first vision" of things is made up of "optical illusions"— but the narrator seems also to be saying that the content of perceptual errors, rather than corresponding to strictly individual histories, is also universal. The narrator's most convincing argument is for the particularity of the artist's vision, whose work would neither be a description of the external world "as it is," nor would it illustrate a point of view on reality shared by all men. But he is constantly tempted by the idea of an art that would be objective and universal. At the end of Le Temps retrouvé, when we see that his decision to write has been inspired by experiences of memory that have made available to him not general truths about human nature but rather specific moments from a unique past, he nevertheless suggests that involuntary memory liberates not merely an individual history, but also "the permanent essence of things, usually concealed." [56] This passage from the particular to the universal seems irresistible: art, the narrator writes, should throw light on "our feelings, our passions—that is to say, the passions and feelings of everyone." [57] The narrator exposes his early illusions about the external world, but his present point of view seems almost more naïve than the young Marcel's; he now finds, for example, a universally valid definition of love in his own peculiar experience of it, and he offers his special, comic point of view on society as an exhaustive report on the vanity and nothingness of social life.

The narrator's contradictory views of what art expresses can partly be explained by certain interests that seem to develop as he writes his work. The first pages of "Combray" create expectations of an entirely subjective narrative, but there is very soon a shift of perspective, and we are reading passages of presumably objective observation. We find later on a similar change of focus from one large section of the novel to another, from, roughly speaking, *A l'Ombre des jeunes filles en fleur* to *Le Côté de Guermantes*.[58] Marcel's curiosity about the world reappears and is, for the first time, fully satisfied, since the difference between himself and others can now be contained within his awareness of what these differences are. The world he sets out to describe is first of all in his own mind, and its existence outside his mind cannot extend beyond his decisions as a writer. Reality is now bearable because, by re-creating it from the perspective of memory, he has made of it, as Gaëtan Picon writes, "an *anteriority* from which aggressions and surprises can no longer come." [59] Marcel thus returns to the world by cutting himself off from it; the questions he asks about other people's lives can now be answered because he creates their lives by asking his questions. The work he writes becomes, as a result, different from the work he often speaks of having decided to write. Rather than present the world only in terms of his self-revealing impressions, he also describes objectively, especially in the volumes in which social portraits are dominant, a world to which he responds not only with the freshness of first impressions, but also with the analytic intelligence of the social scientist and the *moraliste*.

But the presumably transcended self reappears in the "real" external world of the novel: to the extent that characters and situations illustrate the resources of the narrator's metaphorical imagination, we feel that Marcel is inventing the world he describes. He seems to be not only remembering impressions, but also creating novelistic drama in order to provoke his own impressions. We should, however, not underestimate the importance of a world presented as distinct from the narrator's sensibility. Literature is the ideal form of self-possession precisely because it satisfies the Proustian hero's desire not only to absorb the world into the self, but also to discover the self in the world as a surprising new reality. While it may appear to us that it is by

inventing his past that he discovers the accents of what is irre-
ducibly individual in himself, the narrator seems to become more
and more convinced of the objective reality of the world he
creates. He writes with the intention of exploring the self, but
his work curiously affects him as a revelation about the world.
The narrator considers his book much in the same way as we
tend to look at our dreams, as if the various disguises of the self
constituted a world whose existence and nature did not depend
on and express the novelist's and the dreamer's fantasies.[60] It
would seem, moreover, that this process of absorbing the world
into the self and projecting the self into pictures of the world
does not characterize only the inventions of dreams and of art.
The fact that our clearest images of ourselves are often images
of external reality undoubtedly accounts for the ambiguity of
our supposed knowledge of the world and the futility of any
attempt to make definitive distinctions between what is subjective and what is objective. This ambiguity, which Proust's narrator experiences with extraordinary acuity, is, it seems to me,
the profound subject of *A la Recherche du temps perdu.* Marcel's "escape" from life into literature allows him to demonstrate
continuously the processes of novelistic invention that characterize life. If he seems to hesitate between the creation of an external world with distinctly individual characters and the con-
version of all parts of reality "into a single substance, made of
vast, uniformly shimmering surfaces," it is because only a certain
artistic indecisiveness can illustrate the double intention of reducing reality to the "fundamental notes" of his personality and
possessing the painfully elusive world in which the self must
live. We may also recognize that the narrator's illusions about
the world he creates reveal nothing less than the poignant confidence with which we take our own inventions as knowledge
about reality. But this illusion is undoubtedly possible only because the self is ordinarily anything but familiar; Marcel's metaphorical representations of his own sensibility have all the richness and newness which, at Combray, he mistakenly thought of
as belonging only to a world beyond the reach of his imagination.

CONCLUSION

The novel, Maurice Nadeau has remarked, follows a "natural" evolution from encyclopedic description of the world or of passions to an expression of what novelistic invention hides and reveals: "the particular way a man has of living in the world." [1] All the characters in any novel are, of course, aspects of a single point of view on life, but realistic fiction assumes our willingness to forget this, to accept the novelist's fantasies as an accurate description of reality. The illusion of reality obviously depends on the quality and range of the point of view. Cervantes's particular vision includes, for example, different enough visions of the world to make part of what he sees seem not like a vision, but rather like a reflection of life "as it is." The external world in which Don Quixote moves stubbornly resists being shaped by his chivalrous fantasies, and it is largely this capacity for resistance that gives it the prestige of seeming real. When Proust speaks of Flaubert's "subjectivism" and writes that ". . . what was, until Flaubert, action becomes an impression," [2] it is as if he were trying to locate the precise moment in the history of the novel when the novelist's hidden subject becomes his real subject. The importance Flaubert attached to style is only superficially a sign of his ascetic devotion to art; more profoundly, it seems to indicate a fundamental indifference to the external world, an unprecedented absorption on the part of the novelist in the quality and texture of individual responses to the world.

It is this indifference that impressed Proust as the revolutionary aspect of Flaubert's fiction; he acutely saw the assimilation of the most diversified material into the continuously recognizable Flaubertian voice. While Proust himself continues this movement away from the ambitions and conventions of realistic fiction, he is far from indifferent to the realistic novelist's relatively confident hold on the external world. A certain indefiniteness in his own literary ambitions makes of *A la Recherche du temps perdu* an example of that improbable category of novels called novels of transition. The narrator's critical perspective on the motivations of social behavior, his interest in analyzing a certain evolution in aristocratic society are, for example, more reminiscent of Balzac than of Flaubert, and we are reminded, in reading a considerable part of *A la Recherche,* less of the author of *L'Education sentimentale* than of the architect of *La Comédie humaine.* On the other hand, insofar as it points to a primarily introspective narrative, Proust's work prefigures much of twentieth-century fiction. A great deal has been written about the *rapprochement* between fiction and poetry in the modern novel. The novel, because of its double resource of dialogue and narration, can move between the two "purer" forms of drama and lyric poetry. The realism of the great nineteenth-century novelists is in their commitment to images of society as well as to individual characterizations. Their works are dramatic in that they are essentially dialogues: dialogues not merely in the technical sense, but between individual character and social reality. What has been called poetic fiction is fiction in which the main interest is not in conflicts between the self and the external world, but rather in the quality of private inner worlds. In Proust and the later works of Henry James, we have the appearances of earlier novelistic drama; both writers are interested in fully rendering the social contexts that impinge on and transform individual consciousness. But in James's last novels the social world seems increasingly allegorical. Characters are often unconvincing as distinct individuals; they strike us more as representative of moral choices available to the center of consciousness. Densher's ambiguous behavior toward Milly in *The Wings of the Dove,* for example, may suggest to us that James's own moral vision has become seriously deficient until we realize that she is being presented less as a real person whom Densher can harm than as a spiritual choice internal to his own mind. In *A la Recherche*, to the extent that all the characters repeat the patterns of Marcel's psychology, we have the impression that even when he seems to be describing people apparently very different from himself, he is actually engaged in a kind of dream creation. Edmund Wilson has said that Proust's novel "stands alone as a true dream-novel among works of social observation. It has its harmony, development and logic, but they are the harmony, development and logic of the unconscious." [3] The novelist's fantasies have been only partially mediated into convincing images of social life; the self-projection into fictional characters and incidents has kept some of the psychological repetitiousness and metaphorical unity of a dream.

But because the real world Proust's narrator describes has such profound analogies to his inner world, we have the rare chance of following the continuities among the various stages in a writer's progress toward greater and greater objectification of feeling. In other novelists, links may be missing; there is such an impressive range of being among Cervantes's or Tolstoi's characters that we may find them closer to the real world than Proust's characters, and therefore less suggestive of the imaginative process by which sensations, memories, impulses, and feelings can become elements of a convincing literary representation of reality. As I have tried to show in this study, that process is the main concern of Proust's narrator, and not merely because he is a writer and finds his life most meaningful when he thinks of it as preparing him for his artistic vocation. In the fear of being separated from *maman* and the adolescent enthusiasms of Combray, in his jealous love for Gilberte and Albertine, in his life in society, and in his experience of other works of art, Marcel repeats and re-creates, in a variety of dramatic circumstances, both his anxious curiosity about what is different from himself and his effort to reduce the world to a reflection of himself which he would be able to accept as a revelation about the world. Writing his own work is Marcel's most elaborate and most successful attempt to satisfy a fantasy of perfect identification between himself and external reality. His work is experimental, but not in a superficial technical sense; literary creation provides the Proustian hero with the ideal conditions for an experiment in self-dramatization and self-distribution.

I have, of course, been assuming throughout this study that the book we are reading is the book the narrator speaks of writing in *Le Temps retrouvé*. Germaine Brée has taken the opposite point of view, arguing that, until Chapter Three of *Le Temps retrouvé*, the work is written by a man unaware of his vocation as an artist, that otherwise the idea of a "recherche" would be meaningless and the Guermantes *matinée* would no longer have the character of a genuine "revelation." [4] But, if this were true, it would be difficult to see why the work is being written at all; it is, after all, only at the Guermantes *matinée* that the narrator gains the confidence necessary to begin a literary work. Why would Marcel, lacking faith in himself and, much of the time, in art, undertake this immense project of reminiscence without the encouragements and justifications discovered only in the Prince de Guermantes's library? And *is* the work no longer a "search," and the last chapter no longer a "revelation" if we assume that we have just read the book the narrator speaks of beginning to write in *Le Temps retrouvé*? The dramatic quality of the narrative does not seem to me to depend on the narrator's not having yet reached the conclusions of the last volume. Both the search *and* the revelation are, in fact, in the act of writing itself and are, therefore, a continuous part of our reading experience. The discoveries of the Guermantes *matinée* are a kind of theoretical appendix to the more exciting discovery, made throughout the work by both the narrator and the reader, of a style capable of unifying and individualizing an apparently meaningless and fragmentary life. There is no "other" work not yet written because by writing, as I have tried to show, the narrator learns to transform and, largely, to resolve the conflicts and the anguish that explain the urgency and even the sacred character that literary activity has for him. Proust's narrative is constantly dramatic in the sense that it does not merely record the anxieties and disappointments of Marcel's life, but provides at every moment the instruments of combat that transform a discouragingly alien world into the substance of a self-affirmation. It is, therefore, the work we have been reading that reveals to the narrator and the reader how, exactly, the fiction of remembering can be a way to exploit the full creativity of fiction, that is, the possibilities it offers for self-creation.

The narrator's memory of the failures in his life therefore includes a certain sense of the insignificance of these failures; his work allows him to exploit resourcefully the frustrations of the past. When he writes, the gap between imagination and reality no longer causes him the same pain as in the past: in the novel the daydreams have as much weight as the reality, and reality is reduced to a purely verbal existence. He is, apparently, being faithful to his past in presenting his fantasies as fantasies; we are constantly reminded that imagination distorts reality, and in the novel the "real" Madame de Guermantes and the "real" Albertine correct or at least qualify Marcel's images of them. Several incidents support what has now become a philosophical generalization about the impossibility of our ever knowing what is different from ourselves. "Man is the creature that cannot emerge from himself, that knows his fellows only in himself; when he asserts the contrary, he is lying." [5] And yet it is precisely in making this point that the narrator manages to convince us that he is capable of reporting accurately on the external world. For in order to emphasize the extent to which he was incapable of finding in the world a reality that was not essentially a reflection of himself, he creates characters whose function it is to resist Marcel's fantasies about them. It is the presence of a "real" Madame de Guermantes that makes clear the extravagance of Marcel's early impressions of her, and even Albertine is a sufficiently distinct figure to make us aware that Marcel is pursuing a fantasy in his love for her. The novel thus unexpectedly illustrates the impossibility of getting outside of oneself by the most minute observation of a world impressively rich in dramatic variety. The act of writing reveals not only the particular techniques for reducing phenomena to a uniform, self-revealing style, but also the existence of a world that can now be safely detached from Marcel's mind. It is true that what engages his interest in a world that bored and disillusioned him when it did not make him suffer is most often the general patterns he discovers: snobbery and vanity become interesting objects of study in which the narrator recognizes with pleasure the laws of human behavior. And, as I have pointed out, the reader easily recognizes the general as that which is most characteristic of Marcel. But the emergence of the universal laws is most impressive when the appearances of behavior keep their diversity, and the narrator attempts to shape a world that would be monotonously uniform from material that he first presents as richly diversified. Moreover, the variety we find in the appearances of behavior is not only never wholly absorbed into the style of Marcel's perspective on society, or into the leveling perspectives of the general laws; the narrator himself becomes retrospectively interested in the very range of being in the external world which he either feared or despaired of knowing, or found not worth knowing, before his decision to write.

But by insisting on the inability of all men to penetrate the world outside of the self, the narrator necessarily raises questions in the reader's mind about the objective reality of the other characters in the book he writes. He has learned in his life that an authentically dramatic relationship with other people is impossible: his love for Albertine is really the pursuit of an elusive image of himself. And literature is the acceptance and resourceful use of that fact; it does not reveal anything about the nature of the world, but allows the writer to explore his own nature. Whereas earlier novelists attempt to create the illusion that the world they are describing is as objectively real as the world of the reader's daily experience, Proust has his narrator continually point out that in literature the writer willingly—and even joyfully—does what we cannot help but do in life: he substitutes a world of fantasy for the impenetrable world of external reality. And since we usually see Marcel fantasize about people before he meets them, we are trained to accept his characterizations as exercises in self-projections. By remembering in detail the way his imagination constantly distorted reality, he therefore makes it difficult for himself to write a book in which we would easily accept the distinction between the narrator and the other characters. The very point of Proust's novel would seem to be to destroy the illusions novelists usually seek to cultivate.

The narrator himself presents his work both as a faithful report on his past and as an exercise of pure invention. He speaks of his book as one "in which there is not one fact that is not imaginary, nor any real person concealed under a false name, where everything has been invented by me to meet the needs of my story," [6] but he is also obviously encouraging us to believe that he is remembering a past which involuntary memory has recently allowed him to relive long after he had abandoned it as dead. In his theoretical remarks the narrator tends to define the writer as a "translator" of realities that exist first of all outside his book: ". . . to write that essential book, the only true book, a great writer does not need to invent it, in the current sense of the term, since it already exists in each one of us, but merely to translate it. The duty and the task of a writer are those of a translator." [7] But in the same way that Marcel's description of the towers of Martinville and Vieuxvicq gives to an external scene a character that exists only in that description, the imaginative processes that enter into the narrator's remembering of his past create a past inseparable from the act of memory. With individual objects, with people, and with events, the narrator attempts both to convince us of their existence in the past as objective realities independent of his imagination, and also to transform them now into images and allegorical representations of the self. We thus have simultaneously a chronological account of different real moments in his life, and a kind of demonstration of the narrator's ability to *imagine* a past—one that would be completely defined by his creative capacities at the moment of writing. The ambiguity in his contradictory statements that he is writing about his own life and that he has invented everything in his work is not satisfactorily resolved by attributing the first statement to Marcel and the second to Proust. The two points of view become intelligible if we realize that it is only by inventing his past that he can write about himself. The world is remembered in all its otherness; but from the perspective of memory the otherness is contained in Marcel's mind, and changing the facts of his past into novelistic material is a way of changing his images of the world into metaphors for his individuality. The "désir premier" that most profoundly characterizes the narrator is not to be found in the recurrence of favorite metaphors (and it has seemed to me unnecessary to determine statistically what his preferred images are), but rather in the constant effort we recognize in his writing to make every aspect of his experience enter into a metaphorical relation with every other aspect. His ambition is to portray a world in which nothing resists the imagination, in which every object of description has the depth, the *soubassement* of other objects with which it naturally suggests analogies. In this way his own work has the "transparent unity" which Proust defined as the "absolute beauty" of great works of art: ". . . all things, having lost their original appearance as things, are now lined up alongside of one another in a kind of order and penetrated with the same light; everything can be seen through everything else, and not a single word resists or escapes from this assimilation." [8]

It is perhaps only after feeling that the narrator's powers of realistic observation successfully give the lie to his pessimistic theory of the imprisoned self that we realize that, in spite of great diversity in the world he describes, it does, after all, reflect his own psychology. The people he has known repeat, subtly but nonetheless faithfully, his own psychological patterns. But Madame de Guermantes and Swann and Saint-Loup do not express the narrator's psychology in the same way as his first fantasies about them. There is, between the two characterizations of Oriane, for example, all the distance between fantasy as a kind of richly ornamented wish satisfaction and fantasy as an almost impersonal objectification not merely of conscious desires, but of the most profound levels of an individual point of view on the world. It is possible to find that this objectification is never completely convincing in Proust, but, if this is so, what might ordinarily be considered as a creative defect actually sharpens our awareness of different aspects of the creative process. Precisely because the various parts of his novelistic world hesitate between dramatic distinctness and allegorical representations of the narrator's psychology, his work illustrates a passionate and often desperate struggle of the imagination to create for itself a world as convincing as the "other" world, one that would both surprise and appease the anxious self.

NOTES

Introduction

1. Marcel Proust, *Remembrance of Things Past*, tr. C. K. Scott Moncrieff and, for *Le Temps retrouvé*, Frederick A. Blossom, 2 vols. (New York, copyright 1924, 1925, 1927, 1929, 1930, 1932 and renewed by Random House, Inc.; reprinted by permission), II, 1017; Proust, *Le Temps retrouvé*, in *A la Recherche du temps perdu*, ed. Pierre Clarac and Andre Ferré, 3 vols. (Paris, 1954), III, 900–901.

This study is, of course, based on my readings of Proust in French; since, however, many English-speaking readers are familiar with his work through the Moncrieff-Blossom translation, I have decided to use that translation as much as possible for the passages I quote from the novel. For the convenience of readers who know *A la Recherche* in the original, I shall be giving the reference to the French edition immediately after each reference to the Random House edition. I have chosen to keep the French titles of the various volumes of the novel; the English equivalents are: *Du Côté de chez Swann—Swann's Way, A l'Ombre des jeunes filles en fleur—Within a Budding Grove, Le Côté de Guermantes—The Guermantes Way, Sodome et Gomorrhe—Cities of the Plain, La Prisonnière—The Captive, La Fugitive—The Sweet Cheat Gone, Le Temps retrouvé —The Past Recaptured*.

There are passages in the 1954 edition of *A la Recherche du temps perdu* which Moncrieff and Blossom, working with the Nouvelle Revue Française text published from 1919 to 1927, could not include in their translation. Clarac and Ferré, for reasons explained in their notes, have made changes in other passages which are present in both of the French editions. I have therefore translated passages not in the Random House edition and, occasionally, have changed that translation to make it correspond more closely to the latest French edition. I have also provided translations of my own when I have not agreed with Moncrieff's or Blossom's reading of the text. All the passages I have translated are bracketed, and in each case I show briefly in a note why I have not followed Moncrieff or Blossom. From time to time I have also included phrases from the French text; there are, inevitably, spots where no translation can adequately render the sense and suggestiveness of the original.

251

All the English translations from Proust's other works as well as from all the French works I refer to are my own; the reference in each case is to the French edition of the work.

2. *Lecture de Proust*, in *L'Usage de la lecture*, III (Paris, 1963), 21. Picon's book was published after the greater part of my own study of Proust had been written; our analyses of *A la Recherche*, as the following study will make clear, have several points in common.

3. A further distinction could, of course, be made between the narrator and Marcel. (See especially Louis Martin-Chauffier, "Proust et le double 'je' de quatre personnes," *Confluences*, III [juillet-août 1943], 55–69.) Since, as I shall show, the narrator re-creates his past in the process of remembering it, it would seem important to distinguish between Marcel before he writes his book and the narrator who is now writing. I shall, therefore, generally be referring to *Marcel's* experience in the past and the *narrator's* present perspective on that experience, but the point of this distinction would be lost if it were applied too rigorously. The revision of the past which literature allows is dramatically interesting precisely because of the narrator's urgent need to resolve tensions that were apparently unresolvable before he began his work; the distinction between him and Marcel is a continuous achievement of the act of writing.

4. I, 1002; *Le Côté de Guermantes*, II, 397.

5. I shall be using the word "fantasy" to refer to a wide range of inventiveness, to designate not only an irrational fear of being deprived of the self, but also Marcel's images of Madame de Guermantes and Albertine before he meets them and, finally, the novelist's world of imaginary characters and situations. It is, of course, necessary to distinguish between obsessive fantasies that dominate a personality and the richly inventive play of an artist's imagination. But Proust's narrator impressively demonstrates, as I shall show, the novelistic potentialities of apparently limiting and sterile anxieties; his work provides a context in which these anxieties are creatively exploited, but it does not provide an escape from psychology. I shall naturally be making important distinctions between different kinds of fantasies, but my general use of the word should help to underline the psychological continuity among the various aspects of Marcel's imaginative activity.

6. "Quelques aspects nouveaux de la critique littéraire en France," *Filología moderna*, I (abril 1961), 3. I obviously am not presenting the following remarks as an adequate appraisal of contemporary French criticism, and I might add that—especially after struggling with the translations that appear in the Introduction—I am fully aware of how easily a reader accustomed to an Anglo-Saxon critical tradition may be put off by the extravagant language the writers I mention tend to use.

7. *L'Univers imaginaire de Mallarmé* (Paris, 1961), p. 24.

8. Jean-Paul Sartre, *Baudelaire*, in *Les Essais*, XXIV (Paris), 20 and 31.

9. *Des Métaphores obsédantes au mythe personnel: Introduction à la psychocritique* (Paris, 1963), pp. 13, 23, 194–5.

10. *L'Eau et les rêves* (Paris, 1942), *L'Air et les songes* (Paris, 1950), *La Terre et les rêveries de la volonté* (Paris, 1948), *La Terre et les rêveries du repos* (Paris, 1948), *La Psychanalyse du feu* (Paris, 1938).

11. Mauron, in his discussion of Bachelard and thematic criticism, pp. 26–30, writes: "The similarity to psychoanalytic ways of thinking is more or less apparent, but the science itself remains absent or unacknowledged; unconscious processes are ignored as such and ambiguity sets in. Psychologically, what are these themes? At what level are they formed? Do they belong to the author or to the critic? What does such an analysis offer us an image of? If it were the image of a writer's total consciousness, I would understand what disturbs Jean Pommier, who can no longer recognize in the mind being described either normal structures or normal contents. But the image will not satisfy a psychoanalyst either if it is meant to describe a human unconscious. The level being explored still seems to be that of an incipient and confused consciousness; and the investigation itself, which is purely introspective, makes no use of the mental contexts and tools of classical criticism, without benefiting from those which psychoanalysis could furnish or suggest."

12. *Etudes sur le temps humain* (Paris, 1950), pp. 364–404; and *L'Espace proustien* (Paris, 1963).

13. *Mallarmé*, p. 599.

14. *Jean-Jacques Rousseau: La Transparence et l'obstacle* (Paris, 1957).

15. Richard, "Quelques aspects nouveaux," p. 6.

16. *Michelet par lui-même*, in *Ecrivains de toujours*, XIX (Paris, 1954), 5 and 180–81.

17. Mauron, p. 343.

18. *Mallarmé*, p. 32.

19. (Paris, 1954), pp. 162 and 218.

20. *Mallarmé*, p. 28.

21. *La Poétique de la rêverie* (Paris, 1960), p. 4.

22. *Faux pas* (Paris, 1943), p. 212.

23. Richard, "Quelques aspects nouveaux," and Bonnefoy, "La Critique anglo-saxonne et la critique française," *Preuves*, No. 95 (janvier 1959), pp. 68–73. See also Jean Pommier, "Baudelaire et Michelet devant la jeune critique," *Revue d'histoire littéraire de la France*, LVII (octobre-décembre 1957), 544–64.

24. *L'Ecrivain et son ombre* (Paris, 1953), pp. 70 and 31.

25. *Contre Sainte-Beuve*, suivi de *Nouveaux mélanges* (Paris, 1954), pp. 136–7. The Sainte-Beuve passage is from "Esquisse d'une méthode," *Nouveaux lundis*.

26. *Marcel Proust: A Biography* (London, 1959), p. xii.

27. See Justin O'Brien, "Albertine the Ambiguous: Notes on Proust's Transposition of Sexes," *PMLA*, LXIV (December 1949), 933–52. Harry Levin, in a brief comment on this article in "Proust, Gide, and the Sexes," *PMLA*, LXV (June 1950), 648–52, points out that a change

in Albertine's sex introduces more difficulties than it settles, and that, in any case, the effect of narrative art depends on our accepting the novelist's characters and situations as he presents them.

28. See Proust's early letters to the Comte de Montesquiou for a disheartening example of his capacities for shameless flattery (*Lettres à Robert de Montesquiou, 1893–1921*, in *Correspondance générale de Marcel Proust*, ed. Robert Proust and Paul Brach, I [Paris, 1930]).

29. The irritability that seems to have alternated with Proust's extreme devotion to his mother can be seen in some of his letters to her. Toward the end of 1902, for example, he writes: "The truth is that as soon as I am feeling well, the kind of life that is necessary for my good health exasperates you and you demolish everything until I am ill again. . . . But it is sad not to be able to have affection and health at the same time" (*Marcel Proust: Correspondance avec sa mère, 1887–1905*, ed. Philip Kolb [Paris, 1953], p. 204).

30. (Paris, 1953), p. 20.

31. "Proust et le double 'je' de quatre personnes."

32. *The Gates of Horn: A Study of Five French Realists* (New York, 1963).

Chapter One—FANTASIES OF THE SELF AND THE WORLD

1. I, 5; *Du Côté de chez Swann*, I, 5.

2. Not in edition Moncrieff used; *La Fugitive*, III, 466.

3. I, 5; *Du Côté de chez Swann*, I, 5–6.

4. I, 5–6; *Du Côté de chez Swann*, I, 5–7.

5. See especially Chapter IX in *L'Espace proustien*.

6. II, 69; *Sodome et Gomorrhe*, II, 694.

7. II, 837; *La Fugitive*, III, 651–2. Bracketed passage not in edition Moncrieff used.

Proust uses "sentiment" twice in the first sentence of this passage; since I discuss this as a stylistic peculiarity, it has seemed best not to translate the word and to keep the repetition.

8. II, 837–8; III, *La Fugitive*, 652–3.

9. II, 1039; *Le Temps retrouvé*, III, 931.

10. Involuntary memory, the narrator writes, frees us from the effects of the "law" according to which we can imagine only what is absent; the sensations accompanying an involuntary memory are experienced both by the senses in the present and, because these sensations come from the past, by the imagination (II, 996; *Le Temps retrouvé*, III, 872).

11. I, 85–86; *Du Côté de chez Swann*, I, 112.

12. *Etudes sur le temps humain*, pp. 385–6.

13. There are anecdotes about Proust's extraordinary absorption in certain objects; Reynaldo Hahn, for example, describes his sudden "absence," during one of their walks, in front of a rosebush, which Proust stared at for several moments with a devouring attention ("Promenade," *Hommage à Proust*, in *Les Cahiers Marcel Proust*, I [Paris, 1927], 33–4).

14. II, 839; *La Fugitive*, III, 654–5. Bracketed passage not in edition Moncrieff used.

15. I, 141; *Du Côté de chez Swann*, I, 184. Moncrieff translates "je croyais aux choses" as "I used to think of certain things."

16. I, 64; *Du Côté de chez Swann*, I, 84.

17. I, 293; *Du Côté de chez Swann*, I, 384.

18. I, 369; *A l'Ombre des jeunes filles en fleur*, I, 481–2.

19. I, 63; *Du Côté de chez Swann*, I, 84. The narrator speaks of his thoughts as forming "une autre crèche au fond de laquelle je sentais que je restais enfoncé," which Moncrieff translates as "a similar sort of hiding-hole, in the depths of which I felt that I could bury myself and remain invisible." This translation, it seems to me, emphasizes too strongly the idea—certainly implicit in the word "crèche"—of a deliberate and enjoyable retreat from the external world; the sense of pain and frustration, which is at least as important here, is thus lost.

20. I, 507; *A l'Ombre des jeunes filles en fleur*, I, 667–8.

21. I, 8; *Du Côté de chez Swann*, I, 10.

22. I, 693–4; *A l'Ombre des jeunes filles en fleur*, I, 926.

23. I, 308; *Du Côté de chez Swann*, I, 403–4.

24. I, 107; *Du Côté de chez Swann*, I, 139–40.

25. I, 129; *Du Côté de chez Swann*, I, 167–8; and Pommier, *La Mystique de Marcel Proust* (Paris, 1939), pp. 52–3.

26. I, 65–6; *Du Côté de chez Swann*, I, 86–7.

27. I, 500–502; *A l'Ombre des jeunes filles en fleur*, I, 658–60.

28. But, as Picon points out, the Idea in Proust, while it is extratemporal, is always an individual reality; and beauty is located in a personal vision of the world, not, as in Plato and Plotinus, in a general model behind individual expression (*Proust*, pp. 175–6).

29. I, 505; *A l'Ombre des jeunes filles en fleur*, I, 666.

30. I, 506–7; *A l'Ombre des jeunes filles en fleur*, I, 666–7.

31. *Proust* (New York, 1931), p. 8.

32. I, 23; *Du Côté de chez Swann*, I, 30.

33. I, 24; *Du Côté de chez Swann*, I, 31.

34. II, 483; *La Prisonnière*, III, 150–51.

35. I, 119–22; *Du Côté de chez Swann*, I, 155–9. Moncrieff, incidentally, gives "damn" for the untranslatable "zut."

36. I, 140–41; *Du Côté de chez Swann*, I, 183.

37. II, 1122; *Le Temps retrouvé*, III, 1044.

38. II, 122–4; *Sodome et Gomorrhe*, II, 769–71.

39. 3 vols. (Paris, 1952), I, 105–6.

40. II, 800; *La Fugitive*, III, 594.

41. Poulet is especially good in analyzing what he calls the "general principle of discontinuity" in Proust (*L'Espace proustien*, pp. 56ff.).

42. II, 1123; *Le Temps retrouvé*, III, 1047.

43. II, 1116–17; *Le Temps retrouvé*, III, 1037–9.

44. II, 1119; *Le Temps retrouvé*, III, 1041–2. Blossom translates "l'amitié des gens" as "the unfriendliness of people."

45. II, 1120; *Le Temps retrouvé*, III, 1042.

46. II, 1123; *Le Temps retrouvé*, III, 1047.

47. II, 1115; *Le Temps retrouvé*, III, 1036.

48. A certain dread in front of his own strength is suggested in one of Proust's letters to Antoine Bibesco: "I had made my intelligence a slave to my tranquillity. When I undid its chains I thought I was only freeing a slave, but I have given myself a master, one whom I do not have the physical strength to satisfy and who would kill me if I did not resist him" (*Lettres de Marcel Proust à Bibesco* [Lausanne, 1949], p. 132). Dr. Milton L. Miller has linked "the self-sacrificing cultivation of his genius" to Proust's need for approval: he will be loved only if he can convince someone else of his weakness (*Nostalgia: A Psychoanalytic Study of Marcel Proust* [Boston, 1956], pp. 168–9). The real strength necessary to write his work therefore tends to be described as if it were a foreign presence in his body; Proust himself would be only the helpless victim of this terrible invader. The idea that he can be loved only if he is injured in some way is, of course, obvious in the letter to his mother from which I have quoted in footnote 29 in the Introduction.

Chapter Two—THE ANGUISH AND INSPIRATION OF JEALOUSY

1. I, 543; *A l'Ombre des jeunes filles en fleur*, I, 716–17.

2. II, 441; *La Prisonnière*, III, 92.

3. I, 595–9; *A l'Ombre des jeunes filles en fleur*, I, 788–94.

4. I, 605; *A l'Ombre des jeunes filles en fleur*, I, 801–2.

5. I, 616–17; *A l'Ombre des jeunes filles en fleur*, I, 818.

6. II, 649; *La Prisonnière*, III, 385.

7. II, 12–13; *Sodome et Gomorrhe*, II, 614.

8. II, 208; *Sodome et Gomorrhe*, II, 892.

9. II, 745; *La Fugitive*, III, 516.

10. *Sur Proust: Remarques sur "A la Recherche du temps perdu"* (Paris, 1960), p. 198.

11. I, 23; *Du Côté de chez Swann*, I, 30.

12. II, 953; *Le Temps retrouvé*, III, 812.

13. II, 687; *La Fugitive*, III, 435.

14. I, 85–6; *Du Côté de chez Swann*, I, 112.

15. II, 771–2; *La Fugitive*, III, 555–6. Bracketed passage not in edition used by Moncrieff.

16. II, 765; *La Fugitive*, III, 546.
17. *La Fugitive*, III, 550–51. None of this passage is in the 1925 edition of *Albertine disparue*.
18. II, 765; *La Fugitive*, III, 546.
19. II, 649; *La Prisonnière*, III, 385.
20. II, 745–6; *La Fugitive*, III, 517.
21. I, 552; *A l'Ombre des jeunes filles en fleur*, I, 729.
22. I, 833; *Le Côté de Guermantes*, II, 164–5.
23. I, 841–4; *Le Côté de Guermantes*, II, 177–80.
24. I, 838; *Le Côté de Guermantes*, II, 172–3.
25. I, 843; *Le Côté de Guermantes*, II, 179.
26. II, 307–8; *Sodome et Gomorrhe*, II, 1032–4.
27. II, 221; *Sodome et Gomorrhe*, II, 910.
28. II, 413; *La Prisonnière*, III, 51.
29. II, 531; *La Prisonnière*, III, 217–18.
30. II, 529–30; *La Prisonnière*, III, 214–15.
31. II, 453; *La Prisonnière*, III, 106.
32. II, 477; *La Prisonnière*, III, 141.
33. II, 426–8; *La Prisonnière*, III, 70–73. The bracketed passage, which is in the early French edition, is not translated by Moncrieff.
34. I, 979–80; *Le Côté de Guermantes*, II, 365–6.
35. II, 426–7; *La Prisonnière*, III, 70–72.
36. II, 418; *La Prisonnière*, III, 59. See also II, 494; *La Prisonnière*, III, 165.
37. Brasillach, *Portraits* (Paris, 1935), p. 81; Brée, *Du Temps perdu au temps retrouvé: Introduction à l'oeuvre de Marcel Proust*, in *Études françaises*, XLIV (Paris, 1950), 84.
38. I, 186.
39. I, 713; *A l'Ombre des jeunes filles en fleur*, I, 953.
40. II, 395–6; *La Prisonnière*, III, 26–7.
41. "Qu'est-ce que la littérature?" *Situations*, II (Paris, 1948), pp. 101–2.
42. (Paris, 1957.)
43. II, 1028; *Le Temps retrouvé*, III, 916–17.
44. I, 64; *Du Côté de chez Swann*, I, 85.

Chapter Three—THE LANGUAGE OF LOVE

1. II, 685; *La Fugitive*, III, 433. Moncrieff translates "tels hasards" as "similar mishaps."
2. "Le temps, la distance et la forme chez Marcel Proust," *Hommage à Marcel Proust*, p. 293.
3. *Oeuvres complètes de Jean-Jacques Rousseau*, ed. Bernard Gagnebin and Marcel Raymond, II (Paris, 1961), 91.
4. II, 685; *La Fugitive*, III, 432–3.
5. II, 709; *La Fugitive*, III, 465.

6. *La Fugitive*, III, 626. This sentence is not in the edition Moncrieff used.

7. II, 769; *La Fugitive*, III, 552.

8. I, 627; *A l'Ombre des jeunes filles en fleur*, I, 833.

9. I, 670–71; *A l'Ombre des jeunes filles en fleur*, I, 894–5.

10. II, 1014; *Le Temps retrouvé*, III, 896.

11. II, 375; *Sodome et Gomorrhe*, II, 1127.

12. *L'Etre et le néant: Essai d'ontologie phénoménologique* (Paris, 1943), pp. 431ff.; see also "La Transcendance de l'ego," *Recherches philosophiques*, VI (1936–37), 85–123.

13. *La Fugitive*, III, 466. This passage is not in the early French edition.

14. *Par les Chemins de Marcel Proust: Essai de critique descriptive* (Neufchâtel, 1955), p. 91.

15. I, 98–9; *Du Côté de chez Swann*, I, 128–9.

16. I, 644; *A l'Ombre des jeunes filles en fleur*, I, 857.

17. II, 166; *Sodome et Gomorrhe*, II, 831–2. Here is Proust's sentence: "Du reste, dans cette oscillation rythmée qui va de la déclaration à la brouille (le plus sûr moyen, le plus efficacement dangereux pour former, par mouvements opposés et successifs, un noeud qui ne se défasse pas et nous attache solidement à une personne), au sein du mouvement de retrait qui constitue l'un des deux éléments du rythme, à quoi bon distinguer encore les reflux de la pitié humaine, qui, opposés à l'amour, quoique ayant peut-être inconsciemment la même cause, produisent en tous cas les mêmes effets?" Moncrieff dislocates the sentence and thus misses the objection against setting up superfluous mental states to account for behavior: "However, in that rhythmical oscillation which leads from a declaration to a quarrel (the surest, the most certainly perilous way of forming by opposite and successive movements a knot which will not be loosed and attaches us firmly to a person by the strain of the movement of withdrawal which constitutes one of the two elements of the rhythm), of what use is it to analyze further the refluences of human pity, which, the opposite of love, though springing perhaps unconsciously from the same cause, produces in every case the same effects?"

18. II, 709; *La Fugitive*, III, 465.

19. II, 366–7; *Sodome et Gomorrhe*, II, 1114–15. For another suggestion of the matricidal fantasy hinted at in this passage, see the article Proust wrote after learning that Henri van Blarenberghe had killed his mother: "Sentiments filiaux d'un parricide," *Pastiches et mélanges*, in *Oeuvres complètes de Marcel Proust*, VIII (Paris, 1933), 211–24.

20. I, 23–4; *Du Côté de chez Swann*, I, 30.

21. II, 453 and 628–9; *La Prisonnière*, III, 107 and 353.

22. II, 188; *Sodome et Gomorrhe*, II, 862. Moncrieff translates "les traits familiaux" as "our characteristic features."

23. II, 1020; *Le Temps retrouvé*, III, 905. Blossom gives only "one can win release from suffering" for "on sort de la constatation d'une souffrance."

24. II, 367; *Sodome et Gomorrhe*, II, 1115.
25. II, 376; *Sodome et Gomorrhe*, II, 1128.
26. *Essais sur le roman*, in *Les Essais*, LXXX (Paris, 1956), 96–8.
27. *L'Etre et le néant*, pp. 216–17.
28. I, 233–4; *Du Côté de chez Swann*, I, 304.
29. II, 696; *La Fugitive*, III, 448.
30. II, 748; *La Fugitive*, III, 521.
31. II, 774ff.; *La Fugitive*, III, 559ff.
32. II, 367; *Sodome et Gomorrhe*, II, 1116.
33. "La Transcendance de l'ego," pp. 102–3.
34. II, 733–6; *La Fugitive*, III, 499–504.
35. II, 650–51; *La Prisonnière*, III, 387.
36. I, 595; *A l'Ombre des jeunes filles en fleur*, I, 788.
37. I, 624; *A l'Ombre des jeunes filles en fleur*, I, 829–30.
38. Brée, p. 113.
39. II, 752–3; *La Fugitive*, III, 527–8. Moncrieff's version of the bracketed passage ("Now I saw her by the side of the laundress, girls by the water's edge") corresponds to the French in the 1925 edition.
40. I, 625; *A l'Ombre des jeunes filles en fleur*, I, 830.

Chapter Four—SOCIAL CONTEXTS: OBSERVATION AND INVENTION

1. I, 135; *Du Côté de chez Swann*, I, 176.
2. I, 132–3; *Du Côté de chez Swann*, I, 171. Bracketed words not in edition used by Moncrieff.
3. I, 743; *Le Côté de Guermantes*, II, 42. Moncrieff translates "la valeur conventionnelle d'une écriture" as "the conventional value of a written document."
4. I, 255; *Du Côté de chez Swann*, I, 332.
5. I, 256–7; *Du Côté de chez Swann*, I, 334–5.
6. The "Génie" of the family is analyzed in I, 1032ff.; *Le Côté de Guermantes*, II, 439ff.
7. II, 572; *La Prisonnière*, III, 276.
8. *The Magic Lantern of Marcel Proust* (New York, 1962), pp. 81–2.
9. I, 740; *Le Côté de Guermantes*, II, 38.
10. I, 744; *Le Côté de Guermantes*, II, 43.
11. I, 744; *Le Côté de Guermantes*, II, 43.
12. I, 745–8; *Le Côté de Guermantes*, II, 45–9.
13. I, 1069–70; *Le Côté de Guermantes*, II, 494–5.
14. I, 1096; *Le Côté de Guermantes*, II, 532.
15. I, 1103; *Le Côté de Guermantes*, II, 542–3.
16. I, 1103; *Le Côté de Guermantes*, II, 542.
17. I, 1070; *Le Côté de Guermantes*, II, 495.
18. I, 1103; *Le Côté de Guermantes*, II, 542–3.

19. II, 881; *Le Temps retrouvé*, III, 709.

20. II, 888; *Le Temps retrouvé*, III, 718–19.

21. II, 888; *Le Temps retrouvé*, III, 718.

22. II, 577–8; *La Prisonnière*, III, 284–5. Moncrieff translates "des fragments d'un monde détruit qu'on croyait voir ailleurs" as "fragments of a vanished world which seemed to extend round about them."

23. II, 579; *La Prisonnière*, III, 286. Moncrieff translates "leur double spirituel" as "an astral body."

24. I, 1099; *Le Côté de Guermantes*, II, 537.

25. *Par les Chemins de Marcel Proust*, p. 107.

26. I, 11–12; *Du Côté de chez Swann*, I, 14–15.

27. II, 113ff.; *Sodome et Gomorrhe*, II, 755ff.

28. I, 719; *Le Côté de Guermantes*, II, 9.

29. I, 342; *A l'Ombre des jeunes filles en fleur*, I, 445–6.

30. II, 161–2; *Sodome et Gomorrhe*, II, 825.

31. I, 937; *Le Côté de Guermantes*, II, 310. Moncrieff translates "pour lire ses journaux en faisant ses petits besoins" as "to read his papers and do his little jobs."

32. I, 940; *Le Côté de Guermantes*, II, 314.

33. II, 205ff.; *Sodome et Gomorrhe*, II, 887ff.

34. II, 925; *Le Temps retrouvé*, III, 772–3.

35. I, 514–15; *A l'Ombre des jeunes filles en fleur*, I, 678–9. Moncrieff translates "la cloison de ses habitudes" as "the barrier of her private life."

36. I, 1072; *Le Côté de Guermantes*, II, 498.

37. II, 78; *Sodome et Gomorrhe*, II, 706.

38. I, 1116; *Le Côté de Guermantes*, II, 561.

39. I, 1105; *Le Côté de Guermantes*, II, 545–6. Moncrieff gives merely "intense" for "anxieuse."

40. II, 573; *La Prisonnière*, III, 278.

41. I, 901–2; *Le Côté de Guermantes*, II, 259–60.

42. II, 926–7; *Le Temps retrouvé*, III, 773–5.

43. II, 633–4; *La Prisonnière*, III, 361–2.

44. II, 439; *La Prisonnière*, III, 88.

45. II, 624; *La Prisonnière*, III, 347. Moncrieff translates "revirements" as "revulsions of feelings."

46. II, 972; *Le Temps retrouvé*, III, 839–40.

47. "La Vie sociale dans l'oeuvre de Marcel Proust," in Charles Daudet, *Repertoire des personnages de "A la Recherche du temps perdu,"* in *Les Cahiers Marcel Proust*, II (Paris, 1927), xii.

48. II, 969; *Le Temps retrouvé*, III, 833–4.

49. I, 1126; *Le Côté de Guermantes*, II, 575.

50. I, 1139–41; *Le Côté de Guermantes*, II, 595–7.

51. II, 13; *Sodome et Gomorrhe*, II, 615.

52. II, 967–8; *Le Temps retrouvé*, III, 835–6.

53. II, 1032–3; *Le Temps retrouvé*, III, 922–3. In the 1954 edition we read: "ce que peut être devenu l'insecte le plus rapide, le plus sûr en

ses traits." The 1927 edition of *Le Temps retrouvé* (pp. 86–7 in the second volume) has a more confused version—"ce que peut être devenu le plus rapide, le plus sûr en ses traits d'un insecte"—which Blossom translates as "the swift and certain evolution of the characteristics of an insect."

54. II, 1037; *Le Temps retrouvé*, III, 928. Blossom translates "je vis se superposer" as "I saw in imagination."

55. II, 1044; *Le Temps retrouvé*, III, 938.

56. II, 1058; *Le Temps retrouvé*, III, 957.

57. II, 1057; *Le Temps retrouvé*, III, 993.

58. II, 153; *Sodome et Gomorrhe*, II, 813.

59. II, 217–18; *Sodome et Gomorrhe*, II, 904–6.

60. I, 1015; *Le Côté de Guermantes*, II, 416.

61. I, 247–8; *Du Côté de chez Swann*, I, 322.

62. *Marcel Proust: Sa Vie, son oeuvre* (Paris, 1935), p. 281.

63. I, 248; *Du Côté de chez Swann*, I, 323.

64. I, 324; *Du Côté de chez Swann*, I, 426.

65. I, 552; *A l'Ombre des jeunes filles en fleur*, I, 728–9.

66. I, 736; *Le Côté de Guermantes*, II, 32.

67. *The Contemporary French Novel* (New York, 1955), p. 77.

68. Revel, p. 223.

69. See, for example, Charlus's remarks about World War I: II, 941–3; *Le Temps retrouvé*, III, 796–9.

70. I, 206 (see also p. 186 in the same volume); *Du Côté de chez Swann*, I, 268 and 242.

71. I, 67 (see also p. 82 in the same volume); *Sodome et Gomorrhe*, II, 690 and 712.

72. I, 883; *Le Côté de Guermantes*, II, 234.

73. *Proust*, pp. 60–61.

74. I, 392; *A l'Ombre des jeunes filles en fleur*, I, 513.

75. *The Maxims of Marcel Proust* (New York, 1948).

76. II, 420; *La Prisonnière*, III, 61.

77. II, 698; *La Fugitive*, III, 450.

78. II, 680; *La Fugitive*, III, 425.

79. II, 497; *La Prisonnière*, III, 170.

80. "The Nature of the Novel," tr. Evelyn Rugby and Diego Marín, *The Hudson Review*, X (Spring 1957), 39.

81. Levin, pp. 50–51 and 25.

82. II, 429 and 488; *La Prisonnière*, III, 75 and 157.

83. I, 15; *Du Côté de chez Swann*, I, 19.

84. II, 1114; *Le Temps retrouvé*, III, 1034–5.

Chapter Five—MARCEL'S VOCATION

1. I, 1002; *Le Côté de Guermantes*, II, 397.

2. I, 71–2; *Du Côté de chez Swann*, I, 94.

3. I, 420; *A l'Ombre des jeunes filles en fleur*, I, 550.

4. I, 264–70, and II, 553–61; *Du Côté de chez Swann*, I, 345–53, and *La Prisonnière*, III, 249–61.

5. II, 557–8; *La Prisonnière*, III, 255–6.

6. II, 643–4; *La Prisonnière*, III, 375–7. The bracketed passage is not in edition used by Moncrieff.

7. II, 490; *La Prisonnière*, III, 159.

8. II, 641; *La Prisonnière*, III, 372.

9. I, 405; *A l'Ombre des jeunes filles en fleur*, I, 530.

10. In his discussion of Elstir's painting, Proust was undoubtedly thinking of Monet rather than Cézanne, with whose work he seems to have been unfamiliar. In a letter to Jacques-Emile Blanche on January 25, 1919, he speaks of "Cézanne, Degas, Renoir, painters of whom I have only a vague impression and whose works I would have been very anxious to know" (*Correspondance générale*, III [1932], 156). For a discussion of *A la Recherche du temps perdu* as a literary application of impressionistic principles and techniques, see Maurice E. Chernowitz, *Proust and Painting* (New York, 1945).

11. II, 785; *La Fugitive*, III, 573. In the 1925 edition of *Albertine disparue* (p. 194), we find: "Notre tort est de croire que les choses se présentent habituellement telles qu'elles sont en réalité," which Moncrieff translates as "Our mistake lies in our supposing that things present themselves ordinarily as they are in reality." The first part of this passage is "Notre tort est de presenter les choses" in the 1954 edition.

12. I, 496; *A l'Ombre des jeunes filles en fleur*, I, 653.

13. I, 631; *A l'Ombre des jeunes filles en fleur*, I, 838.

14. I, 628–30; *A l'Ombre des jeunes filles en fleur*, I, 835–8.

15. I, 425; *A l'Ombre des jeunes filles en fleur*, I, 558.

16. II, 559; *La Prisonnière*, III, 257–8.

17. II, 1001; *Le Temps retrouvé*, III, 880.

18. "External existence is not promised to books any more than to men" (II, 1120; *Le Temps retrouvé*, III, 1043).

19. I, 34; *Du Côté de chez Swann*, I, 45.

20. II, 995–6; *Le Temps retrouvé*, III, 871–2.

21. The interview can be found in Robert Dreyfus, *Souvenirs sur Marcel Proust*, in *Les Cahiers verts*, LXVIII (Paris, 1926), 285–92.

Unlike Freud, Proust is not interested in the processes by which certain memories and feelings become unconscious; his concern is mainly with the unconscious as an extension of being. And, as Germaine Brée has pointed out, Proust does not consider it as a center of repressed fantasies and anguished conflicts; it is rather of a spiritual nature and contains the "law" of our individuality (Brée, p. 231). The narrator does, however, also speak of an unconscious to which we relegate unflattering self-images or desires, and which we attempt—by no means successfully—to exclude from ordinary social discourse. Marcel, as I have pointed out, is particularly sensitive to those moments in life when impulses absent from our rational judgments of ourselves assert themselves. The attention he gives to the body as a revealer of character, for example, implies his sense of the strategies by which the unconscious defeats the simplifying and dignifying intentions of our conscious will. But essentially the unconscious is, for the narrator, much more than a kind of refuge for unacceptable impulses; it is what we express when we have our richest and most deeply personal impressions.

22. II, 1003; *Le Temps retrouvé*, III, 882.

23. II, 996–8; *Le Temps retrouvé*, III, 872–5.

24. II, 1013–14; *Le Temps retrouvé*, III, 895–6. The bracketed words are not in the 1927 edition.

25. II, 1015–16; *Le Temps retrouvé*, III, 898–9.

26. Blanchot, "Jean Santeuil (II)," *La Nouvelle nouvelle revue française*, No. 21 (septembre 1954), pp. 482–3; and *Jean Santeuil*, II, 229 and 233.

27. *Etudes sur le temps humain*, p. 380.

28. II, 558; *La Prisonnière*, III, 256.

29. II, 642; *La Prisonnière*, III, 374.

30. II, 1001; *Le Temps retrouvé*, III, 880.

31. *Contre Sainte-Beuve*, p. 209.

32. *Lettres à la Comtesse de Noailles, 1901–1919*, in *Correspondance générale*, II (1931), 86–7.

33. *Contre Sainte-Beuve*, pp. 207–9.

34. *Correspondance de Flaubert*, ed. René Descharmes, 4 vols. in the *Oeuvres complètes de Gustave Flaubert* (Paris, 1922–25), II, 28.

35. "A propos du 'style' de Flaubert," *Chroniques* (Paris, 1927), pp. 196–7.

36. Brasillach, pp. 99 and 113.

37. II, 992–3; *Le Temps retrouvé*, III, 867–8.

38. II, 1008–9; *Le Temps retrouvé*, III, 889. The narrator speaks of the relationship between two objects chosen by the writer as "analogue dans le monde de l'art à celui qu'est le rapport unique de la loi causale dans le monde de la science." In the 1927 edition, "de la loi causale" is set off by commas, which may explain Blossom's translation: "analogous in the world of art to the sole relationship in the world of science, the law of cause and effect." The narrator goes on to say that the writer creates a metaphor when, "en rapprochant une qualité commune à deux sensations, il dégagera leur essence commune en les réunissant l'une et l'autre . . . dans une métaphore." The early edition gives just "essence" instead of "essence commune." Blossom translates: "comparing similar qualities in two sensations, he makes their essential nature stand out clearly by joining them in a metaphor." Proust's sentence is not ideally clear, but, by making "qualité" plural, Blossom adds to the confusion: we no longer know whether the antecedent of "their" and "them" is "qualities" or "sensations."

39. I, 137; *Du Côté de chez Swann*, I, 179.

40. II, 1000; *Le Temps retrouvé*, III, 878.

41. "Invention d'un langage," *La Nouvelle revue française*, VII (septembre 1959), 500–513.
42. I, 139; *Du Côté de chez Swann*, I, 181.
43. Tadié, p. 512.
44. I, 139; *Du Côté de chez Swann*, I, 181–2.
45. Tadié, p. 511.
46. I, 106–7; *Du Côté de chez Swann*, I, 138–40.
47. I, 86–7; *Du Côté de chez Swann*, I, 113–14.
48. I, 77; *Du Côté de chez Swann*, I, 101–2.
49. II, 750; *La Fugitive*, III, 523.
50. II, 767; *La Fugitive*, III, 549.
51. II, 1021; *Le Temps retrouvé*, III, 906. "Oeuvre" is the last word in Proust's sentence; the pronoun "la" is used twice before we know the noun to which it refers. Blossom gives the noun at the very beginning of the passage I have bracketed ("comes and adds itself to our work to complete it"); my point about Proust's sentence therefore obviously requires a change in the structure of Blossom's sentence.
52. *L'Espace proustien*, p. 133.
53. *Proust et la musique du devenir* (Paris, 1960), p. 256.
54. I, 629–31; *A l'Ombre des jeunes filles en fleur*, I, 835–8.
55. *Proust*, Studies in Modern European Literature and Thought (New Haven, 1956), pp. 61–2.
56. II, 996; *Le Temps retrouvé*, III, 873.
57. II, 1021; *Le Temps retrouvé*, III, 907.
58. It is, of course, hazardous to speak of any consistent change of direction or style as the novel progresses. By comparing the proofs made by Grasset of the unpublished second volume of *A la Recherche* with the version published by Gallimard after World War I, Albert Feuillerat showed that there is a constant juxtaposition of passages written in different years. On the basis of differences he finds between Proust's early and late styles, Feuillerat then attempts, with the help of the table of contents Proust gave to Grasset, to discover what the third volume would have been. Feuillerat finds that the final version has become less poetic, has lost "all traces of velvety smoothness [velouté], of mystery, all musical qualities"; it is more intellectual and analytic than the early text, and the moral and psychological point of view is more pessimistic. Feuillerat deplores the change and complains of a lack of unity of tone: "The generalizations, the reasoning, the essays continually destroy the atmosphere, similar to a waking dream, which originally pervaded the novel, and the sensuously poetic passages which are still there from the early version are now only gray touches on the grayish background of abstract, often abstruse thought" (*Comment Marcel Proust a composé son roman* [New Haven, 1934], pp. 129–31 and 262).

Feuillerat's findings have, not unexpectedly, been challenged by critics who point to texts written years before *A la Recherche* was begun and in which the presumably later style is very much in evidence. (See especially André Maurois, *A la Recherche de Marcel Proust* [Paris,

1949], pp. 287–8.) But while Feuillerat's reconstruction of the original
third volume is obviously open to criticism, and although I do not share
his annoyance with the "later" Proust, his distinction between two different conceptions of the novel seems to me justifiable, and corresponds,
in a general way, to my own distinction between an impressionistic,
wholly subjective novel and a work of psychological and social analysis
and criticism.

59. *Proust*, p. 121.

60. William Stuart Bell, in *Proust's Nocturnal Muse* (New York
and London, 1962), has found numerous analogies between the characteristics of dreams as the narrator describes them and the form of *A la
Recherche*. Proust himself encouraged such comparisons: his narrator,
for example, writes that he will not disdain the aid of dreams—"this second muse, this nocturnal muse, who would occasionally assume the functions of the other"—in the composition of his work, and he mentions that
dreams have helped to convince him of "the purely mental character of
reality" (II, 1026; *Le Temps retrouvé*, III, 914). The analogy with
dreams accounts inadequately, I think, for Proust's literary achievement,
but his interest in dreams does provide further evidence of his concern
with a more general process of self-dramatization in which aspects of the
self are seen as pictures of the world.

Conclusion

1. "Nouvelles formes pour le roman," *Critique*, XIII (août-septem-
bre 1957), 710.

2. "A propos du 'style' de Flaubert," pp. 196–7.

3. *Axel's Castle: A Study in the Imaginative Literature of 1870–
1930* (New York and London, 1945), p. 179.

4. Brée, pp. 23–33.

5. II, 698; *La Fugitive*, III, 450.

6. II, 976; *Le Temps retrouvé*, III, 846.

7. II, 1009; *Le Temps retrouvé*, III, 890.

8. *Correspondance générale*, II, 86–7.

INDEX

The following names and titles are mentioned in the text or in the notes; for Proust, references are included only for works other than *A la Recherche du temps perdu.*